Beyond Confrontation

Beyond Confrontation: Globalists, Nationalists and Their Discontents

BY

PHIL MULLAN

United Kingdom – North America – Japan – India – Malaysia – China

Emerald Publishing Limited
Howard House, Wagon Lane, Bingley BD16 1WA, UK

First edition 2020

Reprints and permissions service
Contact: permissions@emeraldinsight.com

British Library Cataloguing in Publication Data
A catalogue record for this book is available from the British Library

ISBN: 978-1-83982-563-7 (Print)
ISBN: 978-1-83982-560-6 (Online)
ISBN: 978-1-83982-562-0 (Epub)

ISOQAR certified
Management System,
awarded to Emerald
for adherence to
Environmental
standard
ISO 14001:2004.

Certificate Number 1985
ISO 14001

INVESTOR IN PEOPLE

Contents

List of Figures and Box   *vii*

List of Abbreviations   *ix*

About the Author   *xi*

Preface   *xiii*

Introduction: Global Times   *xvii*

Part 1: A World of Rules

Chapter 1   **Making the Rules-based International Order**   *3*

Chapter 2   **Globalism against Politics**   *21*

Chapter 3   **The Anti-democratic Roots of Neoliberalism**   *41*

Chapter 4   **From Post-war Order to Disorder**   *53*

Part 2: Myths about Trade

Chapter 5   **The Obsession with Trade**   *69*

Chapter 6   **Trade Becomes Weaponised**   *85*

Chapter 7   **Free Trade Illusions**   *99*

Chapter 8   **The Rise and Rise of Protectionism**   *115*

Part 3: Internationalism Starts at Home

Chapter 9   **Internationalisation: Sustaining Atrophy**   *131*

Chapter 10   The Battle Starts at Home   *151*

**Chapter 11   Internationalism, National Sovereignty
and Democracy**   *165*

References   *185*

Index   *201*

List of Figures and Box

Figures

Fig. 0.1	Changing Shares of World Output, 1500–2018	xxvii
Fig. 5.1	Rising Prominence of World Trade: Exports of Goods and Services as % of GDP, 1970–2017	74
Fig. 5.2	Global Annual Real Growth: GDP and Exports (Five-Year Moving Average), 1976–2018	82
Fig. 7.1	US Tariff Ratio to Total Value of Imports, 1891–2018	105
Fig. 7.2	Evolution of Regional Trade Agreements, 1948–2018	111
Fig. 9.1	Global Annual Real Growth: GDP, Foreign Investment and Exports (10-Year Moving Averages), 1981–2018	133
Fig. 9.2	Overseas Earnings as Share of US Corporate Pre-tax Profits, 1948–2018	134
Fig. 9.3	US Intra-firm Trade Shares of Totals, 1992–2018	136
Fig. 9.4	Intermediate Goods as Ratio of World Product Imports, 1988–2017	138
Fig. 9.5	World Trade Growth: Goods and Services (Five-year Moving Averages), 1985–2018	138
Fig. 9.6	Foreign Debt Relative to GDP, United States and United Kingdom, 1976–2018	140
Fig. 9.7	Asia's Rising Share of Inward Global FDI, 1980–2018	145
Fig. 9.8	Global Passenger Car Sales, 2005–2018	148

Box

| Box 9.1 | The West's Dependence on China's Car Market | 148 |

List of Abbreviations

AI	artificial intelligence
AIIB	Asian Infrastructure Investment Bank
APEC	Asia-Pacific Economic Cooperation
BIS	Bank for International Settlements
CFIUS	Committee on Foreign Investment in the United States
ECB	European Central Bank
ECJ	European Court of Justice
ECSC	European Coal and Steel Community
EMU	Economic and Monetary Union (of the EU)
EU	European Union
FDI	foreign direct investment
FTA	free trade agreement
GATS	General Agreement on Trade in Services
GATT	General Agreement on Tariffs and Trade
GDP	gross domestic product
GDPR	General Data Protection Regulation
GSC	global supply chain
GTA	Global Trade Alert
GVC	global value chain
ICC	International Criminal Court
ICJ	International Court of Justice
IMF	International Monetary Fund
IP and IPR	intellectual property (rights)
IPCC	Intergovernmental Panel on Climate Change
M&A	mergers and acquisitions
MFN	most favoured nation
NAFTA	North American Free Trade Agreement
NATO	North Atlantic Treaty Organization
NTB	non-tariff barrier
OECD	Organisation for Economic Co-operation and Development
R&D	research and development
RTA	regional trade agreements
RTP	Responsibility to Protect
TPP	Trans-Pacific Partnership
TRIMs	trade-related investment measures

TRIP	trade-related intellectual property
UN	United Nations
UNCTAD	United Nations Conference on Trade and Development
WTO	World Trade Organization

About the Author

Phil Mullan combines business management with research and writing, primarily on economic topics. He is the author of *Creative Destruction: How to Start an Economic Renaissance* (Policy Press, 2017) and *The Imaginary Time Bomb: Why an Ageing Population Is Not a Social Problem* (IB Tauris, 2000).

Having completed eight years in Senior Management roles with Easynet Global Services, an international communications services company, he is now a Business Consultant and a Charity Trustee. Previously, from 1996 until 2003, he was the Chief Executive of Cybercafé Ltd., running the Cyberia franchise, which had opened the world's first internet café in London in 1994.

Preface

History Accelerating?

Covid-19 was a truly global phenomenon. It started in one country and within weeks had spread all around the planet. Long distance air travel that epitomises the connectedness of our "globalised" world hastened the diffusion of the virus. The equally emblematic international communication systems instantly disseminated awareness of how governments and people were responding, encouraging the replication of actions and behaviours. The sense of a global community, "we're all in this together," had probably never been stronger.

Such extraordinary human crises, like major wars, are thought to bring people together. Certainly there were many, many uplifting instances all around the world of ordinary people supporting their fellow humans during this pandemic. However, at a political level, conflicts and discord were mostly aggravated, not eased, by the impact of Covid-19. Within governing elites, prior political divisions – in and between nations – intensified.

Illustrating a core premise of this book, the twosome of globalist and insular nationalist politicians found more to attack each other for. For instance, US President Donald Trump's suspension of financing for the World Health Organization (WHO) followed his long-running script against globalist multilateralism. No doubt there was also a large element of blame shifting by making the funding announcement at that particular time.

The attack on Trump from other Western governments was similarly consistent with their pre-existing globalist playbook. European Union (EU) and other globalist-leaning leaders condemned his act as destructive "economic nationalism". Their admonishment happened even though the WHO was being widely criticised for its performance by others, including from themselves, far beyond the White House.

This shared censure of the WHO pointed to another feature of the contemporary political climate described in this book. There is often less division between these two political stances than it can appear. Trump's decision itself was not that much of a break from previous official US attitudes to the UN agency. The indifference to its proceedings from his two preceding Oval Office occupants had been well indicated.[1]

---

[1]Powell, P. (2020). How Bush and Obama ceded the World Health Organization to China, increasing risk of pandemics like coronavirus. *Newsweek*, April 14. Retrieved from https://www.newsweek.com/how-bush-obama-ceded-world-health-organization-china-increasing-risk-pandemics-like-coronavirus-1497667.

On conceptual grounds too, commentators from both globalist and isolationist outlooks drew on the pandemic. Globalists called attention to the ease with which Covid-19 moved from one country to another as confirmation that national borders are moribund in our "smaller" world. Fighting such a global disease highlighted for them the limitations of the traditional nation state in dealing with it. The mantra was "global problems require global solutions."

This worldwide scourge was thought to add justification to the case for supranational governance and action. Many globalists adopted the overused Second World War analogy as upholding the need for international institutional collaboration today. The health emergency required something similar to the new international institutions created in the 1940s for today's even more interdependent and, seemingly, fragile world.

Meanwhile isolationists and others of a mercantilist bent turned the globalist perspective on its head. The rapid spread of the disease, they claimed, starkly illustrated the dangers posed by an open globalised world with porous borders. Globalisation, they asserted with extra conviction, had not only been destroying jobs at home, but had also left disease-hit countries at the mercy of global supply chains. Sudden shortages of medical supplies and equipment appeared to expose the risks of offshoring production to lower-cost countries. The pandemic was turned into an argument endorsing the case for inward-looking national self-sufficiency.

In fact, the pandemic experience justifies neither globalist nor isolationist viewpoints. For instance, the previous failure, or incompleteness, of businesses in diversifying their supply lines is neither a repudiation of an internationalised economy, nor an argument for strengthening global governance.

The ordeal of the pandemic repudiated other globalist assumptions. The actions taken by governments vindicated the validity of national state organisation. Only nation states had the authority to impose lockdowns and then provide or, in some countries, try to provide emergency financial aid to compensate businesses and families from the impact. The state could do all this because it retains a legacy of dominion within developed countries that has not been achieved by any of the international and supranational institutions set up during the past 75 years.

Also, there was no objective reason for national state apparatuses to operate only on their own, even if in practice some acted parochially. National science institutions and nation-based pharmaceutical companies worked together across borders in the search for effective treatments, better testing capabilities and vaccines. Nation states could similarly have better pooled their resources for collaborative progress in achieving solutions to the global challenge.

As the alternative to both globalism and narrow-minded nationalism, a third approach also beckoned through the upheavals of the pandemic: a popular internationalist nation-based path as promoted in this book. Just as diseases travel quicker in a more interconnected world than at the time of the Black Death, it is true that solutions can be found much faster, and without erasing the advantages of country boundaries. For instance, the existence of nation states and of national borders did not prevent the attempts to accelerate the discovery of treatments and vaccines through harnessing the wisdom and ingenuity of the global commonwealth.

The early pandemic experience did more than vindicate the possibility of an internationalist alternative to globalism and to insular nationalism. It reinforced the urgency of debating it due to the crisis's dangerous geopolitical repercussions. In particular three pre-pandemic features of international relations that are discussed in the book as together fuelling confrontation were amplified and brought to the surface: the changing economic balance in the world; the unravelling of the post-1945 world order; and crisis-enhanced tensions between the advanced industrial nations.

The crisis also saw many stirring examples of people, businesses and other non-governmental institutions working together to beat Covid-19. The hope is that the positive practical solidarities displayed, within nations and between them, can inspire a new popular internationalism to go beyond confrontation. However, we know that hope is not a sufficient strategy … so please read on.

Phil Mullan, 20 April 2020

Introduction: Global Times

"Be convinced that to be happy means to be free and that to be free means to be brave. Therefore do not take lightly the perils of war."

Thucydides, *The History of the Peloponnesian War*

Blueberry sales have recently surged across Europe. In Britain, they have even overtaken those of the raspberry, the favourite fruit grown domestically. Blueberries' relatively long shelf life for a soft berry appeals both to retailers and shoppers since neither likes to be stuck with punnets of rotting fruit.

Only a tiny share of blueberries sold in Europe is harvested there. Most are imported from Argentina and Chile where the terrain is better suited to acid-loving plants. The durability of the fruit suits the three-week sea voyage to Europe without losing freshness. And with labour costs in South America about one-tenth of those in Western Europe, prices are competitive with fruits produced in Europe.

Blueberries are one of a thriving group of *global commodities*. And while shoppers in London or Berlin buy their fresh fruit from Argentina, many businesses produce across borders too. The Apple iPhone is sold around the world and also involves one of the most internationalised of production processes. Making the smartphone involves operations in many parts of the world.

Many of us will have seen the sign on the iPhone packaging that it is "designed in California". Many are also aware that the phones are mostly final assembled by two Taiwanese companies, Foxconn and Pegatron, in their factories in China. Emphasising the global nature of production, Foxconn has already diversified some iPhone assembly into India, while Pegatron has plans to assemble in Indonesia.

Meanwhile, the individual iPhone parts are not just made in China, Taiwan and South Korea but are mostly imported from manufacturers around the world. Apple uses specialist manufacturers from a multitude of geographies to deliver individual items, including the battery, the lenses, the camera, the glass screen, the liquid crystal display, the various digital chips, the gyroscope, the compass and the phone shell. Factories producing these hundreds of individual components are located in more than 30 countries (Costello, 2019).

Apart from fruit sales and hardware production, other global linkages have proliferated. An email communication from Delhi will arrive in Paris instantaneously. The football FIFA World Cup final in 2014 between Germany and Argentina attracted over one billion viewers. A similar number watched the 2015 cricket World Cup match between India and Pakistan. Movies open on the same weekend in cinemas as far apart as New Zealand and the Netherlands. In so many ways, the world's cultural and economic lives are more *interconnected* than ever before.

Interconnectedness: Deterrent or Stimulant of Conflict?

It is often assumed that this increasingly interconnected world is a less conflict-prone world. With greater economic interdependence, surely governments would be foolish to confront each other. Closer connectedness should herald an era of peace, at least between the prosperous advanced countries that have far too much to lose from war. But the history of the twentieth century is not so reassuring.

That same assumption at the start of that century saw many deny that anything like the First World War could happen. The rapid expansion of the world market from the late nineteenth century suggested the prospect of continued peace, progress and prosperity – at least within the most developed countries.

Norman Angell's 1910 book *The Great Illusion* seemed to capture this mood.[2] The "illusion" he sought to dispel was that nations could gain by military confrontation. He argued that because of economic interdependence, war between the major nations would be futile and counterproductive. He also thought nationalist sentiment could no longer motivate the leaders of industry, because

> the capitalist has no country, and he knows, if he be of the modern type, that arms and conquests and jugglery with frontiers serve no ends of his, and may very well defeat them.

It seems the "global citizen" is an old idea.

Although Angell himself was anxious that disastrous wars could still happen, many who subscribed to his thesis saw it as an argument that war was now impossible. Of course, they were soon disabused. An uncontrolled escalation of rivalries culminated in not just one but two world wars, interspersed by periods of instability, depression, protectionism, militarism and barbarism.

But despite the bloody realities of the First and then the Second World Wars, the notion that interconnectedness guarantees peace persisted. After the second of these wars, a new world order emerged under US hegemony, regulated by a network of institutions and a legal framework conditioned by the experiences of previous decades. This settlement was powerfully legitimised by two phenomena: the outbreak of the Cold War that pitted a free, liberal West against an authoritarian repressive Soviet bloc, and also by the post-war economic boom in the industrialised capitalist nations.

Carl von Clausewitz famously said that war is a continuation of politics by other means. We can go further by adding that politics is often influenced by economic developments. However, politics, and the possibility of war, is *never*

---

[2]The first edition in 1909 had been titled *Europe's Optical Illusion*.

determined solely by economic considerations. In consequence, economic interconnectedness is not a deterrent to conflict. On the contrary, it can become a tense source of friction. Economic troubles and joblessness at home often get blamed on trade and capital flows across borders.

Thus, it is more than coincidental that signs of the crumbling of the post-war world order first become evident from the 1970s alongside the arrival of the West's long economic depression. Slowing productivity, the monstrous expansions in debt and a series of recessions culminating in the 2008 Western financial crash have aroused more aggressive competition between advanced capitalist countries.

Against this rivalrous background, the shift in the balance of economic power from West to East and especially the rise of China has deeply unsettled the old order. In response, the declining powers have clung, pragmatically, to the existing structures and rules that they established and still oversee, though often clashing with each other in the process. Meanwhile, the rising powers, generally excluded from positions of authority in those institutions, have been, selectively, challenging the old framework. This has included setting up international organisations side by side with the existing ones.

As a consequence, conflict between countries is being channelled *through* interdependence, rather than being contained. Closer links provide a means of furthering national interests at the expense of others. For instance, the tool of sanctions uses economic dependence to pressurise targeted nations.

The closer countries become connected, the more weapons are available, ranging today from disrupting global supply chains to controlling international payments systems. Political scientist Abraham Newman has explained that the very networks of globalisation that were supposed to "liberate business and bring peace" have become "a yoke on business and a source of coercion" (Farrell & Newman, 2019).

For instance, alongside the high-profile trade wars launched by the United States against China, in 2019, Japan and South Korea began their own economic war. Japan restricted key chemicals needed by the South Korean information technology industry in retaliation for South Korea's continued demands for Second World War reparations.

Thus, while economics matters a lot to politics, economic integration doesn't make international relations more amicable. Geopolitical confrontation operates alongside and sometimes through, denser economic entanglements. Nevertheless, the old notion that international connectedness is a stabilising influence lives on in today's globalisation thesis. This gives backing to the enormous faith that the globalist leaders who run most Western nations place on the "rules-based international order" as the preserver of peace and prosperity.

Recalling Angell's contention, this book demonstrates that this belief is one of today's "great illusions". We examine how the approaches adopted by Western leaders in pursuit of international *stability* are ironically an accelerant for *instability*. Clinging to an anachronism can be dangerous. We propose an alternative not just to the dominant outlook and practices of globalism but also to its supposed antithesis, mercantilism – the idea that trade generates wealth and that government protectionism contributes to the accumulation of lucrative trade balances.

- Missing cultural / migration impact of Globalisation.

Globalist politicians both stress the importance of established institutions and "weaponise" the existing rules and regulations. Their mercantilist opponents, personified by President Donald Trump, openly resort to trade protectionism. In both cases, defensive measures become aggressive by inflaming hostilities between nations and between regional blocs. The democratic alternative we propose here instead incorporates the possibility of enlightening change, as guided by human agency through the institution of the nation state. In particular, we explain how domestic economic transformations initiated by bottom-up democratic forums are vital to reducing the tendencies towards international conflict.

The Theory of Globalisation

The global developments that impinge on all our lives have fed both the popular and the scholarly belief in *globalisation*. The latter first gained some credibility as a *description* of the more integrated world economy, boosted by technological developments, mass consumption, financialisation and the apparent primacy of market forces. The concept of globalisation expressed the belief that the world – economically, politically, culturally and ecologically – is shrinking fast in its social and physical dimensions (Camilleri & Falk, 1992, p. 1).

Globalisation is a relatively recent term. It was only in 1983 that Theodore Levitt, a prominent marketing professor and émigré from 1930s Germany, popularised this previously little used word. His *Harvard Business Review* article "The Globalization of Markets" triggered a whole new intellectual discourse. Levitt (1983) thought that the latest technologies had brought about a distinct commercial reality: "the emergence of global markets for standardized consumer products on a previously unimagined scale of magnitude". Today, just about everything is viewed through the prism of globalisation (Held & McGrew, 2003).

Despite its ubiquity, perhaps because of it, the word globalisation is without an agreed definition. According to the prize-winning scholar Or Rosenboim (2017b), the "multifaceted, flexible character of the idea of the global enhanced its appeal but also highlighted its weakness" (p. 6). For most of its users, globalisation refers to some aspect of the enhanced integration of international markets and higher levels of trade and capital flows. However, this is just the start of its perceived overarching significance.

Others draw attention to the increasing flow across borders of ideas, information and people and often mark out three main types of globalisation: economic, political and cultural (Hoffman, 2003). It appears that no area of life is now unaffected by it. We also have the globalisation of disease, of ethics, of technology, of wealth, of geography, of ecology, of gender equality, of terrorism and of religion (Conner, 2004, pp. 2–5).

By the end of the last century, David Held, an influential writer on international relations, warned that the term is "in danger of becoming, if it has not already become, the cliché of our times". He and his colleagues then proceeded to provide a definition, which has become the standard one cited in academia:

Globalization can usefully be conceived as a process (or set of processes) which embodies a transformation in the spatial organization of social relations and transactions, generating transcontinental or interregional flows and networks of activity, interaction and power ... (and) can be thought of as the widening, intensifying, speeding up, and growing impact of world-wide interconnectedness. (Held, McGrew, Goldblatt, & Perraton, 1999)

A bit of a mouthful. Helpfully, the authors clarified the historical context:

(C)ontemporary patterns of globalization mark a new epoch in human affairs. Just as the industrial revolution and the expansion of the West in the nineteenth century defined a new age in world history so today the microchip and the satellite are icons of a new historical conjuncture. By comparison with previous periods, globalization today combines a remarkable confluence of dense patterns of global interconnectedness, alongside their unprecedented institutionalisation through new global and regional infrastructures of control and communication, from the WTO [World Trade Organization] to APEC [Asia-Pacific Economic Cooperation]. Driven by interrelated political, economic and technological changes, globalization is transforming societies and world order. (Held et al., 1999)

In short, technological and related development has driven the world's evolution into a distinctive and fast-changing era. The particular emphasis on the institutionalised expressions of globalisation points to the political importance of the thesis as *prescriptive* for how our lives should be conducted. Although "globalisation" is sometimes loosely equated to "internationalisation", this association downplays the crucial political significance of globalisation as an edict of governance.

Far from globalisation being a quantitative, or qualitative, extension of economic internationalisation, politically it is its opposite. While internationalisation relates to links *between* nations, the dominant theories of globalisation *transcend* the framework of nations and nation states. Rosenboim pointed out that the word "international" attributes importance to the nation, or the state, as a "defining, order-creating unit, and explores the relations between nations as sovereign entities". While the "international" assumes mediation *through* states, "globalisation" in contrast assumes the diminution of the state and privileges the political role of the globe as a whole (Rosenboim, 2017b, pp. 3–4).

In political praxis, the globalisation thesis favours technocracy over democracy and the ascendancy of supranational institutions over nation states. This follows from the blame it heaps on nationalism and democracy for the barbaric catastrophes of the first half of the twentieth century. It is this prescriptive, rather than the descriptive, element of globalisation that unsurprisingly has come to the fore as the post-war order has experienced increasing strain.

A Less Controllable World?

While increasing interconnectedness is real, it doesn't substantiate the core premise of most globalisation literature: the idea that impersonal, autonomous global forces dominate humanity. The thesis presents the world as more complex, uncertain and out of control. Political scientists Robert Keohane and Joseph Nye (1977) describe this as "complex interdependence".

This notion of global complexity underpins the most critical and far-reaching of the globalist tenets: that *national political activity* has become much less effective and often detrimental. In her seminal book *The Retreat of the State*, the scholar Susan Strange (1996) explained how global economic and financial developments had rendered the nation state obsolete. Nation states have supposedly become "disempowered co-players" embedded in "irreversibly globalized markets" (Habermas, 2015, pp. 87–90; Hardt & Negri, 2000). This idea – that the nation state has become irrelevant as the prime political mover – is erroneous in fact, self-serving in theory and dangerous in practice.

Globalist thinking assumes that national political activity and national sovereignty are supplanted because they are no longer able to meet today's global challenges. The existence of our global problems is thought to require "global", not national solutions (Mounk, 2018, p. 60). Thus, globalisation theory is much more than a description of internationalised production and trade; it embodies the ascendancy of complexity over mastery, of the global over the national and of supranational institutions over nation states.

The most developed representation of supranational organisation is the European Union (EU). Its genesis was in the European Coal and Steel Community (ECSC) established in 1951. Motivated by the French foreign minister Robert Schuman as a way to prevent another war between France and Germany, the aim of strengthening European economic integration was to make war not only "unthinkable but materially impossible". However, the inter-country clashes within its EU successor over, among other matters, the crisis within its common currency zone, migration flows and interpretations of the rule of law, bring to mind the follies of that pre-1914 complacency about the impossibility of conflict.

The fundamental danger of globalist thinking is that the very discounting of national politics does make the world more out of control and less certain. Belief in the undermining of national authority and power by globalisation reinforces the fatalist component within present-day thought. This is counterproductive to solving the world's real problems.

More than ever, we need collective human capabilities to overcome our biggest challenges. We already have the means: the same technological, economic and social developments that inform the globalisation thesis actually provide us with *greater* capacity to influence and mould our world. Not least a more extensive international division of labour expands humanity's productive capabilities and resources.

Yet regarding the nation state as impotent abandons the only effective, and potentially legitimate, vehicle so far developed for executing human agency. By rejecting the institution of the nation state, globalist politicians give up on the main instrument through which people could take some control of their lives. Collaborative international problem solving is best achieved through *nations acting together*, not by demeaning proven national apparatuses in favour of undemocratic supranational bodies.

National Sovereignty Curbed

The defining political habit of the past three decades is of Western politicians giving away their powers to a multitude of appointed technocratic bodies, both transnational and national ones. National political enfeeblement has thereby become institutionalised. When national politicians outsource their responsibilities to globalist bodies and mechanisms, they make themselves *doubly* ineffectual. They delegate their authority in the first place and then become subordinate to the new globalist arrangements. The rules and boundaries imposed by the international bodies render national governments even less capable of autonomous action.

For instance, at the turn of the millennium, a dozen EU governments accepted the use of the euro in place of their national currencies. They hoped this could bring about improved currency stability, since the new supranational currency would be further removed from the pressures of national economic conditions and policies. Wim Duisenberg, the founding president of the European Central Bank (ECB), stressed this feature by presenting the euro as the first currency to have severed its link not only to antiquated gold but also "its link to the nation state". This was a prototype globalist currency.

Within a decade, the eurozone crisis shattered the illusions of being able to eclipse the national. In reality, national economic problems and differences still mattered a lot. But by then, national governments, not least in Greece, saw themselves helpless in the face of economic chaos. Because of the euro framework, governments couldn't resort to currency devaluation or decide how much to borrow to dig themselves out of the mess. The distress of nation state impotence was the self-produced outcome of globalist initiatives.

Democracy Degraded

Giving up on national sovereignty eviscerates democracy. In place of the national arena comes the formal suggestion that democracy needs to be reinterpreted for the new global times. This proposition is usually expressed as a combination of local, community-based voices alongside supranational mechanisms. But in most matters, local democracy has too little weight to make a real difference to folks' lives, while supranational authority has failed to attain democratic legitimacy.

The same suggested impotence of national politicians is offered as justification for abandoning political accountability. It is "difficult" to see, argued the political scientist Yascha Mounk, what the realistic alternative is to relying to a greater extent on the technical expertise of unaccountable international organisations. We must choose, he argued, between achieving international cooperation on key issues such as climate change and the spread of nuclear weapons "by a troublingly undemocratic path" and "not achieving it at all" (Mounk, 2018, p. 96).

The late German sociologist Ulrich Beck came to the same conclusion. He suggested that the recent scale of social and economic transformation has been so extreme that it amounts to a "metamorphosis of the world". He deduced that if "one acts nationally ... one is left behind". Additionally, Beck thought a continued attachment to the nation *gets in the way* of finding solutions. He drew on what he described as the "common sense" insight that no nation state can cope alone with the global risks of climate change and extrapolated that the principle of national sovereignty is "an obstacle to survival of humankind" (Beck, 2016, pp. 4–5, 9–10,17–18, 35).

But why do states have to act "alone"? Why is inter-nation cooperation not possible anymore to address international challenges? The answers suggested by globalists tend to be vague but imply a loss of faith in ordinary men and women acting with such "common sense".

The globalist disparaging of national politics takes advantage of popular political disconnection. The failure of the old political parties, particularly since the 1980s, to offer compelling visions to the electorate has led to disillusionment. This loss of legitimacy reinforced declines in traditional party membership levels and falling electoral turnouts. When the political class also belittles national policies on the basis that the global arena is now the relevant one, then domestic politics appears even less consequential. Politics seems instead to revolve around careerists and self-important personalities.

Ordinary citizens living far beyond elite circles became even further disengaged, adding to scepticism about what is politically possible. In an inversion of reality, frustrated individuals are seen as the source of the democratic crisis. Mainstream commentators blame them for being apathetic, when it is the failures and excuses of national and globalist politicians that have discredited modern politics.

The anti-democratic propensity within the globalist perspective has recently become much more evident. Since 2016, globalists have rubbished the actions of the populace who voted in large numbers for Brexit, or for Trump as US president, or for "populists" across Europe. The previous aloofness of politicians became contempt for ordinary people who failed to vote as advised. The electorate was patronised as having been duped or, at best, badly informed. Some were described as "deplorable" and imagined to be motivated by racist, xenophobic thinking.[3] In fact, survey evidence confirmed that most of the contrary voters simply wanted things to change for the better (Economist Intelligence Unit, 2018, p. 4).

There is much that is new about internationalisation today that we need to understand. None of it, though, renders the nation state, sovereignty and collective human action as obsolete. Greater global interconnectedness has no determinate consequence for the potential potency of a nation state's policies. Moreover, none of what is novel vindicates putting up with the old status quo. And none of

---

[3]During the 2016 US presidential election campaign, the Democratic Party candidate Hillary Clinton said half of Donald Trump's supporters belonged in a "basket of deplorables" characterised by "racist, sexist, homophobic, xenophobic, Islamaphobic" views. Retrieved from http://time.com/4486502/hillary-clinton-basket-of-deplorables-transcript/.

it excuses the top-down globalist and mercantilist approaches that are exacerbating inter-nation tensions.

Global Frameworks Under Strain

We have entered another unstable era for the world order. Every four years, the US National Intelligence Council produces its *Global Trends* "map of the future": a strategic assessment of how the world might look over the next 20 years. Its January 2017 report anticipated increasing tensions between countries and heightening of the risk of interstate conflict during the ensuing five years. It concluded with a picture of increased international tension:

> The near-term likelihood of international competition leading to greater global disorder and uncertainty will remain elevated as long as *a la carte* internationalism persists. As dominant states limit cooperation to a subset of global issues while aggressively asserting their interests in regional matters, international norms and institutions are likely to erode and the international system to fragment toward contested regional spheres of influence. (National Intelligence Council, 2017, p. 44)

This is an accurate description of the state of the world: international fragmentation around fluid regional groupings. It is telling that this official American assessment of global fragility was prepared *before* Trump entered the White House. It is, therefore, unhelpful to concentrate, as so many commentators do, on Trump's impromptu and arbitrary overseas policy initiatives as being the source of international conflict. His mercantilist actions don't help, but they are not the underlying cause of confrontation.

Instead, today's impending geopolitical rupture derives from the unusual collision between two epochal developments. This is the distinctive feature of modern international relations. First, the centre of global wealth creation has shifted from West to East, specifically from the United States to China, while the distribution of power within international institutions still reflects the very different economic world of 1945. This incongruity is bound to foment tension.

Some anticipate a Thucydides moment. In his history of the Peloponnesian War 2,500 years ago Thucydides wrote that "What made war inevitable was the growth of Athenian power and the fear which this caused in Sparta". Today, we appear to be on the same path as old and new powers clash.

Just as Sparta could not expect always to be on top, so America, and the West in general, should not expect always to be the dominant powers. The problem is that a rising China is bringing out the anxieties within declining America and Europe. West-East animosities are heating up over trade, technology, investment and geopolitical influence around the world. The EU and the United States agree in officially describing China as not only an economic competitor but also as a systemic threat.

But a second phenomenon exacerbates this flux. Escalating strains *within* the old Western world add to the disruptive mix. International rivalries reminiscent of a century earlier are sharpening, aggravated by these advanced industrial countries' collective failure to recover after the crash and recessions of 2008 and 2009. In particular, transatlantic ructions between the United States and EU countries have turned bitter.

Thus, mounting West–East tension is interacting with chronic intra-West tensions. While all the major nations will seek to avoid a frontal military confrontation between each other, this is not the way a world war is likely to begin. An escalation in one, or several, of many hotspots around the globe – including the Middle East, the South China Sea, the Balkans or Sub-Saharan Africa – could see the big powers finding themselves on opposite sides. Actual fighting could break out. If this happens, it might appear the outbreak of global conflict is "accidental", but the roots will be these two big international trends.

Either one of the two could on their own precipitate confrontation. Their fusion brings even greater danger because each makes it harder to deal with the other. The West's economic decline relative to the East reinforces frictions between the leading industrial economies as each vigorously seeks to reap advantage from world markets. When one Western power sanctions China, this creates competitive opportunities for others (Rosenberg & Saravalle, 2018). For instance, the US threat in 2019 to extend financial sanctions against Chinese companies encouraged Britain's authorities to double down on promoting their service offerings to these same firms (UK Government, 2019).

Meanwhile, the malaise and disunity within exhausted and fearful Western countries makes it more difficult for them to negotiate together a new international set-up with the world's rising nations. Also by providing a convenient foreign scapegoat for the West's economic troubles the rise of China helps Westerners evade that the real roots of economic decay are at home. These problems should be addressed domestically rather than dodged by assigning false blame on other countries.

The combination of these two trends also means the West can no longer confidently impose its geopolitical agenda on the rest of the world. The current international regime as inherited almost unchanged from the end of the Second World War no longer corresponds to the economic realities. The rise of Asia has decisively flipped the location of production and new wealth generation.

At the end of the Second World War, the United States and Western Europe accounted for the lion's share of global production. America was by far the supreme nation. Not only had it led the Allied victories over Germany and Japan, it produced about two-fifths of the world's output.[4] The rest of the advanced Western nations produced another third.

The global economic hierarchy is very different today. For the first time since the industrial revolution, a greater part of world production happens outside the advanced industrial economies than inside. Fig. 0.1 shows that the US national share of world output fell below a quarter by 1970 and has been below a fifth, and falling, since the 2008 crash.[5] Western Europe taken collectively was the biggest

---

[4]At market exchange rates.
[5]Measured by purchasing power parity (PPP), a metric that adjusts for the local pricing of services.

region between the mid-nineteenth century and the Second World War. It fell just behind the United States after the war and has since tracked America's steady decline.

On the ascending side, China has now overtaken the United States and Western Europe to become the world's largest economy.[6] India is in third position as a nation. On present trends, until at least the late 2020s, more than two-thirds of global economic growth is expected to come from the non-advanced countries.

These economic shifts should not be surprising to any Western government since balanced development across all countries would be exceptional. Nevertheless, tension derives from the mismatch between where economic power now lies and which national authorities politically dominate international institutions.

Even when international regimes are promoted in the language of universal equality, as was the case after 1945, the reality is an uneven world with inequalities

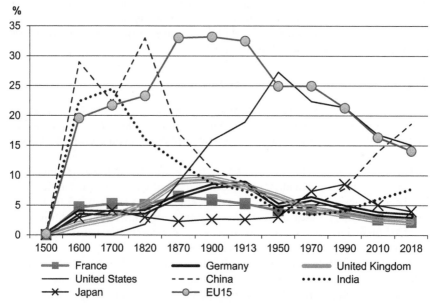

Fig. 0.1.   Changing Shares of World Output, 1500–2018 (Years 1500–1990: Maddison, 2003; Years 2010 and 2018: World Bank World Development Indicators, 2020: GDP, PPP (Current International US$)).[5]

---

[5]The figures are in PPP terms. EU 15 (pre-2004 members): Austria, Belgium, Denmark, Finland, France, Germany, Greece, Ireland, Italy, Luxembourg, Netherlands, Portugal, Spain, Sweden and the United Kingdom.

[6]In *nominal* terms, the United States' share is bigger, and it remains the largest economy. Its share has still been falling, to one-third by 1970 and to below a quarter since 2008. China is second in size and is projected to overtake the United States by the end of the 2020s.

of national power. The more powerful countries imposed their wills on the less powerful. Hence, the international arrangements agreed at the end of the Second World War expressed the balance of forces in the world then. Now, the material basis of that order has irretrievably gone.

Those on top will always try to extend their dominion. The Western powers today though seem unusually reluctant to let go. This doggedness to perpetuate the past is significantly reinforced by internal unease within Western elites.

The Enlightenment belief that a better system is worth striving for has lost its appeal. Aspiration to lead change is enfeebled. The idea of progress itself has become tainted through the cumulative impact of the daunting experiences endured since the First World War (Furedi, 2014). This informs today's peculiarly pervasive sense of uncertainty, inducing an impulsive attachment to the status quo.

For the past three decades, "TINA" has increasingly dominated the Western outlook. "There is no alternative" to how things are has become the stock leadership response to the fear of change. It is as if they all want to freeze the world as it was, with them in charge. So, the mercantilist Trump argues for technology wars to preserve America leadership. Meanwhile, the globalist school holds that there is no alternative for maintaining stability to retaining the liberal international order and the pre-eminence of Western values.

The Battle Over Rules and Institutions

It is true that universally agreed multilateral rules and institutions are helpful in some circumstances. They can smooth international working arrangements. For example, when foreign investment regulations provide a common framework it facilitates new cross-border ventures.

However, such benefits are secondary to the question of the legitimacy of the overarching arrangements. For many years, consent to the post-1945 order has been withering, especially among developing countries inspired by a more dynamic China. The tarnishing of Western authority was further reinforced by the 2008 financial crash, specifically the damage done to the reputation of the US economic model from being at the epicentre of the crisis.

The next geopolitical transition will adjust how world order is maintained. When any international hierarchy is no longer materially justified, the process of change is usually protracted and disruptive. But changing a *rules-based institutionalised* system creates particular challenges because it has embedded the authority of the dominant powers at the time of its establishment. This mode of order provides political leverage to the incumbent countries.

Authority that is derived from a depoliticised rules-based order arises precisely because it is not subject to the whims of political contestation. To retain dominion the rules don't even need to be enforced that often, nor does everyone have to fully grasp their specifics. The fact of established rules, especially judicially overseen ones, gives the system an objective validity that discretionary balance-of-power arrangements couldn't possibly match. Appealing to the authority of this type of order is often sufficient for the national governments presiding over its institutions to get their way.

The predicament today is that this formal authority continues even when the original leaders no longer warrant being leaders on the basis of economic strength. The legitimacy of the rules and the institutional structure gives the old order an aspect of permanence that benefits the founding states. The difficulties Britain had in leaving the institutionalised order of the EU illustrates this wider problem. The inertia built into formalised regimes makes them less adaptable, including being unfitted to incorporate rising nations on equal terms.

Nations inheriting authority from earlier times use that very authority to sustain a status quo even when it no longer corresponds to the reality of the world. They are able to use their presiding rank to resist any change that they perceive would disadvantage them.

For instance, although they can't justify it on the basis of economics or international fairness, the United States and Europe have continued to run the two most important international economic agencies. They have been insistent in perpetuating the archaic custom that the United States appoints the head of the World Bank, while Europe, now in the form of the EU, selects the head of the International Monetary Fund (IMF). Similarly, Britain and France jealously protect their permanent positions on the United Nations (UN) Security Council (alongside the United States, the Soviet Union (subsequently Russia) and China), when other countries – from both north and south – exert bigger influences in the world.

As a consequence, the international system itself becomes a source of dissension and rivalry. Rising nations question why shouldn't an Asian or an African lead the IMF or the World Bank? Why does India or Brazil – or Germany or Japan – not qualify to be a permanent member of the Security Council? National differences are expressed and sometimes inflamed through opposing or supporting the existing format of institutions and rules. The rules-based order and its institutions become weapons, used especially by the leadership of those countries who want to hang onto the way things were.

Most countries, ascending or descending, are unlikely to reject the rules-based order wholesale. Few rising nations will want to abandon a system under which they have been able to develop. It is clear that China and other emerging powers have become much stronger economically within the "liberal order" (Stuenkel, 2016, p. 184). Hence, the peculiarity of China criticising the American government for "undermining the rules-based order" that the United States was instrumental in establishing in the first place (Zhong, 2019).

Instead, differences between countries are manifest over the *interpretation* of rules and over *how* institutions apply them. For instance, what is meant by the "rule of law" has become an area of national difference, as seen currently with Germany and France clashing with Poland and Hungary over what it means in practice.

The EU spelt out the significance of *interpretation* when in 2019 it first described China as a "systemic rival". It pointed out that "China's engagement in favour of multilateralism is sometimes selective and based on a different understanding of the rules-based international order". Future cooperation with China would be on the EU's terms (European Commission, 2019, p. 2).

Conflicting interpretations of rules are also manifest on the other side of the Atlantic. With bipartisan support, the Trump White House has been highly critical both of China and of the WTO for the way trade, investment and state aid rules are being implemented. China is attacked for supposedly "cheating" the WTO system, especially the rules that favour developing over developed countries. The United States says China is now a "rich" country and shouldn't present itself as not being developed. At the same time, the WTO is blamed for interpreting the rules to the disadvantage of the United States.

These differences can quickly escalate because there is no definitive way to defuse disputes over interpretation. The United States claims it is being treated "unfairly" by China and the WTO. But what is "fair" and "unfair" is in the eye of the aggrieved party. Is it fair or unfair to preserve order by stunting the rise of less developed countries? What is a "fair" measure of economic convergence: the absolute size of an economy or relative living standards that remain uneven between mature and emerging countries despite the latter's much faster growth? Country-by-country answers to these questions will differ.

Challenges to the old order will most likely be indirect. Rising nations will establish *parallel orders* that don't necessarily involve them leaving or openly confronting the longer established structures (Stuenkel, 2016, p. 11). A prominent example is China's Belt and Road Initiative that offers countries in Asia, Africa, Eastern Europe and even South America, alternative sources of infrastructure funding to the World Bank and other established Western-led multilateral facilities. Given these entities have usually started on a regional – mostly Asian – basis, one of their consequences is to institutionalise the world's fragmentation, exacerbating tensions between regional power blocs.

In particular, countries will take different approaches to developing *new* international rules and regulations. This applies especially to emerging technologies. The country that sets the standards in a new technology usually gives its own companies a big advantage. Clashes are already evident over cyber security and digital privacy rules, where China and the West have different priorities and goals.

Countries, or regions, don't even need to be strong in a technology to try to assert themselves through setting rules. The EU, for example, has been seeking to set standards in car emissions and in data protection, even though its electric car industry and information technology sectors are relatively weak. The expanding international influence of the EU's General Data Protection Regulation (GDPR) owes more to the EU's particular expertise in rule-making than it does to European technology companies being world leaders.

Rule setting also becomes a tool for commercial competition. For instance, GDPR rules constrain international businesses from sending customer data collected in Europe into the United States. Data flows are even further restricted into China. This can hold back the development of both American and Chinese headquartered firms. Meanwhile, Chinese companies leading global technology in sectors like electronic payments and bike sharing systems are unable to operate freely in developed countries without falling foul of stricter Western regulations (Beattie, 2019).

The weaponisation of rules and standards leads to specific international organisations becoming battlegrounds between nations. Recently, the United States has been citing "national security" imperatives to exclude Chinese companies from its technology supply chains in areas from 5G mobile networks to surveillance cameras. In response, China has been working through existing international organisations such as the International Organisation for Standardization and the International Telecommunication Union to extend its influence and challenge United States restrictions on its products and equipment.

Even when countries succeed in getting their national standards agreed as the global norm, nothing is permanently settled in today's febrile climate. Other countries might still go their own way. We can anticipate the *regional segregation* of rules, standards and institutional structures over some newer technologies: not only probably 5G but also possibly the internet-of-things, artificial intelligence (AI), facial recognition, payment systems, drones and driverless cars. The regionalisation of rules through parallel institutional systems is likely to be a significant way that global fragmentation and friction spreads.

The Choices: Mercantilism, Globalism or Democracy

In these strained conditions, how can prosperity be secured and the drift to war averted?

Mercantilism

Certainly, mercantilist trade protectionism, with import controls and export subsidies, is not the answer. Original mercantilist thinking goes back to the early pre-industrial phase of capitalism. The huge Europe-centred mid-millennium expansion in international trade led thinkers at the time to view exporting as the source of wealth and importing as a waste of resources.

Being successful in trade was associated with the accumulation of wealth often in the form of precious metals. Economic prowess was identified with a positive trade balance. This motivated the use of national protectionist procedures to limit profligate importing and stimulate exporting. Trump's tariff wars echo these mercantilist propositions.

Modern mercantilism lacks much practical support or intellectual backing. Economists from most of the main contemporary schools of thought condemn this style of traditional trade protectionism. They justifiably identify it as an ineffective as well as divisive response to economic problems in the advanced countries.

Today, though, *protectionism* has extended far beyond a way of policing trade with which the word is conventionally associated. More broadly, it operates as an extensive programme that seeks to protect existing economic arrangements. Modern varieties of protectionism, often not even proclaimed as being protectionist, are just as problematic as mercantilism. And these problems hurt the imposing countries to a greater extent than those targeted. All protectionist policies eventually undermine domestic prosperity in the places where they are initiated. This is because they cover up the necessity for economic restructuring and renewal.

In consequence, protectionism should not be understood narrowly as the tool of mercantilists like "Tariff Man" Trump. It is now more about non-tariff barriers (NTBs) like regulation, subsidies and public procurement policies. Much present-day state intervention acts to sustain domestic businesses and, de facto, discriminates against those located elsewhere.

Globalism

The historical record is that globalist bodies have used these protectionist policies extensively, especially of the non-tariff variety. A regulationist rather than tariff-led style of protection conforms to the globalist affinity for rules. For instance, a core feature of the EU is its regional customs union and rules-based single market. These protect its producers from the rest of the world by tariffs, and even more, by NTBs. Protectionist support for the economic activities of EU member states reaches far beyond the well-recognised French farmers and German car producers.

The shared attachment to protectionism indicates the error in seeing mercantilism and globalism as opposites. Although their respective advocates often attack the other, they have much in common. Ultimately, globalism and mercantilism are both *status quo doctrines*. In particular, they both seek to hang on to their existing businesses and industries by propping up their domestic economies. They both fear the disruption of economic renewal. Both approaches want to put the interests of their own geographies above those of the rest of the world, and both also have the contrary effect of stunting economic possibilities.

The concurrence between mercantilists and globalists is further illustrated in the consensus between them that China's state-led industrial policies are a huge threat. It has been widely noted, even by Trump's critics, that a desire to put additional pressure on China is "not simply a Trump phenomenon. Indeed, it's one of the few areas where there's bipartisan agreement in the United States and among its traditional allies Japan, Canada, and Europe" (Edel, 2018). Globalism and mercantilism both try to hold on to a past when the advanced Western countries were able to translate their economic dominance into geopolitical power, individually and collectively. Their mutual antipathy to Chinese economic ascendancy reveals that they can both inflame an already strained international situation.

There is though, one big political difference between mercantilism and globalism. The former has been exposed by historical experience as damaging at home and abroad. The other retains a largely benign reputation in the West.

The world has already experienced the tragic consequences of a mercantilist defence of the existing order in the 1930s. The beggar-thy-neighbour method is associated – crudely – with the bloodiest conflict in human history. That image provides some assurance today against mercantilism's uncontrolled exacerbation.

In contrast, the globalist proposition developed in reaction to that earlier global conflict has yet to be fully tested in the heat of geopolitical metamorphosis. We have to scrutinise and lay bare the dangers of globalism primarily intellectually, rather than through drawing on established experience.

The pitfall with both the mercantilist and globalist outlooks is that change is already happening, yet pursuing their respective programmes only makes the change less orderly. Trying to hold on to the past makes the future more dangerous.

Acting to preserve how things used to be represents an imperious path, provoking the nations and populations who were not part of the old supremacy. In consequence, the West's institutional procedures for maintaining stability are having the unintended effect of fuelling international instability.

When societies are in trouble, finding others are at fault is common. As Trump blames the Chinese and the perfidious Europeans, the political classes in the rest of the world mostly blame Trump and his revival of mercantilism. Meanwhile, the Washington establishment condemns the parochial, nativist Americans who voted for Trump. On the other side of the Atlantic, commissioners in Brussels pillory Eastern European governments for refusing to follow EU directives.

Scapegoating other people never works out well, either at home or abroad. It incites confrontation. The blame game is also a distraction from domestic problems: a low-investment US economy, an out-of-touch Washington establishment and an increasingly crisis-prone EU project seeking "ever closer union". Identifying foreign culprits is a chimera that raises the temperature further. It is not hard to see how one or more modern anxieties – such as climate change, AI or cyber security – can be blamed on others and become triggers for serious conflict between countries.

The common intellectual flaw of mercantilism and globalism is the failure to appreciate that capitalism has always operated simultaneously on *both* a national and international basis. A long time, 150 years ago, Karl Marx (1973) noted that the "tendency to create the *world market* is directly given in the concept of capital itself" (p. 408). This drive is amplified in periods of sustained stagnation. Global market relations assume a primary importance in coping with economic atrophy within the Western nations.

The common counterposition of the national to the international by both mercantilists and globalists is spurious. The practical implications of this essential dualism of capital help clarify some frequent misunderstandings. It explains why there has never been fully "free" trade: national interests always trumped completely free and open borders. It accounts for the difficulty of neoliberal thinkers being consistently anti-state, because their support for capitalism necessitated tolerating a role for the state's backing of national capital. Similarly, it reveals why globalist and mercantilist politicians both rely on protectionist practices and policies out of their common, though backfiring, consideration for their national capitals.

There is Another Way: Democratic Rule

This book argues that the roots of modern international disorder are fundamentally domestic. Upon this base, we suggest what can be done to avoid things becoming more dangerous and, eventually, militarised. Our main conclusion is that we have to reject any proposals that try to preserve the existing anachronistic order. The composition of the world has changed so much that acting to hold on to the status quo stokes the very international conflicts everyone says they want to avoid.

We have a choice. We can choose between the haphazard and uncontrolled change, exacerbated by mercantilist and globalist policies, or change that is guided by human judgement. Neither option avoids disruption. But change that engages with and is ultimately directed by ordinary men and women increases the prospects of containing instabilities. This approach can also make the most of the accompanying opportunities.

The greater recognition of capitalist malaise since the financial crisis informs our alternative to mercantilism and globalism. The material problem for the advanced industrial countries does not derive from the rise of new economies in the East. Internationalisation and stormier economic tensions are a *consequence* not a *cause* of the West's productive sickness. We will delve into how the extension of international economic connections since the 1970s is largely a response to the compounding domestic problems of Western capitalism.

The real economic problems we need to address lie *within* the national Western economies. Primarily, it is within those five that have dominated the post-1945 economic world: the United States, Japan,[7] Germany, France and Britain. Each has lost its economic mojo, expressed in slowing productivity growth, bringing about weakly rising or stagnant levels of prosperity. As a result, we have seen the extension of uneven economic development between countries, underpinning the escalation of international rivalries.

Just as the real problem is at home, the only durable and effective solution also starts at home. It doesn't finish there: for example, the best long-term response – in both economic and geopolitical terms – to the fear of falling behind techno- logically is to invest extra resources in collaborative ventures. These should not be confined to the old West, but extended globally including with, not against, China.

But the foundation for such mutually beneficial international cooperation is a shared dynamic of technological advance in each of the partner countries. This allows everyone to make a positive contribution and avoids the perception of being an errant free rider. Rather, countries could establish national specialisa- tions to partake in a more extensive international division of labour.

Just as there was nothing natural about British, or American, or Western eco- nomic and technological leadership in the past, there is nothing natural about the West's economic and technological malaise and decline today. These mature economies could reinvigorate themselves. The precondition for this scenario is an extensive shake-up in the mature economics. The existing apparatus of produc- tion needs dismantling, rather than preserving, in order to facilitate the creation of productive sectors and improved employment appropriate to the twenty-first century.

Our conclusion is that until effective economic solutions are pursued *inside* Western countries, neither of the two epochal economic trends – and the tensions that go with them – is likely to be mitigated. Economic revival at home can reverse the intensification of inter-country competition that has so strained international relations. This would also offer a stronger grounding for independent nations

---

[7]Although Japan is located in the *geographical* East, this book shares its conventional inclusion as part of the post-war political and economic West.

working together to establish an international regime appropriate for today. The way would be opened for durable international economic cooperation between the West, China and the rest of the rising East, as well as with other so far less developed parts of the world. Such cooperation would strengthen each party individually as well as collectively.

Domestic renewal will not come about spontaneously through market mechanisms. Instead, we require public dialogues within Western nations about implementing a long overdue phase of creative destructive change. This can be focussed around launching an *economic transformation programme* to replace outdated and, today, mostly futile industrial strategies. The goal is to drive innovation and create the conditions for new productive sectors and better jobs.

To bring this about, Western nation states need to act in three main areas:

(1) Stopping the policies and mechanisms that have been reinforcing zombie economies. In particular, low-productivity firms, being sustained by cheap debt and providing insecure and inadequately paid employment, should be allowed to contract or close down.
(2) Catalysing investment in innovation, in new businesses and in new sectors to provide future sources of productivity growth, prosperity and better employment.
(3) Providing income and other support for workers and their families during the transition from their existing inadequately paid, insecure employment into high-productivity better paid jobs.

Because economic renewal is bound to be a painful process, its successful implementation requires both popular commitment and government answerability. At a time when many citizens have understandably become suspicious of existing politicians, the precondition for economic transformation is a political transformation that connects the demos to the polity it elects. Successful programmes for renewal need to be bottom-up, democratic and accountable, not top-down, autocratic and technocratic.

Ordinary men and women on the ground in local communities and workplaces are best placed to appreciate how to rejuvenate their areas. They will still need the collective resources of larger society to implement these plans. This is why a production transformation strategy needs national funding and coordination. The nation state remains the only effective channel for democratic engagement and genuine accountability. This brings us back to the core reason the globalist influence is reactionary. Despite globalism's democratic claims, its dismissal of the nation state and national sovereignty is essentially detrimental to invigorating democracy.

Without restoring active participatory democracy, society loses the necessary means for changing the world for the better. Stopping the drift to war relies on strong, autonomous, democratic, national polities cooperating together. In contrast, weak societies where there seems to be no escape from depression and where most people feel ignored and estranged from politics are prone to international conflict. Fears and desperation can be easily exploited towards blaming the foreigner, whether the migrant from Syria, Ghana or Venezuela, or the "Yellow Peril" Beijing regime.

The scholar Graham Allison has explored the "Thucydides' trap" across the centuries (Allison, 2017). He found that in 12 of 16 historical precedents of rivalry between established and rising powers, the trap ended in conflict. Can the United States and China, the West and the East, today escape this fate? A successful, peaceful transition to a new international settlement *can* happen, but it needs reasoned humans acting through their nation states to bring about some vital changes. The immediate priority in the mature parts of the world should be their domestic political, cultural and economic metamorphosis. This can provide the platform that is fit for forging the democratic internationalism capable of realising genuine worldwide collaboration.

Part 1

A World of Rules

Chapter 1

Making the Rules-based International Order

Globalists are committed to the ascendancy of a rules-based institutional international order over the powers of individual nation states. The subordination of the nation state to a global framework was the legacy of the economic and political turmoil of the mid-twentieth century. Early theorists of globalisation attributed this disorder in large part to the turbulent impact of mass democracy.

Restricting the scope of national sovereignty reflects a fatalistic outlook towards the domination of global market forces and a lack of confidence in human agency in commanding economic factors. The elevation of the rule of law and the power of the judiciary – in both national and supranational bodies – over the authority of democratically elected national governments has become a pervasive feature of governance in the advanced industrial societies.

More than 70 years after the end of the Second World War and the subsequent codification of a new framework of global authority, the shifting balance of international economic power is a cause of growing tensions within the established order. In response to a long period of stagnation and political exhaustion, the West's status quo powers are inclined to cling to the structures within which they flourished in the post-war decades, using the rules selectively and pragmatically to protect their enfeebled positions.

It is symptomatic, for instance, that it was the United States and the EU that brought about the collapse of the reforming Doha round of international trade talks by refusing to reduce their agricultural subsidies at the expense of developing countries (Amadeo, 2019). The old powers also frequently promote their "universal" standards that they have previously defined, which just happen to protect their national interests and hold back the rise of emerging nations (Wijen, 2015).

As a consequence, the rising powers in the rest of the world become frustrated by the restrictions imposed by the prevailing rules and the established institutions. While reluctant to challenge the existing arrangements openly, these advancing countries are starting in a piecemeal and tentative manner to develop parallel systems. This heralds the end of the old order.

In the first part of this book, we examine the emergence of the current rules-based international order, the dogma of the "rule of law", the anti-democratic

Beyond Confrontation: Globalists, Nationalists and Their Discontents, 3–19
Copyright © 2020 by Phil Mullan
All rights of reproduction in any form reserved
doi:10.1108/978-1-83982-560-620200001

roots of neoliberalism and the growing tensions within the old framework. Later, we go on to consider the potential for the nation states of the industrialised powers – and more broadly for political activity – to play a constructive role in reducing the rivalries among these states.

Creating the Post-war Order

War creates as well as destroys. Out of the barbarism and chaos of the twentieth century's world wars, international order was created. Now, the strains within it could precipitate the next conflict. The structures established at the end of the 1939–1945 war were seen as enablers of peace. In practice, they were also the continuation of warfare by non-violent means. The post-1945 order reflected the hierarchy consolidated during wartime. It is now outdated.

What was most distinctive about the post-war system was the way its institutions were built on rules. Its architects sought to outlaw aggression and instead promoted the judicial resolution of international disputes (Anghie, 2004, p. 124; Kennedy, 1987, pp. 282–289). This rules-based approach has permeated international relations ever since (Claude, 1984, p. 57; Williams, 1929, p. 67).

The core presumption behind elevating the role of international law was the belief that law was separate from politics. The post-war planners were attracted to international law as a procedural way to manage relations between nation states and ultimately within them. As an "independent variable", law was not only detached from politics. The post-1945 architects hoped it could constrain the "wrong type" of politics (Trimble, 1990, p. 823).

The attraction to political leaders of an institutionalised rules-based order does not derive from breaches to the rules being easy to prosecute, or the rules' details being simple to comprehend. Authority is derived from the very existence of a *depoliticised* rules-defined order detached from the uncertainties of political contestation.

Furthermore, the apparent autonomy of international law and its accompanying organisations allows them to extend their reach and authority. They feed on themselves (Camilleri & Falk, 1992). Governments are then able to exert influence by drawing upon this authority. This offers the leading countries a less costly and, they hope, non-confrontational way for exercising power, certainly compared to the direct political domination of pre-war colonialism or the mandated territories.

For example, the UN began as an alliance of the victorious nations embedded inside a notionally "universal" organisation (Mazower, 2008, p. 7). Its sympathisers today brush over that there were only 51 original members in 1945, with large parts of Africa and Asia excluded. Such revision helps the UN today to still exert great moral authority on a number of issues.

Although the UN's own website accentuates its core universal principles of "individual liberty", "democracy" and "the rule of law", it is telling that none of these phrases can be found in its founding Charter. At the time it was written, it was easier for critics to expose the rhetoric about international equality as a veil that masked the consolidation of a great power directorate. It was clear then that the bigger countries controlled the UN through the Security Council, the only component with the authority to issue binding resolutions.

League of Nations as Precursor

The earlier response to the end of the "Great War" had been different. That conflict had been precipitated by the breakdown of the late nineteenth century arrangement of global power (Kagan, 2018, p. 26). By the turn of the century, the British hegemon was well in decline and being challenged both by old rivals like France and Russia and the newer industrial economies of the United States, Germany and Japan.

The First World War famously failed to resolve those global imbalances. In 1918, it was not even obvious which of the big powers would in future be adversaries and which would be allies. A month after the fighting ended, US President Woodrow Wilson was frustrated with its wartime partner Britain's refusal to grant the United States freedom of the seas. He warned that if Britain would not come to terms, America would

> build the biggest Navy in the world, matching theirs and exceeding it … and if they would not limit it, there would be another and more terrible war and England would be wiped off the face of the map. (Tooze, 2015, p. 268)

Antagonistic feelings were mutual. Two years later British Prime Minister David Lloyd George was so irritated with America's uncooperative stance in Europe that he considered strengthening the Anglo-Japanese alliance instead. The US secretary of state had a "blue fit" in response (Tooze, 2015, p. 395). Meanwhile, London and Paris clashed over the German reparations question with France adopting a more punitive position partly because of its experiences of German, and previously Prussian, land invasions. France's unilateral invasion of the Ruhr as its enforcement of the Versailles Treaty made United Kingdom–French relations particularly fraught. An expanded Royal Air Force was agreed by the UK parliament in 1923 with the principle mission of deterring a *French* attack on Britain (Howard, 1972, pp. 81–84).

Subsequently, the big three victor nations were unable to agree how to incorporate a potentially resurgent Germany, a rising industrial Japan, or a Mussolini-led Italy. For example, when in 1931, US President Herbert Hoover proposed to freeze all political debts to alleviate the pressure on a Germany in emergency economic conditions, France initially vetoed the plan. London and Washington were outraged. This was symptomatic of the abject weakness of the inter-war system (Eichengreen, 1992, p. 278). Hoover speculated that he could see the possibility of an Anglo-German alignment, possibly including the United States, against France (Tooze, 2015, p. 496).

Such national divisions were aggravated by the shell-shocked state of the leading ruling classes, especially of the major European countries. The fighting had not only physically devastated large regions of the continent but also severely weakened Europe's claims to moral superiority (Anghie, 2004, p. 138).

Writing while the bloodshed continued, the anti-colonial writer Henry Brailsford summed up the profound impact on the political classes. The war "struck us with surprise as the thing it is, an anachronism, an absolute barbarity, a blot on civilisation" (Brailsford, 2012, pp. 1–2). The warfare itself, reinforced by the punitive "peace" imposed on the losers, tarnished trust in Enlightenment values. Millions of lives had been lost, but for what? For a "botched civilization" as Ezra Pound put it, "for an old bitch gone in the teeth" (Kagan, 2018, p. 18).

The confidence of the political elites of all combatant nations was so shaken that it destroyed belief in the normality of international peace (Kennedy, 1987, p. 901). This sense of disarray and loss of control stimulated desperate efforts to try to avoid the return of armed conflict. War was the impetus driving mankind to absolve itself by establishing superior arrangements (Mangone, 1954, p. 167). The League of Nations that ensued was the first time leading powers had proposed a permanent *world organisation* to address the classic dilemma of war and peace.

In contrast to what followed later in the century, this experiment in international governance was not launched as an antidote to nationalism but as its expression (Mazower, 2019). Promoted most actively by Wilson, this novel departure in international affairs garnered support not just from the leaders of Britain and France but also, as the bloodshed dragged on, from those of Germany and Austria. The objective of the League was to prevent nations fighting, while guaranteeing national territorial integrity and political independence (Mazower, 2013, pp. 116–117).

Also in contrast to the approach taken with post-Second World War international institutions, Wilson sought to keep power with the *politicians*, rather than give it to lawyers. Departing from the legalist tradition in America Wilson envisaged the League as a forum for quasi-parliamentary deliberations, rather than a judicial court to deliver judgements. What mattered were "values", not legal codes. He preferred to put his trust in people and their political representatives, rather than in abstract law (Mazower, 2013, pp. 119–122).

Although in late 1919, the US Senate famously rejected American participation, the League broadly followed the Wilsonian non-legalist format (Wertheim, 2012). Lloyd George and the other British politicians who took over leadership mostly shared Wilson's distrust of law not least because they worried international law might constrain British colonial activities (Mazower, 2013, p. 128). When an international court was eventually set up in 1922 under the League's auspices, it was an insubstantial body with meagre enforcement mechanisms over inter-country disputes.

Lessons for the 1940s

The failure of the League's relatively loose system to prevent conflict encouraged a different approach in the 1940s. In the aftermath of fascism, the Holocaust, urban aerial bombing and the atomic bomb, the victorious political classes' moral purpose and authority was further eroded. Their deeper gloom was offset by a stronger determination to achieve an effective international organisation (Claude, 1984, p. 57).

Influenced by emerging globalist ideas, they favoured a strict *rules-based regime* further removed from the sway of national politics than the League had been. A robust international authority was proposed with the power to make and enforce rules and laws (Mazower, 2013, p. 187; Patrick, 2008).

While governing through rules has been the globalist norm since the Second World War, it had precedents. The inter-war desire by Britain, France, Germany and other developed countries to return to the pre-1914 gold standard expressed the pre-existing political affinity for rules. Despite John Maynard Keynes presciently calling it a "barbarous relic" in 1923, in the immediate post-1918 period rejoining a gold standard was a mostly uncontentious goal. By the end of 1925, 35 currencies were either officially convertible into gold or had been stable against it for at least a year (Tooze, 2015, p. 465). Return was seen as pursuing a rule that had in effect only been "suspended" because of the emergency contingent circumstances of war.

Re-adoption of the standard was thought to impose some necessary political "discipline" through binding fiscal and monetary policy actions. In this spirit, Montagu Norman as Governor of the Bank of England saw the return to gold as "knaveproof" (Crafts, 2018). A common adherence to the gold standard by developed countries created a de facto international rule.

It is pertinent for an appreciation of the deeper significance of rules today that the essence of the gold standard rule was a *domestic* commitment mechanism. Alignment limited discretionary state policies at home. It tied the hands of government, thereby shielding the political class from democratic pressures to abandon "hard-money" deflationary policies. In fact, the earlier breakdown of the gold standard in 1914 has been partly attributed to the rise of democracy. The newly enfranchised masses had been suffering the most from the austerity imposed to adhere to the rule (Bordo & Kydland, 1995, pp. 430, 457, 459).

The stubborn inter-war adherence to following the gold standard rules contributed to the tensions that resulted in the resumption of global conflict in 1939. Nevertheless, this lesson about the dangers of rule following was not learnt. Efforts were redoubled in the aftermath of the 1939–1945 bloodbaths to govern through a rule-organised regime.

Peace after the war became associated with neutral, non-political institutionalisation. The new architects of order thought the League's incapacity to fetter sovereign authority had been a core deficiency. The inter-war system was perceived as having allowed too much scope for the political process at the expense of international law. The objective now was to find a legalistic organisational means of channelling the pursuit of national sovereign interests into international cooperation.

For instance, majoritarian voting was initially favoured in the UN instead of the previous practice of unanimous voting. The latter was regarded as an earlier error derived from sovereign autonomy that had stymied inter-war efforts at cooperation[1] (Kennedy, 1987, pp. 862, 931–933, 964).

---

[1] By the 1960s, the fashion shifted again to favour "consensus" decision-making. This followed decolonisation and the more than doubling in the number of member states. Majority voting was now regarded as problematic by the big powers as it left them likely to be outvoted in the General Assembly by the less developed countries.

This depoliticised rules-based approach to international order was reinforced by the elites' greater antipathy to politics in general. It was foreshadowed by late 1930s literature that attributed the failure of the League to its emasculation by the intrusion of ideology and power politics (Kennedy, 1987, pp. 876–877). Alongside concerns about great power manoeuvrings, the other large influence on the institution makers of the 1940s was their distrust of *popular* politics, which they associated with fascism and violence. They were motivated by the thought of nationalism stirring people up into frenzied fears and taking inhuman actions against others.[2]

Their plainspoken reaction to the horrors of combat and the Holocaust identified German nationalism as the cause. Denunciations of it morphed into an intellectual suspicion of nationalism in general and especially the nationalism driving mass movements. This represented a distinctive and thoroughly hostile approach to nationalism.

Following this particular antagonistic interpretation of nationalism, those planning the international post-war systems assumed that sensible national political elites, like themselves, could be managed through institutionalised cooperation. They sought to reverse the inter-war privileging of politics over law with the opposite: the dominance of law over politics. They turned to rely on rules-based institutions that could regulate and control relations not only directly between countries but also, indirectly, within them. Deferring to international rules and decisions insulated national politicians from their own people. This set in process the mode for elites not only delegating their powers to supranational organisations but also using these institutions to uphold their authority at home as well as abroad.

This post-Second World War denigration of domestic politics was not simply the product of the founders' will. It was more easily realised because of the seachange in political life compared to the end of the First World War. Then, inspired by the Bolshevik Revolution of 1917, working-class revolts were taking place all across Europe. The idea then that politics could be sidelined might have appealed to elites, but it would have been fanciful.

In contrast by the end of the Second World War, mass politics had been neutered or incapacitated in most places. Across Europe radical politics and working-class organisations had suffered huge defeats inflicted by fascism and militarism. Working-class resistance that survived the conflict was soon brutally suppressed, as in Greece. The new international order was made possible by a more quiescent political environment, which it then helped consolidate.

The new institutional regime secured the position of the victorious national elites domestically as much as it sought to maintain peace. It acted as a "safe repository for our cultural fears". At the same time, the post-war institutions seemed to "express an elaborate anti-intellectualism, constantly enslaving our thought ... allowing us to forget what we know to be true about the law and

---

[2]This prefigures the way many globalists today seem agitated to a greater extent by people being "duped" by populists than they are by intensifying geopolitical tensions.

politics of our situation" (Kennedy, 1987, p. 988). The elites were mitigating their diminished confidence and purpose through a reliance on institutional security and cohesion.

The Juridification of International Relations

It used to be uncontroversial in the modern age, at least before the EU, that domestic authorities make domestic laws. Meanwhile, stronger countries made the international law, something Immanuel Kant had criticised in his influential essay on "perpetual peace" more than two centuries ago (Kant, 2016). Over the passage of time, and especially since 1945, the line between domestic and international law has blurred. International law has come to assume a higher status than the national. As a result, international legal obligations can override national political accountability.

Throughout modern times, the use of anti-war and universal ideals to justify international law has been common. Even today, international law is often presented as facilitating the management of relations between equal nations. In practice, though it has always expressed relations of power between countries. As a result, the political domination of one country by another has often been obscured or even justified through the language of international law. This has been simply taking different forms with changing political and cultural circumstances (Anghie, 2004, p. xi).

In the late nineteenth century, for instance, international law embraced the "civilising mission" of colonialism with regard to native peoples, justifying occupations by the imperialist countries. Subsequently, the League of Nation's Mandate System was established, primarily for the ex-colonies of Germany and the Ottomans. Using less racial language than had been the norm before 1914, the system was motivated as protecting and guiding the interests of backward peoples as a "sacred trust of civilisation".

The victors of 1918 would agree which advanced nation would be the mandatory power in a particular territory, sometimes on a shared basis. The chosen country was tasked to provide tutelage and promote the people's welfare and national development. Although this was a modification to nineteenth century interventionism, it was also its continuation.

The Mandate System experimented with new legal techniques and instruments to govern the dominated territories from outside. These experiences were highly influential in extending the project of international justice after 1945. The UN Trusteeship System was the strict legal successor to the League's Mandate System. However, in terms of the expansion of international jurisprudence, it was the Bretton Woods institutions of the IMF and the World Bank that were its ideological successors (Anghie, 2004, pp. 120, 146, 191).

International judicial bodies have increasingly been granted authority to override national legislation, especially in the economic arena. The greater internationalisation of capital during the twentieth century gave a further impetus to codifying international law. In the 1920s, Lord McNair, later an International Court of Justice (ICJ) judge, anticipated that the more "important international economic interests grow, the more International Law will grow" (McNair, 1928, p. 103).

After the Second World War, the victors had more pressing concerns than cross-border capital flows. They wanted to prevent a recurrence of the unilateral military incursions of the 1930s. Making all countries abide by international law seemed to provide a fix. Law offered an autonomous body of rules that could serve as a mechanism of restraint against unruly and potentially violent governments.

International Judicial Institutions

At the end of the Second World War, the Nuremburg and Tokyo war crimes trials offered a practical example of how a globalist supranational judicial process could get results (Sellars, 2010). From these precedents, the juridification of international relations has produced multiple legal bodies operating across borders. As a consequence, international institutional action is increasingly "cleansed of politics" (Kennedy, 1987, p. 986). Political considerations are literally over-ruled, undermining sovereignty.

One significant judicial mechanism has been the extension of dispute resolution. When in 1995 the General Agreement on Tariffs and Trade (GATT) was transformed into the WTO, this included more powerful Disputes Settlement and Appellate bodies. These dispute resolution procedures attain the status of trade law, thereby infringing national sovereignty and limiting the democratic control of a country's trade policies.

Jan Tumlir, an international law theorist and long-serving director of economic research at GATT from 1967 to 1985, had previously summed up "the crucial weakness" of the GATT system as its inability to provide an authoritative interpretation of its rules (Tumlir, as cited in Slobodian, 2018, p. 256). The constitution of the WTO sought to rectify that deficiency. It established new commercial norms and the means to enforce them through stronger arbitration procedures (Mazower, 2013, p. 361).

For instance, under GATT, a losing party in a dispute still had an effective veto over an adverse recommendation, stopping it from having the force of law. Instead under the WTO regime, it takes a consensus to *block* adoption of a Disputes Settlement Body recommendation. This effectively gives the winning party control over any attempt at blockage (Murphy, 2004, p. 50).

The victor in a WTO dispute also has the power to veto any move to reject a decision by the Appellate Body. This extended disputes settlement system transformed GATT's predominantly advisory role into a stronger legalistic, rules-orientated mechanism. Through this shift, the WTO gains a "quasi-judicial and quasi-constitutional aura" (McBride, 2011, p. 28).

One of the most developed and active examples of international juridification is the European Court of Justice (ECJ). The distinguished political scientist Gerda Falkner has explained that the ECJ's "judicial policy-making" is almost irreversible through political processes. She characterised this as a "court-decision trap" meaning that courts increasingly act in place of politics accelerating the erosion of political decision-making (Falkner, 2011, pp. 5, 220, 251).

When based on the ECJ's interpretation of an EU Treaty provision, it takes an extremely high hurdle to overturn one of its decisions. Unanimous agreement by all the heads of government is required, subsequently ratified by every member state's parliament. As a result, the ECJ is able to exercise "enormous political influence" on substantive policies, more than the highest domestic court could (Falkner, 2011, pp. 5, 247).

This illustrates how supranational law can override national law within the domestic courts. The high-profile operations of the ECJ illustrate how European law always take precedence over any norms of national law, including the constitutions of member states. The principle of European law prevailing over national law has actually been around since 1964 when it was decided that otherwise "the legal basis of the community itself (would be) called into question" (ECJ, 1964).

But this doesn't mean globalists are always dismissive of the domestic courts. On the contrary, many recognise that domestic courts have the advantage over international ones of a greater semblance of legitimacy. More importantly, domestic judges are believed to be more reliable than democratic governments for enforcing international law (Tumlir, as cited in Slobodian, 2018, p. 254). This indicates that for globalists, the denigration of the political by the law assumes even greater importance than the promotion of the supranational *per se*.

The "Rule of Law" or the Power of the People

Globalists often demonstrate their liberalism through their support of the "rule of law". However, the meaning of this phrase is probably "less clear today than ever before" (Fallon, 1997, p. 97). When we hear these words so often today, we should consider this malleability. Law reflects power so, which law rules? A leader of the critical legal studies movement has suggested that through elevating procedural justice, appealing to the rule of law enables the powerful to "manipulate its forms to their own advantage" (Horwitz, 1977, pp. 561, 566).

Historically, there is no doubt that the rule of law principle *was* a crucial element in the spread of liberty and freedom. This juridical view of freedom was well captured by the eminent inter-war Supreme Court Justice Louis Brandeis. He observed that "the history of liberty is to a large extent the history of procedural observances"[3] (Tumlir, 1983a, p. 79).

The key feature of the principle was that everyone is equal before the law. Officials, as well as ordinary citizens, should be subject to its dictates (Murphy, 2004, p. 2). Nobody – the richest businessperson or the foremost politician – should be "above the law". In this meaning, the rule of law guards against the arbitrary exercise of power. In the past, it has certainly helped to promote a healthy scepticism towards the rulers by those ruled.

Historically too, the "rule of law" was associated with democratic advances. With its origins in ancient Athens and the Roman Republic, it was re-introduced

---

[3]Possibly, Brandeis was quoting his close colleague Justice Felix Frankfurter, to whom this statement has also been attributed.

in modern times through Britain's Revolution of 1688. By removing the "divine" rights of kings and the political privileges of the aristocrats, this episode sowed the seeds of the beginnings of political democracy. Political power could only be exercised according to procedures and constraints prescribed by publicly known laws. The rule of law required all persons, including governmental officials, to obey the laws and to be accountable through the courts.

Furthermore, laws could be changed only through constitutional procedures and could not be nullified nor overridden by individual fiat. This principle still provides an important protection against oligarchy and despotism and the defence of minority rights. However, that positive role has been offset over the past century as it has been used to a greater degree to limit democratic practices.

Regressive, anti-democratic consequences from pursuing the "rule of law" are not new. It was evident, for instance, in the context of the British colonies and neo-colonies. The colonial administrator John Sydenham Furnivall described how this worked. After a 30-year career in Burma, he left service in the early 1930s to become a scholar critical of Western imperial policies. Dubbed a "reluctant imperialist", he challenged the then-conventional view that economic development was the precondition for self-government and democracy in colonised territories. He argued the reverse: begin with autonomy, and social and economic development would follow.

From his pro-democracy perspective, Furnivall (1948) assessed that the "rule of law" imposed by Western powers on their colonies was mostly designed simply to promote commerce. He explained how this approach to the rule of law could not empower and unite people. Instead, it expanded economic activity at the expense of the social and political integrity of colonial society (Anghie, 2004, p. 193).

Thus, the rule of law cannot be regarded as universally progressive because it means different things in different social and political contexts. Consider a definition of liberalism suggested by the political scientist Francis Fukuyama: having "generally accepted rules that put clear limits on the way that the [nation] state can exercise power" (Fukuyama, 2017). This sounds like a sensible check on authoritarianism, but the emphasis on "clear limits" embodies the potential for counterposing the rule *of* law to rule *by* democratic will.

With the spread of mass suffrage in the twentieth century, the idea of putting constraints and limits on what rulers can do turned into putting constraints and limits on the actions of elected governments. This could justify overriding a government's democratic mandate. In this context, the meaning of the rule of law shifts to take precedence over rule by law – that is, by law-making that is politically accountable to the voters.

In the 1930s, US President Franklin Delano Roosevelt (FDR) came up against this potential judicial block to liberal democracy. Roosevelt had been elected in 1932 with a mandate to combat the effects of the Great Depression. The Supreme Court, however, ruled against some of his New Deal measures as being "unconstitutional" and only narrowly endorsed others by a five to four spilt decision (Acemoglu & Robinson, 2012, pp. 325–328).

After being reelected in 1936 with an even larger majority, Roosevelt accused the Supreme Court as having been "acting not as a judicial body, but as a policymaking one". His proposed remedy of replacing Supreme Court justices could not get legislative approval – another part of the American "checks and balances" system. However, because of his renewed electoral mandate, the Supreme Court felt compelled to back down and approve his earlier New Deal policies.

Roosevelt's clash with the courts in the 1930s anticipated the anti-democratic tendencies in the post-1945 evolution of the rule of law. By appealing to the sanctity of the rule of law, juridified institutions can see themselves as justified in overruling the wishes of the people expressed through popular votes and elections. The responsibility of governments to act on their electoral mandates is devalued by insisting on their overriding responsibility to the law.

To take a recent example, Paul Tucker, former deputy governor of the Bank of England, described how since the 1980s economists have openly argued that the rule of law should have priority over democracy. This is motivated as avoiding the "volatility and excesses of majoritarian policy making" imperilling property rights (Tucker, 2018, p. 175).

This use of the law defends stability and "free market prosperity" from interference in economic matters, even when it is democratically decided. Tucker pointed out that this conception of the law as rules that outweigh the political accountability of government is one that unites classic neoliberals with social democratic liberals like John Rawls.

The Law-based Erosion of Sovereignty

Appeals to the *international* rule of law draw out the dangers to democratic popular sovereignty. Early in the new millennium, the UN Secretary-General described the rule of law as:

> (A) principle of governance in which all persons, institutions and entities, public and private, including the State itself, are accountable to laws that are publicly promulgated, equally enforced and independently adjudicated, and which are consistent with international human rights norms and standards. (UN, 2004)

Again, on the surface, this does not sound undemocratic. Institutions of government *should* be bound by the rule of law. Governments should not be free to flout laws that apply to others. But another essential democratic principle is that governments should be accountable to their electorates. The laws to be followed should be those that the people agree with. If enough people did not vote for a law, or subsequently disagreed with it, they can at the next election replace the government and mandate change to the law.

However, this relationship is at best blurred or subverted when non-elected UN officials assert that the law they want governments to follow has to be in accord with "international" standards. When those often vague and imprecise international norms and standards are given an effective veto over domestic legislation, people's decision-making capacities are being overridden.

National government deference to the international institutional regime becomes corrosive to democracy. Privileging unelected international authority undermines the accountability of national authority. Citizens' diminished role in decision-making is reinforced when we are continually told that international organisations are the real peacemakers and the true engineers of prosperity. Criticising or challenging these institutions appear almost sacrilegious.

Pursuing the international rule of law can also justify militaristic denials of sovereignty. When national governments are deemed to have fallen short of meeting internationally set criteria, external intervention in the affairs of sovereign states becomes legitimate. Many nations have been invaded because of claims they were in "breach of the law", including in recent times Somalia, Serbia, Iraq, Libya and Syria. The appeal to law becomes a "vocabulary of permissions, a means of asserting power and control that normalizes the debatable and justifies the exception" (Mazower, 2013, p. 404).

The assumed authority of international institutions *over* national governments obscures from where their power derives. These organisations are strong or weak depending on the dynamic of relations between their member states. An institutional order can only reflect the forces and pressures of its member nations. The appearance of autonomy ignores that institutions cannot do much when the most powerful member states evade them.

For instance, the League of Nations could not prevent the Second World War not because of an institutional defect but because the most advanced industrial nations were on a collision course. This developed out of the economic and geopolitical conflicts of the time, which institutional commitments could not prevent.

Indicative too of the inter-war balance of national forces was the fate of the General Treaty for Renunciation of War as an Instrument of National Policy of 1928, usually known as the Kellogg–Briand Pact. Its many signatory nations included all the leading Second World War combatants pledged to use only peaceful means to settle disputes. But particular signatories simply ignored this. For instance, only three years later Japan invaded Manchuria.

Such anti-war legal agreements embody an intrinsic paradox of enforcement. Do the agreements justify military intervention to reverse militaristic acts by member states? "Stopping" a war would become a pretext for war. In addition to exposing the naivety of a legalistic bloc to war, this particular pact helped blur the distinction between war and peace. Countries retained their League membership through waging wars without declaring them.

The continuing national essence of international organisation explains a conundrum about the international rule of law. Given the frequent weakness of enforcement sanctions, some legal scholars ponder why it is that national governments *ever* comply with it. The academic discussion on the reasons for compliance has usually focussed on the nature of relations between states and on factors like international reputation (Guzman, 2002). This misses the important *domestic* driver for national compliance, with even graver implications for the status of sovereignty.

The system of international law appeals to so many national politicians because the insistence on legalistic process helps governments take difficult decisions. They can avoid having to explain and uphold the substance of their actions to the public. Instead, they are able to say, "we have to implement international law".

Governments that feel unable to win arguments at home are still able to impose their authority via their acquiescence to rightful international institutions. Showing respect for the "rule of international law" can legitimate the practical exercise of national state power, even when there is no domestic mandate. The appeal to international law confers validity on government decisions just because it is "the law", in the same way that people obey most domestic laws. In both instances, a permanent fear of punishment is not necessary (Trimble, 1990, pp. 833–834, 839).

National politicians can invoke international law to *take precedence* in domestic affairs. When the international rules restrain, or appear to restrain a government from doing something that it would prefer not to do, it can give politicians a way out: an international law *excuse*. This happened frequently in Britain within the EU.

British governments of all stripes would decline to take action on the basis that they were constrained by EU regulations. For instance, they often invoked EU state aid rules to preclude certain industrial policy measures. This became known as the "EU excuse" (Heartfield, 2013, pp. 66–70). The state aid and other EU rules were, in fact, less restrictive than British governments suggested (Morris & Kibasi, 2019). Regardless, citing them provided cover for politicians who had become remote from their electorates.

This affirms how it has often been national politicians, rather than globalist technocrats, who have done most to torpedo people's sovereign rights. The more infringing, or apparently infringing, upon sovereignty that an international agreement is, the better it can serve the national officeholders who subscribe to it. Sometimes, this is even the *motivation* behind signing new international treaties. An early instance covered an unusual policy area: the hunting of birds.

Soon after being passed in 1918, several US states challenged the constitutionality of federal law that regulated the hunting of migratory ducks. In order to get around domestic opposition, the federal government signed an international treaty with Britain. Britain went along with this on the pretext it was acting on behalf of its imperial possession, Canada, the source and destination of the migrating waterfowl. This treaty required the American government to enact laws regulating the protection of migratory birds, an obligation that it just happened to fulfil through its existing law.

In a famous 1920 US Supreme Court ruling Missouri v Holland,[4] the Court effectively ruled that international treaties took precedence over constitutional arguments in taking domestic political actions (Murphy, 2004, pp. 83–85). Despite later congressional attempts to reverse this, and subsequent ambiguous court rulings, this remains the legal position within the "isolationist" United States.

---

[4]Holland here was the name of an American game warden, not the country.

This illustrates that American lawmakers can fall back on their international "obligations" as much as governments of smaller nations.

The prime casualty of international juridification is not national legislators but popular sovereignty and democratic accountability. It is true that governments that enter into international agreements and transfer some power to international institutions are doing so *through* the exercise of formal national sovereignty. And when they give away some of their authority, it is only "lent". A government is able to take it back by rescinding a particular treaty or leaving an organisation. In 2019, for instance, the Japanese government withdrew from the International Whaling Commission that had banned commercial whaling in 1982 in order to resume it. Today, it still remains quite feasible to restore legal sovereignty.

But when a government hides behind international agreements to avoid engagement with its electorate, popular sovereignty is weakened in substance. This undermining of democracy is compounded when the increasing reach of international jurisdiction interweaves it so closely with domestic law as to blur responsibility. It becomes harder to demonstrate the primacy of domestic law, which used to be one of the cardinal premises of sovereignty. The overall effect of national politicians outsourcing their power and authority to diverse international institutions is a practical reconstitution of sovereignty, whatever its legal status (Camilleri & Falk, 1992, pp. 33, 99).

Although globalists discuss respect for international law as almost synonymous with the exercise of democracy, it differs qualitatively from the democratic process of domestic law-making. Compared to the national law of modern democratic states, international law lacks even a semblance of democratic legitimacy. There is no elected international legislature to make it, nor popularly accountable international executive to enforce it. In the EU, for instance, the European Commission, not the European Parliament, is responsible for planning, preparing, proposing and implementing European law. Nevertheless, international "non-political" judiciaries increasingly interpret and thereby develop the law.

From the perspective of the 2010s, it has become clearer that one of the most troubling features of the post-war rules-based order has been the watering down of sovereignty. This tendency, though, had been implicit from the start. The rules-driven approach adopted in the shadow of war always had the potential for international law and institutions to take precedence over national decision-making and thereby encroach on sovereignty.

Human Rights as a Tool Undermining Sovereignty

This was not immediately evident: support for nation states remained the dominant convention. The founding Charter of the UN endorsed the principles of "self-determination of peoples" and "sovereign equality" for all its members. However, contrary to a common presumption, the Charter did not establish self-determination *as a right*, only as a "principle" to aspire to. The long-term ramifications, whether intended or not by all the drafters, was that national self-determination and sovereignty were later trumped by international obligations, such as human rights or environmental stipulations.

Another reason this possibility wasn't quickly realised was that for a long time, supranational bodies seemed to lack the clout to do much intruding on national rights. In particular, the UN, as the supreme international governance institution, was frequently hamstrung. It was common for one or more of the big five to veto Security Council resolutions decisions, often in line with Cold War objectives.

In practice though, the top nations soon adopted an equivocal stance on sovereignty, whether acting through the UN as the "blue helmets" or directly. In particular, a humanitarian appeal to human rights became particularly compelling in justifying outside intervention in a country's sovereign internal affairs. The preamble to the UN Charter anticipated this by affirming its faith in "fundamental human rights, in the dignity and worth of the human person". The universal appeal of human rights provided a positive connotation to the authority of the "global" that remains significant to the present (Sellars, 2002).

A well-meaning humanist pledge soon turned into a seemingly innocuous *commitment* to international law. A series of human rights treaties and agreements developed into an imposing body of international human rights legislation. Few countries failed to sign up because the vast majority did want to be castigated as "renegades" on human rights. Once they enlisted, countries were expected to act in accordance with international law, giving away sovereign rights in this area. Their obligations became monitored and implemented by a range of international institutions including the UN Human Rights Council, UN treaty bodies, the Council of Europe and the European Court of Human Rights.

By the 1980s, the encroaching on sovereignty through human rights had become clearer. At the end of the previous decade, US President Jimmy Carter's search for a post-Vietnam foreign policy saw him seize on the concept. Within a decade, the UN General Assembly passed resolution 43/131 that established a "right to intervene" in sovereign countries in dire human rights emergencies.

This shift cannot be explained by the novel discovery of people's rights being violated by their own states. There had been much of this previously – think of slavery, the 1819 Peterloo Massacre, the Irish famine, the legal discrimination against ethnic or religious minorities and many more such happenings. What *was* new was that such events had become the pretext for "humanitarian" intervention by foreign powers.

This was the first time that "victims" had the right to be looked after by someone other than their own national authorities. A couple of years later in 1990 resolution 45/100 asserted the right to create "humanitarian corridors" to aid people in distress (Berman, 2007, p. 249). Granting moral authority to the victims of aggression delegitimised the nation state with the contradictory consequence that ordinary people have less scope to assert their own sovereign rights.

By 1999, drawing on the brutal events in Rwanda, Kosovo and East Timor, the then-UN Secretary-General Kofi Annan gave a seminal interview delineating "Two Concepts of Sovereignty". Arguing for adapting the international system to a different world, he explained that there was greater reason than ever that the UN Charter should protect individual human beings, rather than protect the states that abuse them. By this interpretation, the "individual sovereignty" that he saw enshrined in the UN Charter should now be privileged over state sovereignty that had anyway been redefined by the forces of globalisation (Annan, 1999).

Indicating the bipartisan nature of globalism, former left-wingers like Joschka Fischer, a 1968 radical who became Germany's foreign minister, were instrumental in promoting this type of interventionist "liberal internationalism". Fischer described this as "positive" globalisation. World security, he argued in 2003, could not rely on a globalised economy alone. It depended too on the "globalization of fundamental values, such as human rights ... cultural tolerance ... the rule of law and democracy" (Berman, 2007, p. 285). While right-wingers were often to the fore in welcoming economic globalisation, leftists were most enthusiastic about the cultural globalisation of human rights.

Under the auspices of humanitarianism the UN drew up a "Responsibility to Protect" (R2P) in response to the wars of the 1990s, not least in Bosnia and Rwanda. In the shocked aftermath of the 9/11 terror attacks on the United States, Annan further spelt out the new thinking on state sovereignty. "Today's real borders", he said as he accepted the Nobel Peace Prize in Stockholm, "are not between nations, but between powerful and powerless, free and fettered, privileged and humiliated" (Berman, 2007, pp. 259–260).

With the 2005 adoption of the R2P, the UN was openly overriding national self-determination by sanctioning the use of outside force to intervene in the internal affairs of countries. Sovereignty had becoming conditional upon a government demonstrating to the "good" countries of the world that it was looking after its citizens properly. Governments that failed in this ran the risk of military intervention.

Although armed actions with formal UN Security Council backing remained rare, humanitarian-based UN resolutions provided justification for the West's military incursions, from the Balkans to Iraq, Libya and Syria. When these "bad" governments were attacked, their people not only suffered the most but also found themselves profoundly disempowered.

The shibboleth of human rights has also legitimised the extension of international law into other mundane areas of national public life. Legal scholar Antony Anghie astutely identified the "monumental significance" of international human rights law is that it has enabled international law and institutions to "enter the interior, to address the unconscious and thereby to administer 'civilizing therapy'" to the body politic of the sovereign state (Anghie, 2004, pp. 135, 149).

It is striking that as early as 1948 the UN-inspired Universal Declaration of Human Rights contained language about health care, employment, vacations and other domestic matters that had never before been regarded as within scope of international treaties. International law has now extended to many fields that previously were regulated mostly, or even solely, by domestic law including crime, the environment and family life (Murphy, 2004, p. 6). When areas formerly regarded as within the accountable, domestic jurisdiction of a state are redefined as humanitarian concepts, national sovereignty is further undermined (Anghie, 2004, pp. 114, 250).

Legal intrusions into domestic affairs have established the concept of "universal law". This is when some states explicitly claim jurisdiction over people whose alleged humanitarian crimes were committed outside the boundaries of the prosecuting state, regardless of the nationality of the accused.

This situates the legalisation of human rights as a modern version of the nineteenth century's "civilising mission". Even the notorious former US secretary of state Henry Kissinger baulked at this extension of juridification. He argued that "universal law" substituted "the tyranny of judges for that of governments" (Kissinger, 2001). Old-style militarists criticising the way global relations were being juridified brings home the qualitative transformation of the role of international law.

Ironically, it was left-wingers holding liberal values, not traditional right-wingers, who were now to the fore in imposing their values on others in a manner reminiscent of imperial hegemons. Alongside the appeal of human rights, climate change has also become a mainstream focus for revoking sovereign rights. In 2019, when the Brazilian government seemed to be doing little to stop fires destroying the rainforests, there were suggestions of external UN-sanctioned intervention on behalf of "humanity at large" (Silva, 2019).

These types of interventionist conclusions are typical these days given that there is such widespread disregard for national sovereignty among Western elites of all political shades. We now turn to explain the rise and consolidation of the globalist outlook that has spearheaded this disdainful approach to democratic rights.

Chapter 2

Globalism against Politics

Pretty much every Western country today appears uneasily divided and polarised. Especially since the 2016 votes for Brexit and President Trump, the consensus is that present-day divisions are of a novel type. In this chapter, we agree that countries are divided and examine how a lot of the mainstream commentary has actually contributed to the latest rifts.

Few disagree that the left-versus-right confrontation familiar for over two centuries is no longer defining political debate. The left-right substance came from the essential divide of capitalist social existence, between the working class and its bossing bourgeois class (Caryl, 2016). While we still have social segmentation, it is more muddled than 50, never mind 200, years ago. Both the main classes have lost social coherence and are no longer associated with distinctive political thinking. Competing left-right visions of a better society have dissipated replaced for a time by blurred "third way" managerial governance (Babones, 2018).

Today's schisms are assessed variously as between the "people" and the "elites", between the "haves" and the "have-nots", between "liberal internationalists" and "populist isolationists", and between the "Anywheres" and the "Somewheres" (Goodhart, 2017, p. 66). The *gilets jaunes* movement in France from late 2018 well characterised these new times. Begun as a protest against fuel tax increases, it soon evolved into a movement opposing President Emmanuel Macron and the whole Paris-based establishment.

This had parallels to the British and American votes two years earlier, and subsequently to how many German voters from the east of the country have been rejecting the mainstream German Christian democratic and social democratic parties. The big drivers of these shifts in allegiance are not economic. Instead, the revolts all expressed popular discontent with the status quo, though taking different forms in different circumstances. Sometimes, it appeared as a rural backlash against urban elites, between less-educated rural populations and better-educated urbanites. A common feature is of ordinary people showing resentment towards metropolitan elites because of being ignored, looked down upon and feeling like second-class citizens (Zakaria, 2018).

One of the recurring contenders for describing the new dividing line in Western politics is between globalists and nationalists, between globalism and nationalism. Soon after Trump's election victory *The Wall Street Journal* described how

Beyond Confrontation: Globalists, Nationalists and Their Discontents, 21–39
Copyright © 2020 by Phil Mullan
All rights of reproduction in any form reserved
doi:10.1108/978-1-83982-560-620200004

> From Brexit to Trump to the rise of nationalist parties across
> Europe, the old division between left and right is giving way to
> a battle between self-styled patriots and confounded globalists.
> (Ip, 2017)

The battle between nationalism and globalism is thought to have a "new intensity" (Bremmer, 2018, p. 12; Eatwell & Goodwin, 2018).

"Nationalists" and "nationalism" are familiar terms, even though as noted in the previous chapter they embody different connotations for people. In contrast, the terms "globalists" and "globalism" are of later origin. Some identify globalists as the "Davos crowd", the people who gather in Switzerland every January at meetings of the World Economic Forum. Many fly in by private jet, signifying they are the crème de la crème of the global elite. They lead big corporations and run international institutions like the IMF, the WTO and the EU. But there are many more globalists than attendees at Davos.

These include also most of the people running *national* governments, official organisations and other state institutions within the advanced industrial countries. Macron personifies this overlap between the global and the national (Momtaz, 2019). He identifies himself as the most self-avowedly globalist of the Western leaders and Europe's strongest bulwark against "xenophobic populism". Attacking Trump at the UN General Assembly in 2018, Macron claimed that nationalism "always leads to defeat" (Pavia & Philp, 2018). He presents himself as a free trader, an economic liberal and an internationalist (Collins, 2019).

But he's also a French nationalist and an EU protectionist, seeking to support the needs of French capitalism. Macron wants to reform the EU and the eurozone to make it stable. This just happens to serve France's national interests, especially if the wealthier Germans pay out extra funds. While described as a "neoliberal", he has eagerly used the state apparatus to pursue French capitalism's interests at home – including changes to labour legislation – as well as abroad (Fassin, 2019). The Mirage and Rafale fighter jets Macron sent to bomb Syria in April 2018 were not "global" planes. They had the French tricolour on their tails.

Globalists comprise politicians, commentators, business people, central bankers and academics. They follow Keynesian, monetarist or free market economics and come from across the political spectrum. For instance, presidents of the European Commission have hailed from communist and from conservative backgrounds. José Manuel Barroso, the president for a decade from 2004, was a former Maoist leader, while his two successors, Jean-Claude Juncker and Ursula von der Leyen, originate from right-wing Christian democracy.

Globalists are not a fixed group and are united by their sympathy to the outlook, values and opinions that have dominated Western culture and politics since the 1980s. They are distinguished by their focus on the *transnational* as being decisive in recent economic, social and cultural developments. They are committed to the post-war international order and institutions.

It is striking that it has been globalists who have emphasised the new divide as one between nationalism and globalism. Sometimes, they describe it as between "closed" and "open" (*The Economist*, 2016a), between anti- and pro-globalisation electorates (Haugh, Kopoin, Rusticelli, Turner & Dutu, 2016, p. 26), and between opponents and supporters of the "liberal, rules-based world order" (Sandbu, 2017). This underscores that globalism has achieved meaning mostly through what it sets itself against: nationalism.

The Second World War and the struggle against fascism were globalism's formative experiences. As described earlier, Western elites have increasingly attributed the destructiveness of the twentieth century's world wars to the force of extreme nationalism rather than to conflicts between imperialist countries. This antipathy to nationalism made the political classes receptive to the modern notions of globalisation. In turn, the globalisation thesis gives their discomfort with the national an intellectual rationale.

In globalist thinking, to be "nationalist" has become a term of abuse. For instance, when Juncker lamented Europe's slowness in going beyond an underdeveloped "club of nations", he proclaimed that "nationalism is poison". Reiterating his revulsion with nationalist thinking, he alleged that "historically, when nationalist drives are reborn, Europe usually ends up at war" (Pérez, 2017).

Nationalism is not only condemned as the source of the horrors of the previous century but also as a clear and present danger now. Previously alerting us to similarities he saw between today's nationalism and that which brought about the First World War, Juncker (2013) warned, "The demons haven't been banished; they are merely sleeping".

Some people who self-describe as nationalist *are* insular and narrow-minded. But others are tolerant and internationalist. Not only is nationalism not the opposite of internationalism, it is often its consort. This didn't used to be a controversial point. Winston Churchill, for example, a staunch British nationalist, forged an *international* wartime alliance alongside America and the Soviet Union. Today's globalists forget that political nationalism was contemporary to the first wave of "globalisation" at the end of the nineteenth century. Lots of nationalists then were internationalist-minded.

Dictionaries tell us that the original meaning of nationalism, from the late eighteenth into the twentieth centuries, had a significant overlap with patriotism: devotion to one's country. Ideologically, nationalism went beyond patriotism to stress the "autonomy, independence and sovereignty of the nation" (Halikiopoulou & Vasilopoulou, 2011, p. 1). Politically, nationalism also incorporated the goal of advancing a common national interest through the vehicle of the state.

The concepts of reason and rationality emanating from the Enlightenment had inspired a fresh spirit of progress. The accompanying turn towards the state was most strikingly articulated in the work of Hegel, who represented the nation state as the realisation of human reason (Furedi, 2016). The nation state became the institution through which popular sovereignty gained meaning.

Initially, it was the achievement of national autonomy in the eighteenth and early nineteenth centuries that brought out the progressive democratic aspects of nationalism. People gained a voice over their futures through the establishment of political communities defined by recognised national borders. With the creation of many new nations, first in the Americas and then in Europe, the positive political connotations of nationalism became evident through the aim of securing and then maintaining a nation's sovereignty.

The objectives of national unity and freedom from outside domination infused a succession of movements from the late eighteenth century onwards. Starting with the American war of independence from Britain, this liberal spirit spread across Europe over the next 100 years. The French Revolution and its "Liberty, Equality, Fraternity" motto brought together the close relationship between consolidating nationhood and freedom. At the time these struggles had a democratic essence in overthrowing feudal hierarchies, even if actual democratic institutions followed later.

As Liah Greenfeld, the "great historian of nationalism" (Brooks, 2006), explained "Democracy was born with the sense of nationality. The two are inherently linked" (Greenfeld, 1992, p. 10). The original idea of the nation was as a sovereign people: nationalism was the form in which democracy appeared in the world. In the aftermath of the English, American and French revolutions, the nation was the way that the general popular will was expressed. Whether immediately or potentially, space was being marked out to enable democratic advancement.

Before that potential was widely achieved, intrinsic challenges to capitalist progress in the most advanced countries built up during the late nineteenth century. Expressed through the emergence of the imperialist epoch, nationalism adopted a range of reactionary features. Although the rise of racism and anti-Semitism within the industrialised countries was mostly geared to justifying domestic repression and domination, it took the form of demonising foreigners (Anderson, 2016, p. 150).

Imperialism brought a division of the world between oppressor and oppressed nations. The leading capitalist countries were driven to political domination of other countries as a means of coping with their economic and social problems at home. This pervasive feature of advanced capitalism gave national struggles for self-determination a doubly progressive content. Countries that successfully overcome external domination secured the autonomy to pursue their own objectives independently, while also striking a blow against oppressor imperialist powers.

At the same time, rivalries between the leading imperialist nations ratcheted up as each sought to preserve themselves at the expense of the others. National elites whipped up chauvinism and jingoism among its people to justify its militaristic adventures against other imperialist countries, eventually culminating in the barbarism of the First and Second World Wars. The legacy of such open reaction, at home and abroad, emanating from the advanced capitalist nations a century ago is a vital factor in sustaining the modern-day appeal of the globalist predisposition to oppose the nation state.

Today, many globalists interpret anyone endorsing national borders as being necessarily anti-internationalist and parochial, if not overtly racist. Nationalism is being criticised less in old-fashioned political terms than in cultural terms, to do with people's sense of identity and security. It should not be surprising that the hyperbole in such condemnations of nationalism has stirred domestic divisions. Being branded as "backward nationalists" has contributed to many people voting against the recommendations from globalist political leaders (Eatwell & Goodwin, 2018). Such cultural divisions are far more polarising than previous divides, where over a range of public policy options, there was greater scope for compromise.

The Rule of Rules

With globalists identifying the nation state as outdated and often counterproductive, they argue that it needs to be constrained with a set of rules. This is what drives their disposition to rules-based bodies from the various UN agencies to independent central banks and to entities like the EU. In fact, the defining globalist ethos can be summed up as a *devotion to a world of rules*, embedded within their various institutions (Ikenberry, 2004).

Indeed, many globalists illustrate their "liberal" credentials to a far greater extent through their affinity to rules than through actively pursuing liberty and freedom. The WTO exemplifies this approach with its judicial processes. We've noted in the previous chapter that the WTO trade body is distinguished from its GATT predecessor by its regulatory intrusiveness. In particular, its national founders granted it greater authority to broker and enforce agreements between countries. In 1996, Renato Ruggiero, the second Director-General of the WTO, enthused that "we are no longer writing the rules of interaction among separate national economies. We are writing the constitution of a single global economy" (United Nations Conference on Trade and Development (UNCTAD), 1996).

In principle, everyone following rules seems a sensible way of avoiding the disruptiveness of arbitrary actions. However, this is overtaken by the disruptiveness *caused* by entrenching an outdated rules-based order that much of the world sees as a Western "club" dedicated to perpetuating itself (Frankopan, 2019, p. 124). Demanding that others "follow the international rules" that they had little or no part in creating is sure to inflame tensions between the declining and the ascending powers.

A formal devotion to rules does not mean globalist politicians always adhere to them. Institutionalised rules express power, rather than control it (Chalmers, 2019, p. 3). Globalist governments of powerful countries break their rules with relative equanimity when they think circumstances require it. This is what happened when the United States unilaterally dismantled the Bretton Woods currency exchange system in 1971 because it could no longer follow the rules it had earlier approved. Domestic interests simply assumed greater importance for the United States than continuing its core commitment to the international monetary system (Bordo & Kydland, 1995, pp. 458–459).

Ironically, it is the United States, historically the leading post-war rules maker, which has been increasingly perceived as bending, breaking or abandoning the rules (Frankopan, 2019, p. 167). In the words of one international relations specialist, as the "ordering superpower, the United States did not bind itself with the rules of the system. It upended, stretched, or broke liberal rules to shape a putatively liberal order" (Porter, 2018, p. 2).

Especially in military and strategic matters, and long before Trump entered the White House, the United States as the global hegemon has regularly ignored or violated the rules that it wanted others to follow. It has strenuously opposed potential intrusions by the International Criminal Court (ICC) in its own affairs. Having led in creating the WTO's disputes settlement procedures, the United States then reiterated its "right not to comply with WTO rulings" (General Accounting Office, 2000).

The United States has also conducted numerous unauthorised military interventions and covert operations without the sanction of international regimes (Kagan, 2018, p. 52). Overtly too the United States, under President Ronald Reagan, weakened ties with the ICJ. Later, in the absence of a UN Security Council resolution to justify military action in the Balkans, the Clinton administration turned instead to the alternative rules of the North Atlantic Treaty Organisation (NATO) to give cover to the US bombing of Kosovo.

Subsequently, George W. Bush's national security doctrine of pre-emptive war applied to the Iraq invasion of 2003 repudiated the principles on which the UN had been founded. The United States led the invasion without UN approval (Mazower, 2008, p. 2). Barack Obama's administration was also inconsistent in his approach to multilateral rules, breaking WTO rules when it imposed an earlier set of trade tariffs on China (Miles, 2018).

Following in these steps, Trump has simply been less diplomatic in the way he has pursued America's traditionally self-interested approach to international rules (Ganesh, 2018b). He has continued to violate various WTO obligations, and announced domestic policies in breach of the 2015 Paris Agreement on climate change (before formally announcing the United States' withdrawal in June 2017). The United States also withdrew from the UN's Educational, Scientific and Cultural Organization in 2017 and from its Human Rights Council in 2018.

It is fair to conclude that there has been "a substantial degree of inconsistency" in the US record on observing the international rule of law (Murphy, 2004, p. 349). Rules are used or abused, not least by the United States, depending on what best serves perceived national interests. Benefitting from its large size and greater self-sufficiency, as well as its hegemonic legacy, the United States has tended to pursue its interests with less concern given to its own adherence to rules.

However, the US practices just illustrate clearer than elsewhere that attitudes to the international legal process are dictated by national political considerations. European countries too have broken international rules over tariffs and state subsidies. The WTO has found against the EU over several food-related issues from sugar subsidies to restrictions on beef imports containing hormones.

Globalist organisations also share this discretionary approach to following or ignoring their own rules. The European Commission has treated the powerful larger states that break its budget or state aid rules a lot more leniently than other smaller ones (Falkner, Treib, Hartlapp, & Leiber, 2005, p. 20). For example, Germany and France are among many other EU countries that have frequently broken the EU's stability and growth pact rule to limit public deficits to 3% of gross domestic product (GDP) but without being meaningfully sanctioned. Meanwhile, for similar actions, smaller European nations including Greece, Ireland and Portugal have felt the weight of Brussels enforcements.

Globalist Paradoxes

Globalists do not intend to be divisive, but this is the outcome of promoting rules even when to the detriment of the interests of people. Condemning nationalist-minded people is part of a broader pattern of globalist thinkers who identify with the principles of *democracy, reason, openness* and *progress*, yet have increasingly been unable to live up to these values. Paradoxically, popular expressions of democracy are in practice rejected, reasoned arguments are scorned, economic openness is rolled back by protectionist policies and regressive policies are unashamedly pursued.

These unintended consequences express the classic contradictions within political liberalism. Liberalism's identification with the enlightened ideas of freedom, sovereignty and the power of reason first flourished alongside the emergence of industrial capitalism. That same socioeconomic system though blocked realising them fully and consistently. Liberalism's ideals have always being frustrated within the confines of capitalist ways.

We've noted that the social classes no longer manifest themselves in the same politicised way as in earlier times. However, capitalism remains a socially segregated system with unequal power relations. This intrinsic social inequality stalls the fulfilment of liberalism's promises.

One feature is that ever since the dawn of the Enlightenment, liberalism has always had an ambivalent view of democracy. A fear of ordinary people acting unreliably – the "tyranny of the majority" – has fuelled liberalism's suspicion of democratic arrangements. Its rejection today of popular nationalism follows this tradition of violating democratic values. Especially since the 1980s, fear of public opinion has crept back into liberal thought. As political commentator Edward Luce explained in *The Retreat of Western Liberalism*, "The feelings of the elites have become progressively more sceptical of democracy since the fall of the Berlin Wall" (Luce, 2017).

Rejecting Popular Democracy

Despite globalists' self-presentation as guardians of democracy, it is striking how their institutions often lack the basics of democratic accountability. The European Commission that runs the EU is regarded as probably the most powerful "independent agency" in the world. But it is not elected by, or accountable to, the European populace (Mounk, 2018, p. 66).

Former Commission leader Juncker was rarely reluctant to sideline democratic decisions, arguing that those who govern in Europe have to pursue the "right" policies "even if many voters think they are the wrong ones". Of course, he preferred that politicians respect the will of the people as much as possible but only "provided they adhere to the European treaties" (Juncker, 2013). Two years later with its intervention in Greece, the European Commission illustrated how treaties can override democratic will.

In league with the ECB and the IMF, the Commission imposed austere bailout terms despite their rejection in a Greek general election and in a referendum.

The economics writer and former Greek finance minister Yanis Varoufakis (2016) recalled how Germany's finance minister Wolfgang Schäuble brazenly told him, "Elections cannot be allowed to change an economic programme of a member state".

Democracy is a place where the people themselves monitor and hold accountable the authorities (Tucker, 2018, p. 197). Yet it seems that globalists are unable to endorse democratic exercises when they produce unwelcome results. A common liberal reaction to the 2016 election of Trump and the vote for Brexit was to say that people had voted the wrong way, possibly through ignorance or manipulation. Subsequently, attempts were made to bypass democratic decisions.

The Economist Intelligence Unit described how

> an assortment of pro-European lawyers, politicians, journalists and educational professionals fought a rear-guard action in the courts, the House of Commons and the House of Lords to delay, amend or stymie government legislation aimed at implementing the referendum vote to leave the EU.

In the United States, there was a similar refusal to accept the presidential election outcome by "Democratic Party activists, sections of the media, university professors and students" amid demands that the president be impeached on the grounds that he was unfit to occupy the White House (Economist Intelligence Unit, 2018, p. 4).

Democracy is negated whenever it is made conditional upon getting the "right" result. Trying to prevent the *implementation* of something democratically decided is necessarily undemocratic. Instead, the essence of the democratic conviction is faith in people to engage in reasoned discussion and make considered judgements. This includes accepting the possibility of defeat for one's views and an alternative view being put into effect. Democracy also allows people to *continue* to argue for and win support for something different to the majority decision and potentially come to a different decision in the future. But this does *not* mean blocking a democratic result from being *carried out*, while making people vote again until they come to the opposite conclusion.

Scorning Reason

Anxiety about how ordinary people vote is closely linked to thinking that many of them are limited in grasping the complexities required to make reasoned judgements. While highly educated groups are thought better placed to think the "right" things, the less educated are presumed unable to understand fully today's fast-changing and uncertain world.

This informs the refrain that voters often don't appreciate the damaging consequences of their decisions when they fall prey to lies, manipulation and fake news. Rather than being guided by reason, the poorly educated are regarded as subject to such psychological pressures. This has even brought about a revival of liberal interest in "epistocracy" – a system of decision-making that privileges the most informed citizens (see Brennan, 2016).

Such prejudices against the less educated have become acceptable in some quarters because of the way "reason" is now understood: it is often identified simply with a mastery of the facts. To act or vote *reasonably* is to recognise the facts of an issue and draw the appropriate conclusion. To oppose the conventional view is to "deny" the facts.

The globalist attraction to rule following is paralleled by the propensity of modern Western politicians to reduce difficult political questions to technical ones. Instead of thrashing out tough arguments before the public, and then reaching and defending decisions based on good reasoning, they take the easier route of following expert direction on "the facts". Technical claims, often based mostly on projections modelled by technocratic advisors, are presented as non-controversial "evidence-based" truths that only idiots, or people with disreputable agendas, could dispute. By default, reason is belittled. This really betrays a loss of confidence by many politicians in their *own ability* to reason and argue with the public, not the abilities of lesser mortals.

Reasoning used to be understood as not merely an appreciation of facts. It involves reflection, consideration and judgement, which often include *questioning* the conventional facts. Is movement faster than the speed of light possible? Is sluggish productivity growth inevitable in an ageing society? Will climate change bring humanity's demise within a dozen years? These are issues of judgement, not of adhering to the accepted facts.

However, today, facts, and economic facts in particular, are regarded as the trump card in many discussions. As a result, economists have gained greater influence on policy-making and popular culture. Economic claims have assumed a higher stature in making decisions.

For example, the economicisation of reason was prominent during the British debates over leaving the EU. Would Brexit be good or bad for the economy? Prominent Leave campaigners claimed how so much additional money would be available for the health service as an argument for leaving. Meanwhile, leading Remain campaigners forecast a substantial hit to national output, with the government predicting an immediate recession and a surge in unemployment. For them, it followed that the "reasoned" position was to vote remain.

To be "rational" was to be led primarily by financial or economic criteria, rather than an appreciation of broader aspects – political, cultural, moral as well as economic. In practice, the elevation of economic and financial matters relegated the validity of other considerations. Opponents of Brexit sometimes stressed that British people hadn't voted to be poorer. That was literally true – to be richer or poorer was not the question on the ballot paper. However, this attitude dismissed the non-economic factors behind people's reasoning and conclusions.

Exit polls seem to confirm that Leave voters made up their minds not on economics but from concerns about democracy and sovereignty. In a survey taken as people left the voting stations, nearly half of Leave voters said the biggest single reason they voted as they did was "the principle that decisions about the UK should be taken in the UK". Another third said their main reason was that leaving "offered the best chance for the UK to regain control over immigration and its own borders". Just over one in eight said remaining would mean having no choice "about how the EU expanded its membership or its powers in the years ahead".

All of these reasons were to do with matters of sovereignty and control, not economics or financial well-being. Only 1 in 20 Leave voters said their main concern was economic, that "when it comes to trade and the economy, the UK would benefit more from being outside the EU than from being part of it" (Ashcroft, 2016). Thus, most people did not vote Leave because of their wallets, which was why the economic scare stories failed.

The many people who voted to leave while aware of the catastrophist economic forecasts were not being irrational. In a previous age, it might have been concluded that hearing the alarmist economic predictions and *still* voting to leave was rational. People were exhibiting a more all-rounded understanding of the United Kingdom–EU relationship than the intellectuals who sought to reduce it to pounds and pence.

The problem with the economicisation of discussion is not the use of economic facts or projections *per se* but that they are presented as a substitute for proper reasoning. The state of an economy is important for many issues, but it is not pre-eminent with regard to making judgements. Reaching a decision should never exclude wider non-economic considerations. People of all levels of education have proved time after time they are fully capable of reasoning about such matters.

Globalist Protectionism Outdoes Openness

A perennial dilemma for those suspicious of the "national" is that while advanced industrialisation embraces an international division of labour, its base of operation remains robustly national. Industrial capitalism has always operated both nationally and internationally at the same time.

A practical consequence of this dual nature of capitalism is that policies from globalist politicians can be as protectionist as those from mercantilists. This is because national state policies all have the potential to discriminate against foreigners. When economic policies have been primarily conserving existing business arrangements – as has increasingly been the case since the 1980s – their protectionism is clearer. Measures propping up domestic businesses inevitably discriminate against competitors located outside the state's territory.

For example, despite the EU's commitment to free trade, according to the WTO *World Tariff Profiles*, it imposes import tariffs at above world average levels. Particularly, high tariffs protect its agricultural producers, averaging, for example, 36% for dairy produce. Meanwhile, it also protects its core German, French and Italian car manufacturers from American and Chinese imports with 10% tariffs. Globalists also deploy extensive non-tariff and technical barriers to trade. For instance, the EU further protects its farmers with substantial subsidies under its Common Agricultural Policy. Meanwhile, its food standards regulations keep out foodstuffs from cheaper foreign producers.

As it grapples with a less stable world, the EU has been extending its protectionist policies pitting itself against the United States and China, thereby helping fragment the world economy. While EU leaders denounce mercantilist protectionism from Trump, simultaneously they justify protecting their region from external threats. This brings stronger controls at EU external borders and firmer actions against alleged unfair economic competition by other nations. Tony Barber, the Europe editor of the globalist-leaning *Financial Times* acknowledged that such "Fortress Europe" measures are undermining the EU's pretensions to lead the world in "openness, liberalism and fairness" (Barber, 2019).

Progress Abandoned

The EU's eurozone crisis vividly illustrated how far the globalist approach has in practice departed from the liberal ideal of progress. When this crisis hit in the early 2010s, German and French governments insisted on austerity elsewhere in order to defend their own national interests, not least to protect the loans made by their banks to other EU countries. The measures the European Commission subsequently enacted held back or cut living standards for many citizens of member states particularly in the south: Portugal, Spain, Italy and, to the greatest extent, in Greece.

These hardships cannot be attributed to mistaken policies or to the malign intentions of German politicians or Brussels bureaucrats. Rather they derived from imposing a supranational rules-based structure onto countries at very different levels of economic development. Applying the rules during the crisis simply aggravated economic unevenness.

Furthermore, this sparked acrimony between people living in different EU countries. Southern Europeans resented austerity forced on them by outsiders over whom they had no control. Meanwhile, northern Europeans, not least ordinary German and Dutch people, resented suggestions that they pay higher taxes to help out other countries that were described as profligate.

This inflaming of antagonisms as a result of implementing EU procedures has contradicted the progressive possibility of people working closer together across borders. The euro-crisis experience revealed the liberal ideals of prosperity, progress and peace being expressed as the opposite: hardship, regression and enmity. It is telling that the most tangible European divides today result not from a conflict of ideologies but from the *consequences* of globalist-inspired political arrangements.

Change and No Change

Globalism as a political philosophy is often perceived as a natural corollary to a globalised economy. The growing interdependence of national economies since the late nineteenth century certainly spurred the emergence of globalism. But it was not sufficient. Globalist thinking is moulded from political as well as economic developments.

It has filled a space created by the hollowing out of traditional politics. Politics used to promise change. These days, political leaders rarely promote alternative visions of an improved world. Having given up on popular political deliberation and considered action, a legalistic following of rules substitutes for their own creative thinking about a better future. This is far removed from Kant's outline of the path to world order that rejected relying on international law (Kant, 2016).

Kant regarded law as an apologia for power and argued that the cause of world peace could only be based securely on freedom and reason. He was confident that humanity not only possessed reason but also would ultimately be guided by it (Mazower, 2013, pp. 17–18). How did such Enlightenment thinking become so distorted today? What accounts for today's political myopia?

This is much more than a failure of imagination. It derives ultimately from Western cultural anxieties about the future. The ubiquitous sense of unsettlement is not psychologically founded. A world where the advanced countries are stuck in economic depression and where international power structures fail to reflect relative economic weights is one that is pregnant with change. One way or another, through the force of crisis or ambition, the future will be different.

However, a fear of uncertainty and disruption has been driving leading politicians to stick instead with the status quo. Their predominant goal is stability. Of course, they would prefer to live in a genuinely secure and stable world, but they lack the courage to make the big changes that are required to bring this about.

It is common that the initial impulse to any challenge is to avoid change because the perception is that change will simply introduce instability. We saw this, for instance, in the resistance to Britain's attempts to leave the EU. We see it too in the Trumpian desire to sustain failing US industries while doing little to upgrade their old technologies. We see it also in the globalist defence of a "liberal world order" that was created to reflect very different power relations to those in play today.

The deep appeal of the status quo reflects a loss of belief in our collective capacity to act responsibly and make things better. In place of risking attempts to create a better future, the inclination is to manage the present better, including mitigating the effects of uncontrolled changes. The surge in environmental concerns and in anxieties over new technologies like AI illustrates this thinking. Similarly in the sphere of economics, "de-growth" is now fashionable (D'Alisa, Demaria, & Kallis, 2014). And in politics, technocracy has replaced ambition.

This preservative mindset reinforces the four paradoxes of globalism. Democracy is tainted because it can lead to decisions that disrupt the established order. Reason is suspect because it is unable to stop ordinary people's actions from upsetting the present ways. Protectionism emerges because economic change is thought to be too damaging. And progress is exhausted because the world has become too uncertain: pushing forward only risks making things worse.

The displacement of globalism's liberal ideals is more than a casualty of this shift in thinking. Globalist perspectives have also helped consolidate the conservative mood. The theory of globalisation provides the intellectual justification for accepting diminished aspirations. Globalisation appears as a nature-like force that establishes how the world works and takes change out of our hands.

A statement made as Obama's presidential election campaign was getting underway in 2007 captured this succinctly: Alan Greenspan, the then recently retired Chairman of the US Federal Reserve, was questioned by a Swiss newspaper. Who would be the next president of the United States? He replied, we

> are fortunate that, thanks to globalization, policy decisions in the US have been largely replaced by global market forces. ... (I)t hardly makes any difference who will be the next president. The world is governed by market forces. (Greenspan, as cited in Streeck, 2014, p. 213)

Greenspan was drawing on the conventional political corollary of ascendant globalisation: that the theory and practice of national sovereignty and the nation state is undermined by a world in the process of rapid change. The diminishing of the value of democracy by Greenspan reflected globalism's long-standing antipathy to politics and especially to mass democratic politics.

Notions of globalisation became an alluring explanation for assumptions about receding human capability. Living under the dominance of global market forces appeared to justify the fatalist perspective that "change" is less what we do, than what is done to us: a noun rather than a verb. Expressing this sentiment the former Democratic President Bill Clinton called globalisation "the economic equivalent of a force of nature, like wind or water" (*The Economist*, 2016b).

British Prime Minister Tony Blair said something very similar at the Labour Party conference in 2005. In reply to the charge that economic globalisation didn't seem to be delivering for everyone, he answered, "I hear people say we have to stop and debate globalisation. You might as well debate whether autumn should follow summer" (Blair, 2005). Comparing globalisation to nature's seasons implied it was irresistible and unresponsive to human influence. Just as we have to conform to the seasons, so we have to accommodate to globalisation.

It is poignant that globalists' increasing attraction to rules illustrates that globalisation is anything but a natural process. Today's interconnected world has been shaped by an alliance of politicians, other elites and experts, including the likes of Greenspan, Clinton and Blair (Tooze, 2018, p. 574). For instance, the form taken by the 2008–2009 financial crisis exposed globalisation as resting upon the making and unmaking of particular rules. The modern world is the product of multiple human decisions and actions. It is illusory to present globalisation as a "quasi-natural process" divorced from politics. Rather, it is "an institution, an artefact of deliberate political and legal construction" (Tooze, 2018, p. 575).

The Impoverishment of Politics

However, according to globalist thinking, strengthening globalisation and the diminishing scope for politics are symbiotically related. The politics of choice loses meaning when the momentum of globalisation appears to dictate how life unfolds. Hence, globalist commentators stress the shrinking of the power of nation states. Policies pursued by national politicians are deemed to be pretty ineffective; that is, when they don't make problems worse by interfering with global markets.

Even before the post-war boom had ended Raymond Vernon, the international affairs economist who had earlier helped develop the Marshall Plan, had anticipated the globalisation paradigm. It had seemed to him that sovereign states were "feeling naked". Concepts such as national sovereignty and national economic strength "appear curiously drained of meaning" (Vernon, 1971, p. 3). This type of thinking spread during the 1970s as state apparatuses became evidently less effective in dealing with the return of capitalist crisis.

It is not coincidental that the term "globalisation" came to prominence alongside the discrediting of the pre-eminent twentieth century political doctrines. By the early 1980s, it was widely thought that the drawbacks of socialism, Keynesianism and welfarism overwhelmed their earlier promise. The breakdown of Keynesian "pump-priming" policies in the face of economic recession seemed to confirm the diminishing of nation state power. Not only was the state less able to stimulate economic growth: its efforts were seen as counterproductive. Debt-financed spending was blamed for stagflation: fast rising prices alongside anaemic growth.

Free market thinkers saw this as confirmation that state intervention always made things worse, but social democratic leaders had already come to similar conclusions. The left-right consensus around the merits of a Keynesian mixed economy was replaced by a shared intellectual disillusionment with interventionist economic policy. This thinking became the new conventional wisdom. Misleadingly, many on the old left labelled this a "neoliberal renaissance", even as, in practice, state intervention ratcheted up, broadening in response to every extra economic challenge since.

The globalisation discourse expanded significantly a decade later with the collapse of the Soviet Union and the withering of Cold War certainties. Pronouncements about the "end of ideology" and the "end of politics" became commonplace. A thesis imbued with fatalism, uncontrollability and state impotence appeared to make sense of this unsettling time.

Belittling the potential of the contemporary nation state emptied national sovereignty of meaning. Why defend national self-determination and sustain national borders if the national political unit is outdated in a globalised world? Alongside denigrating the nation state, the same theory elevated the status of cross-border corporations and other non-governmental bodies in global affairs.

Christine Lagarde, the former head of the IMF and subsequently president of the ECB, explained that power has diffused, "extending to a whole host of networks and institutions that inhabit the fabric of global society". "Think", she suggested,

> about the rising nexus of non-government organizations, which can use the communications revolution to extend their reach and amplify the voice of civil society. ... Think about the growing power of multinational corporations, who now control two-thirds of world trade. (IMF, 2014)

National states still existed but it seemed that other organisations now had greater influence because they were operating easily across borders.

Governments of all political stripes assimilated the globalist outlook and thereby helped reproduce their own diminished power. Sceptical that national economic policies could be effective became a justification for governments failing to enact them. In the aftermath of the West's financial crash in 2008, many political leaders took protracted stagnation – lacklustre productivity growth, flat personal incomes, expanding precarious employment – to be the "new normal".

But a truly hands-off, laissez-faire approach is impossible for modern capitalism. In practice, markets cannot operate spontaneously. They always rely on the support of the collective apparatus of the state. This explains the most important political development of the 1980s: not the perceived diminution of state activity but the reorganisation of how the state operated.

Governments increasingly transferred their authority to other bodies and agencies, including courts, regulators, quangos, central banks and supranational organisations. Piece by piece, public responsibilities have moved away from the democratic realm. Not least, state banking: during the course of the 1990s over 50 countries, including most of the advanced industrial ones, gave their central banks "independence" from political accountability.

"Globalization pressures" were perceived to have encouraged governments to make these operational adjustments (Polillo & Guillén, 2005, p. 1770). The implications of a globalised world were thought to vindicate this depoliticisation of policy.

However, the anti-politics of technocracy has limits too. Without an alternative, democratically legitimate authority to take responsibility, genuine accountability to the electorate is inexorably weakened. People put up with that for a time, but as voting in recent years shows, eventually at least some people seek greater control over their lives. This is what globalists find really troubling today.

Anti-politics Outdoes Anti-state

Returning to Greenspan's statement from 2007, three other points are pertinent. First, what he said well sums up the fatalist ethos of globalism. He claimed that it makes little difference who will be the next president since the world is governed not by politicians but by "market forces". The implication is that since nation states don't control anything there is little we can do to influence things by voting. The market determines our circumstances.

Second, there is an extra significance of this statement because of who made it. Until his retirement a few months earlier, Greenspan had been regularly feted as "the most powerful man in the world". He was speaking before the financial crisis hit, after which his reputation and that of other central bankers became somewhat tarnished. We have the incongruity of the former leader of the world's most powerful central bank asserting *powerlessness* in the face of globalisation. That counterposition between the establishment's levers of real power and the claim of impotence is not an incidental quirk of globalism: it is intrinsic to it.

Third, Greenspan's association, at least before the financial crash, with "free market" ideas points to the important influence of classic neoliberalism on the development of globalist thinking that we explore in the next chapter. Two narratives about globalism can be read into Greenspan's answer to the journalist's question.

The standard and most popular narrative is of globalism as the twin of neoliberalism, expressing the "market fundamentalist" view that state intervention is bad for the economy. The government interferes too much with the self-regulating power of markets, thereby undermining prosperity. This perspective would explain why Greenspan regarded it as "fortunate" that globalisation was rendering the government as redundant. We call this the *anti-state* narrative.

An alternative narrative is actually considerably more germane: an *anti-politics*, specifically an *anti-mass politics* narrative. Greenspan's statement incorporates the conventional presumption that the West has reached the exhaustion of traditional politics: politics has lost its efficacy in the face of global forces. As a result, making policies, especially economic policies, is now pretty irrelevant if not detrimental, because everything is driven by – determined by – the impersonal force of globalisation.

This second narrative highlights the centrality to globalism of the denial of human agency. The American historian Quinn Slobodian charted this anti-politics narrative in his superb book *Globalists: The End of Empire and the Birth of Neoliberalism* (2018). This chapter, and the next, draws on Slobodian's thesis. He well characterised globalism as the belief that "politics had moved to the passive tense" with the "global economy" the only actor remaining (Slobodian, 2018, p. 1).

The conventional anti-state narrative is actually misleading. Globalists are not really *against* state activism. Operating within various national and international institutions they do not remain idle by cause of their supposed aversion to state intervention. In fact, baulking at disruptive change, globalists have become the main proponents of pro-stability state policy initiatives.

For example, in spite of their suspicion of nation state policy-making, globalists have promoted the "unconventional" monetary policy of quantitative easing and ultra-low interest rates. They come up with new regulations, both national and international, in the attempt to stop or at least delay another financial crisis. They also experiment with new forms protectionism to protect jobs at home. They regard these sorts of activities as sensible economic management, in place of the redundant left-right ideological agendas that held sway before the 1980s. Thus, what globalists are really hostile to is not the state but *political* control of what the state does.

They worry about unreliable politicians who engage in activities that break from the "liberal model". This also means they are suspicious of democracy because they assume the masses are not all as rational and clear-sighted as they are. Instead, ordinary people are susceptible to being swayed, misled or duped into electing unreliable politicians. Economists Engelbert Stockhammer and Severin Reissl point out that it is well known that prominent neoliberal individuals have at times been quite hostile to the idea of democracy. Instead of relying on democratic outcomes, they view the "freedom of markets" as the quintessential way to achieve personal freedom (Reissl & Stockhammer, 2016).

Even self-identified neoliberals among the globalists are not against the state as such. Certainly, they will often denounce planning and the state control of business. But underlying this, they are even more concerned about what they see as the *destabilising* impact of politics. In particular, they criticise what they call "discretionary politics". These are political policies that they think interfere with the free operation of spontaneous market forces. Nevertheless, they are quite open to the *state* helping to fulfil their ideal of a free-from-politics market order.

For instance, Lionel Robbins, one of Britain's leading neoliberal economists of the twentieth century, sympathised with the emphasis of the classical liberal conception of national order based on a strong and energetic state. Increasingly from the 1930s, he suggested the same principle should also apply on an international scale, in some form of federal authority (Robbins, 1963, p. 136).

Similarly, the Austrian neoliberal Friedrich Hayek in his 1979 book *Law, Legislation and Liberty* explicitly rejected the mischaracterisation that he was an advocate of a "minimal state". He argued that it was

> unquestionable that in an advanced society government ought to use its power of raising funds by taxation to provide a number of services which for various reasons cannot be provided, or cannot be provided adequately, by the market. (Hayek, 1979, p. 41)

His book was no small-state manifesto.

Coincidentally, he published this denial of being an anti-state purist around the same time that the new British Prime Minister Margaret Thatcher was telling her cabinet colleagues that Hayek's earlier 1944 book *The Road to Serfdom* should be compulsory reading. Despite her "free market" reputation too, given the expansion of the state during her premiership, the obituary of Thatcher in *The Economist* magazine was appropriate. This mouthpiece of globalism indicated that the essence of Thatcherism was "a strong state" *alongside* her commitment to a "free economy" (*The Economist*, 2013).

A couple of years later Hayek reinforced this perspective in an interview with the Chilean newspaper *El Mercurio* during that country's continuing military dictatorship:

> When a government is in a situation of rupture, and there are no recognized rules, rules have to be created in order to say what can be done and what cannot. In such circumstances it is practically inevitable for someone to have almost absolute powers ... It may seem a contradiction that it is I of all people who am saying this, I who plead for limiting government's powers in people's lives and maintain that many of our problems are due, precisely, to too much government.

> However, when I refer to this dictatorial power, I am talking of a transitional period, solely. As a means of establishing a stable democracy and liberty, clean of impurities. This is the only way I can justify it – and recommend it. (Hayek, 1981)

Temporary or not, Hayek is explicit in supporting a strong, even authoritarian state to set the rules. Neoliberalism's most famous figure was in practice, as well as in theory, not a "minimal statist".

So, when globalists allude to being anti-state, they are really expressing their opposition to the politicised nation state, rather than state intervention *per se*. When they are critical of the nation state, they are not even really against the "nation" as an existing political entity. Rather, they are mostly against the idea of political nationhood subject to popular control.

Most globalists feel politically and culturally estranged from their own national institutions. This can make them inconsistent in pursuit of national interests, even doubtful about them. Elites find it easier to get things done through international networks because they are already increasingly detached from the lives and outlooks of their citizens at home.

Politicised nations are suspect to elites because of their intrinsic association with the ordinary people of that nation. Their underlying concern is that common people, many of whom do not share their "advanced" thinking, can influence what the state does through the democratic process, potentially against what the elite wants. And since democracy exists in the national form, this concern underpins their belittling of the "nation state".

Thus, it is a misleading caricature to claim that globalists seek a "borderless" world, or a "zero-state" society (Slobodian, 2018, p. 267). A few eccentrics do, but what really unites globalists is a yearning for a world insulated from *popular democracy and accountability* (Gill, 1998, p. 23). States actually remain relevant for globalists, but they are thought to operate best through actions delegated to expert bureaucrats and regulators, not accountable legislators and politicians.

This is what drives the constitutionalist and legalist impulse within globalism that seeks to constrain national economic policy-making by rules-based disciplines. The legal regulation of commerce is removed from domestic democratic controls in favour of following rules that limit legislative autonomy. Legalism is a way for politicians to try to absolve themselves of responsibility and even to pass the blame when things go wrong: "We were only following the rules".

Following rules avoids having to make judgement calls in how to act. In this manner, rules complement the depoliticising implications of globalisation theories. If global forces denude the nation state, adherence to the rules provides a modest fig leaf for practical governing.

In a special report on the changing role of the state in 1997, the World Bank summed up mainstream thinking when it motivated the need for both domestic and international restraints on governments. The report asserted that it is now "generally accepted" that some areas of public decision-making require "insulation from political pressure". It wasn't clear by whom this was "generally accepted". No doubt among globalists, rather than among the people who are being insulated against.

In this spirit, the Bank suggested countries strengthen "formal instruments of restraint" through an effective separation of powers and "judicial independence" (World Bank, 1997, pp. 109, 117). It spelt out that in the "technical and often sensitive area of economic management", some protection of decision-making from the pressure of political lobbies was "desirable" (World Bank, 1997, pp. 8, 116–117).

This proposal for shielding economic policy-making from democratic influences expressed not a "retreat of the state" but the aspiration for a more effective state through a "redefinition" of global governance (Gill, 1998, p. 38). For the World Bank "reinvigorating public institutions" means designing effective rules to check "arbitrary" state actions (World Bank, 1997, p. 3).

"Reinvigorating" sounds positive, but in this context, it implies limiting democratic control by people. The World Bank has even complimented tough states well known to repress the public. For instance, despite the Augusto Pinochet regime in Chile being a military dictatorship, the Bank applauded it for its regulatory reforms of the telecommunications industry in the early 1980s (World Bank, 1997, p. 6).

The World Bank is not alone among the globalist institutions in belittling democracy. It has become a common feature for technocratic objectives to take precedence over political accountability. The next chapter explains that as legacy of the neoliberal tradition, the derogation of democracy eclipses its conventional association with so-called "free market" practices.

Chapter 3

The Anti-democratic Roots of Neoliberalism

Some critics of "globalisation" use the same word interchangeably with "neoliberalism". This is mostly because "neoliberal" has become a ubiquitous swearword (Hartwich, 2009). High executive pay, public spending restraint, wealth inequality and many other objectionable features of economic life are routinely attributed to the hold of neoliberalism. Applying this pejorative label to anything acts as a dismissive term. For those anxious about global economic developments, an association with "neoliberalism" smears "globalisation" too.

However, quite separate from this modern name-calling, there is a genuine intellectual association between the classic neoliberal ideas that developed in the inter-war years and the emergence of post-war globalism. In this chapter, we explore how globalists from both left and right have absorbed the anti-democratic leanings of classic neoliberal thought.

Today, neoliberalism is usually seen as an Anglo-American economic theory emerging in the 1970s from Chicago school economists, such as Milton Friedman. In fact, it is predominantly a *political* theory, with economic articulations, that emanated from Central and Eastern Europe in the inter-war years.

Carl Menger, who died in 1921, was the founder of the Austrian school of economics that became the cradle of neoliberalism. He had been born in present-day Poland. The two leading Austrian school figures that succeeded him were also from this part of the world: Ludwig von Mises was born in Lviv, in present-day Ukraine, and Hayek was born in Vienna. This geography gave them particular formative political experiences due to their proximity to Czarist autocracy, to the 1917 Russian Revolution and, later, to Stalinism and Nazism.

Although overtaken in economic influence by Keynesianism during the post-war boom, neoliberalism helped consolidate the programmatic political response to the turmoil of the first half of the twentieth century. Its ideas helped address three pressing post-1945 concerns: containing conflict between nations, avoiding a return to economic slump and curbing the power of ordinary people to take matters into their own hands.

Neoliberalism emerged politically from a critique of the spread of national sovereignty coming out of the post-First World War dissolution of empires.

Beyond Confrontation: Globalists, Nationalists and Their Discontents, 41–52
Copyright © 2020 by Phil Mullan
doi:10.1108/978-1-83982-560-620200005

The German, Russian, Ottoman and Austro-Hungarian Hapsburg empires all came to their end with lots of new nation states rising in their place. Many who were involved in setting up the neoliberal Mont Pelerin Society in 1947, not least Mises and Hayek, had grown up destined to serve the now deceased Austro-Hungarian empire (Slobodian, 2018, p. 122). They justified their hostility to national sovereignty because it got in the way of the "universal economic freedoms" they championed. Their favoured alternative to the nation was some mix of "world government", alongside "individual consumer sovereignty".

Most neoliberal thinkers were realistic that the nation state was not just going to disappear. Instead, they proposed "double government": there would be both national *and* supranational states. What they called "cultural" issues could still be managed at the national level, while the running of the economy would be separated from the nation and pursued at a world level. This "double government" system was seen as a way to institutionalise the separation of politics from economics that they so desired.

Double government would detach the rule of nation states from the rule of capital and private property. This represented a division between what neoliberals called "imperium" (to do with the rule of people) and "dominium" (to do with the rule of things). Their aspiration was that the economy would be permanently depoliticised, in the sense of freed from the interference of politics and people.

Neoliberals thought it best for the economy to be overseen by a non-political supranational state. Their ideas anticipated the depoliticisation of economic policy that has become so pronounced over the past three decades. The limiting of the role of politics and people evolved into a generalised anti-democratic bias. Its influence continues to pervade modern times, including endorsing international interventions in national domestic affairs.

Neoliberal Influences

By the 1930s, neoliberals were among the most clear-sighted in favouring supranational state intervention to preserve and secure the private property-based capitalist order. In the absence of their esteemed empire, instead they proceeded to promote the inter-war League of Nations as a model for international federation. Such cross-border organisations, they believed, could help bring about economic unity across countries and secure the benefits from a wider division of labour.

Towards the end of the Second World War, Mises suggested reforming the League of Nations as an international government. He hoped it could ensure the free movement of goods, services, capital and people, thereby anticipating by half a century the EU Single Market's "four freedoms". Mises undoubtedly believed in the "invisible hand" of the market. But he also thought it needed, to borrow an evocative phrase from Slobodian, an "iron glove" of a supranational state to give it protection (Slobodian, 2018, p. 111).

Neoliberalism's inter-war ideas appeared to fully anticipate the post-Second World War framework. The realisation of a limited "double government" conception saw the reaffirmation of the nation state alongside the creation of a set of international bodies including the IMF, the International Bank for Reconstruction and Development (subsequently renamed the World Bank), GATT and, later, the European Community that went on to become the EU. The objective was for a controlled world of states far superior to that the League had achieved. However, when these institutions were actually set up, many neoliberals thought they were flawed. Too much economic power, they argued, was *still* being retained at the national level.

However, this intellectual reaction didn't stop neoliberals becoming active in the new regime. The German version of neoliberalism – which in 1950 was renamed "Ordoliberalismus" or "ordoliberalism" – was probably the most explicit in spelling out the state's necessary responsibilities. Before the war, its founder Walter Eucken, from the Freiburg school, called for a "strong state" to be able to stand above the interests of lobbies.

Thus, the political scientist Werner Bonefeld summarises ordoliberal thought as conceiving the relationship between market and state as a free economy and a strong state. In the 1950s, another ordoliberal leader Wilhelm Röpke spelt this out; he was one of the first globalists actively to pursue the concept of capitalism as a "doubled" system, dependent on the free international flow of goods and capital while partitioned into bounded national states (Slobodian, 2018, pp. 10–11).

Continuing this way of thinking Lars Feld, as director of the Walter Eucken Institute (set up in the mid-1950s following Eucken's death in 1950), described "classic neoliberalism" as the government providing a rules-based, constitutional and legal framework to shape markets. Seeking to hold onto the term "free market", he cautioned that government should not intervene in day-to-day economic decisions. Feld described the state as the "concentrated force" of the system of liberty. Appropriately, Bonefeld (2017) suggests that ordoliberalism is best characterised as an authoritarian liberalism, an approach that has since been realised in the EU.

Jan Tumlir, the senior GATT secretariat official, and, born in Czechoslovakia, another East European neoliberal theorist, praised the EU for its radicalism in this respect. By deploying uniform supranational European law, Tumlir claimed that the "protection of the private economy from the government was the eminent idea" behind European federation (Tumlir, as cited in Slobodian, 2018, p. 256; Tumlir, 1983b, p. 36).

Hayek adopted the same stance in arguing for global institutions to safeguard capitalism. For him, this meant protecting what he called the "negative right" for foreign investments to have freedom from expropriation, and the right to move capital freely across borders (Slobodian, 2018, p. 123).

It was consistent that many subsequent neoliberal thinkers welcomed the EU's Economic and Monetary Union (EMU) and an independent ECB as constituting what they called an "economic constitution" for Europe (Slobodian, 2018, pp. 4, 256). For similar reasons, some free marketeers have supported the controversial Investor-State dispute settlement provisions in recent mega-trade arrangements, since they give businesses operating in foreign territories legal rights over the host nation state (J. Roberts, 2017).

Triple Concerns

While US global hegemony was a precondition for establishing the new post-1945 order, continental European figures were prominent in influencing the form it took. This reflected how the inter-war calamities, from insurrections to Weimer to the slump, were felt most sharply in previously German-occupied and war-torn Central Europe. Three profound concerns emanated from these harrowing experiences, each of which neoliberal ideas helped address.

The first concern was of a return of international conflict and, ultimately, of another world war. Second, worries about the collapse of the economic system, as had nearly occurred in the 1930s depression. And third, an anxiety about the power of the masses taking matters into their own hands. This last fear had been felt with greater dread ever since the Russian Revolution. It was later reinforced by the conventional (though misleading) notion that Hitler and the Nazis were elected fairly and democratically in 1933.[1] The fusion of these three anxieties helps explain the globalists' policies and behaviours throughout the post-1945 period.

Preventing Conflict

The immediate worry was about a resumption of international conflict. It is unsurprising that the term *globalism* first emerged during and immediately after the experiences of world war. Rosenboim in her excellent book *The Emergence of Globalism: Visions of World Order in Britain and the United States, 1939–1950* explained how the word "global" began to gain intellectual currency for the first time soon after the outbreak of the Second World War.

The year 1939 marked the onset of the first truly *global* war. Until then, the war of 1914–1918 had mostly been called the "Great War". Although there had been some action in Asia and Africa, this earlier war had been fought predominantly on European soil. *Time* magazine is reputed to have coined the term "*World* War I" only in its issue of 12 June 1939 as war between the great powers loomed again. From this new sentiment of *global* warfare, minds soon turned to the need for a *global plan* for the peacetime order.

This was when the globalists first gave priority to the global at the expense of the national. Rosenboim describes how a transnational network of globalist thinkers emanated from the traumas of war. As we've shown already, the brutal consequences of the actions taken by Germany and Japan overwhelmed for many the earlier appreciation of the benefits of national sovereignty. After 1945, political authority on the scale of the nation state seemed to lose much of its claim to "optimality" (Scharpf, 1988, p. 240).

From that time, politicians from various creeds decried "self-interested" sovereign states as the cause of war (Rosenboim, 2017b, p. 177). The value of the

---

[1]For instance, Kershaw (2001) refutes this view by describing the peculiar anti-democratic circumstances leading up to the March 1933 elections.

national state as a standalone political unit was questioned. Since a federation of democratic nations had been necessary to defeat fascism, a similar collective seemed an appropriate vision for a durable post-war order.

The globalists' most pressing impulse was to prevent a recurrence of war between nations. It seemed clear that simply reintroducing a loose League of Nations-type grouping would not be sufficient to preserve peace. Instead, they took the technocratic route of adopting rules and institutional systems to try to cement international cooperation.

Hence, the priority the new globalists gave in 1944, even as the bloodbath continued in Europe and Asia, to the Bretton Woods international monetary system for regulating currency rates and setting up the IMF and the World Bank. These international arrangements were forged to prevent a recurrence of the chaotic inter-war relations. The UN was launched in San Francisco in June 1945. In Geneva, a year later, Lord Robert Cecil, who had addressed the first assembly of the League of Nations in 1920, declared at its final meeting: "The League is dead. Long live the United Nations".

The creation of GATT in 1947 embodied one of the preferred post-war narratives about what had brought about the conflict. This emphasised economic factors, blaming the conflagration on an escalation inflamed by the use of discriminatory trade policies, primarily through tariffs. As a result, the first Article of GATT committed its members to *non-discrimination*. Known as the "most favoured nation" (MFN) principle, trade concessions granted to one member were to be applied immediately and without conditions to all other members. Adherence to this provision was aimed at prohibiting the trade policies that had raised the international temperature in the 1930s.

Expressing similar aspirations, at the forefront of the UN's founding Charter was that its members act to "save succeeding generations from the scourge of war" caused by nationalistic behaviours. Collective problem solving sounded attractive for leaders who twice in their lifetimes had seen fighting bring "untold sorrow to mankind" (UN Charter, 1945).

However, as we've noted, this appeal to the responsibilities of member states meant that some mid-century globalists were sorely disappointed that the Charter of the UN continued to tolerate national state sovereignty. Intellectuals such as H. G. Wells and Barbara Wootton, as well as Hayek, expressed misgivings about the establishment of an international organisation that depended upon and reinforced the sovereignty of its member states (Rosenboim, 2017b, pp. 12, 273).

In this regard, the Charter was reflecting the decisive part that nation states played in collectively prosecuting and winning the war. The planning that underpinned the success of the Allied effort had even impressed some right-wing thinkers. This tempered suggestions for completely curtailing the nation state's role. Just as wartime victory had been state organised, it seemed likely that lasting peace would need to be organised around states too. It was agreed though that in the new global political space, the nation was too limited to be effective on its own (Rosenboim, 2017b, p. 36).

Instead, some form of international organisation was required, even though this incorporated a role for refashioned nation states. In the end, most globalists went along with constructing a new order around the extant nation states. States would not be abolished but their powers limited (Rosenboim, 2017b, p. 279). In his classic American college text first published in 1956, international relations scholar Inis Claude reiterated the notion that equated nationalism with reckless passions. Only through effective international organisation could this irresponsible tendency be subdued (Claude, 1984, pp. 32–33).

Containing the Capitalist Crisis

The second big concern behind the post-war order was the anxiety of capitalist breakdown. Linked to their first objective, post-1945 leaders saw that the inter-war "derangement of the international economy" had contributed significantly to the resumption of global conflict. Before the end of the war, the future US Secretary of State Dean Acheson pointed out that international peace depended upon "economic peace, as well as a political and military peace" (Kagan, 2018, pp. 29–30). But the concern was domestic too, to prevent tendencies to economic collapse at home.

The new international settlement was hoped to protect capitalism from another economic depression. The slump of the 1930s shook Hayek and his Austrian school colleagues just as severely as it did Keynes and his fellow thinkers. Hayek and Keynes simply adopted different routes in their ideas about how to save capitalism. Significantly, the paths taken were not *that* different.

A famous exchange of multi-author letters in *The Times* in 1932 – three with Keynes as a co-contributor and one from Hayek and some of his colleagues – did express differences over the *means* of economic intervention. However, there was also common ground between them. Both accepted the need for timely intervention on the part of the state when the self-adjusting processes of market experimentation failed (Hingstman & Goodnight, 2011, p. 13). Areas of agreement between Hayek and Keynes were illustrated further at the famous Walter Lippmann Colloquium in Paris in 1938.[2]

This was where the German economist Alexander Rustow, alongside Mises, Hayek and others, adopted the label "neoliberalism" for their anti-socialist and anti-Nazi ideas (Hartwich, 2009). Proceedings at the Colloquium incorporated the same thinking that Keynes did in rejecting nineteenth century laissez-faire ideas. Their prime objective was not to eliminate state intervention but to rethink the type necessary for safeguarding the market from collapse.

Many at the Colloquium recognised, as had Keynes, that the self-regulating market was a myth. They knew from bitter experience that self-correcting capitalism didn't work. The economy needed state support. From their early days,

---

[2]Providing a personal link to the theme of international order, the man behind the conference was Walter Lippman. An influential American journalist and political commentator, he had earlier been research director for President Woodrow Wilson's Great War board of inquiry preparing for peace negotiations.

neoliberal thinkers endorsed an economic role for the state beyond that of the metaphorical "night watchman".

Today's narrative fiction that globalist neoliberalism is firmly "anti-state" is able draw selectively on elements of the Colloquium proceedings. Some participants strongly critiqued what was called the "illusion of control". While neoliberals wanted the state to preserve capitalism, they vehemently rejected state socialist proposals for the "overhead control" of the economy by "intelligent authority". They repudiated such suggestions as naive and damaging. Instead, the Austrian school neoliberals saw the economy as driven by millions of individual responses to prices. It was far too *complex* for any economist or any central authority to fully assimilate, comprehend and control.

The attention drawn to "complexity" even before 1939 is revealing for what's new, and isn't new, today. The pre-war discussion contradicts current globalisation theorists who claim that complexity is a relatively *recent* arrival, resulting from our unusual fast-moving world. They assert that this phenomenon necessitates rethinking how to handle democracy today because democratic governance was only really feasible in those simpler times before the 1980s. From the Colloquium discussions, we see that notions of complexity go back much further in justifying the limiting of democratic practices.

The conclusion the original neoliberals drew was that although the modern economy was too complex to be *controlled*, it could at least be *ordered*. Either implicitly or explicitly, "ordering" implied a role for the state. "Ordering" could not just cement international cooperation, but it could also help curb the destabilising tendencies of capitalism and avoid economic breakdown. Hence, the yearning for rules to encase capitalism. In order for the market to be able to exert "discipline", it itself needed to be protected by an "extra-economic framework" in the form of a legal, constitutional, regulatory structure. The state would be the agency for "ordering".

The US leadership in the post-war revival of the European and Japanese economies illustrates that international capitalist restructuring did not exclude national state activism. Far from it. The international organisations and nation states worked in tandem. This relationship between the state and international capitalism is captured well by the term "embedded liberalism"; the phrase coined in the early 1980s by the political scientist John Ruggie to describe the international expression of the Keynesian mixed economy.

National governments working within these international bodies after the war were not prevented from acting. They were required to act. Indeed, they were expected to take much greater state responsibility for market stability and economic growth. For instance, countries that signed up to the Bretton Woods system committed to new multilateral rules of fixed but adjustable exchange rates in parallel to them aiding their own domestic economies. The new international regime openly reconciled multilateralist economic initiatives with national state intervention (Ruggie, 1982, p. 393). In contrast to current globalist arguments sceptical of politicised states, international and nation state activism was then seen as complementary.

Controlling the Masses

The third motivating concern behind globalism was a distrust of the masses, revealing its anti-democratic inclinations. The political elites of Western Europe and America finished the Second World War determined to avoid the unsettling social unrest of the inter-war years (Hall, 2013, p. 133). The almost immediate onset of the Cold War, with "communism" expanding its territorial dominance, ensured this anxious memory remained pronounced (Maier, 1981). Concerns about class conflict were a heavy influence not just on the extension of domestic welfare statism but also for the establishment of the new international regime.

Globalists see order of some type as required to contain the inherent unreliability and rancour within the populace. They interpret history as demonstrating that ordinary men and women can't be trusted to do the right thing since people often seem to favour authoritarianism over liberalism. Globalists conclude that the absence of international order in the inter-war years enabled these populist sentiments to be expressed in the rise to power of Mussolini, Hitler and Franco. Perhaps, the neoconservative foreign policy scholar Robert Kagan suggested, if the United States had first established a liberal world order in 1919, not 1945, we might never have known the Hitler of our history books (Kagan, 2018, pp. 144–145).

The concern about popular democracy going astray accounts for the ardour with which neoliberals like Hayek opposed Keynesianism. Their antipathy derived from associating Keynesian policies with socialism and the unruly masses. As we've noted, far from denying state activism in principle, neoliberals were a lot more concerned about the influence of Marxism and the Soviet Union – as well as the National Socialist fascism many of them had had to flee from. They recoiled from the post-war mixed economy as another variant of the state socialism of the masses that they hated. Their rejection of these forms of state control reinforced their scepticism about democracy and, for some, stoked outright hostility to mass democracy.

California University political theorist Wendy Brown suggested that the original neoliberals from the inter-war years were not all subjectively anti-democratic. But they were influenced by their reaction to the inter-war revolutionary struggles across Europe. Their intellectual emphasis on keeping politics separate from economics spread to keeping politics insulated from the "emotional demands of the uneducated masses" (Brown, 2018).

These anxieties about democracy reinforced the institutionalised character of the post-war settlement. One account of political decision-making in post-war Europe explained how,

> Insulation from popular pressures and, more broadly, a deep distrust of popular sovereignty, underlay not just the beginnings of European integration, but the political reconstruction of Western Europe after 1945 in general … the "postwar constitutional settlement" was all about distancing European polities from ideals

of parliamentary sovereignty and delegating power to unelected bodies, such as constitutional courts, or to the administrative state as such. (Muller, 2012, as cited in Furedi, 2018)

A technocratic, anti-political approach to post-war international coordination suited the US agenda too. Instead of a "League" based on a presumed shared popular faith in civilised values, the United States stressed the benefits of collective scientific and technical expertise. Building upon and expanding the work of the League's apparatus of technical services, the Americans could see the military benefits of a permanent rules-based machinery. This soon went beyond security into areas of economic, welfare and social affairs.

Especially in the early Anglo-American discussions, it is true that an idealistic motivation of "serving democracy" remained vocal for the new international organisations. However, it was evident from the start that in practice smaller nations, and the demos in general, would have little say in how these organisations operated. Under the UN's Article 2 even *non*-members were expected to obey decisions of the Security Council (Mazower, 2013, pp. 201–213).

Generally, the term "democracy" often had a self-serving meaning for the dominant powers. According to the post-war British government, colonialism was justified as a "practical illustration of democracy under tuition". In line with such thinking, the UN Charter avoided any clear commitment to full independence of colonies – a minimal necessary foundation for national democratic rights. Instead, it merely bound the colonial powers to promote "to the utmost" the interests and well-being of the inhabitants of these colonies, now rebranded "non-self-governing territories" (Mazower, 2013, pp. 251–253).

The US political leadership also retained a highly qualified appreciation of democracy with its talk of an "evolutionary" approach to self-determination. In the 1950s President Dwight Eisenhower's Secretary of State John Foster Dulles explained that the United States supported national political independence only when a country's people had proven themselves "civilised" enough. They needed to be "capable" of sustaining independence and discharging national responsibilities in accordance with the "accepted standards of civilized nations" (Van Dyke, as cited in Mazower, 2013, pp. 262–263). What was "acceptable" was of course defined by the US government at the time, not by the people in those countries.

This top-down conditional approach to democracy was well illustrated at an agenda-setting US conference in 1958 on the topic of Africa's development needs. No African attended. The organisers assumed that Africans would be too poorly educated, partisan and narrow-minded to make a helpful contribution, unlike the Western experts there (Mazower, 2013, p. 285).

The Post-war Expansion of Democratic Worries

The irony of successfully excluding ordinary people from post-war institutions is that it failed to temper anxieties about democracy and the masses. By the 1980s while at GATT, the neoliberal official Tumlir succinctly summed up the rationale for rules-based international systems: "international rules protect the world market against governments" (Tumlir, as cited in Slobodian, 2018, p. 250). The rules established by international elites apparently represent best how the market economy can work. But he went on to explain that rules don't only put shackles on what governments can do. They also justify the refusal to engage in political debate with the demos.

Tumlir argued that whenever you have democracy you have the possibility that the masses can capture the state. The state then "ceases to be a government and becomes an arena for gladiatorial combats of organized interests". The big risk with democracy, he concluded, is that it can lead to people power and even to socialism. As a result democratic governments could act against the vital interest of their own societies. A formal constitution was needed to "structure", that is constrain, political discussion. He reiterated a core purpose of the liberal international order as "protecting the world market" from popular pressures (Tumlir, as cited in Slobodian, 2018, pp. 250–252, and Tumlir, 1983b, p. 32).

Rules and democracy don't mix well. Rules can be used to back up the insistence on "TINA". When rule following takes precedence then "there is no alternative". There is no purpose in even discussing alternatives because the rules need to be honoured. Slobodian unearths Tumlir explaining that international rules could help save national politicians from internal pressures: "The international economic order [could act] as an additional means of entrenchment protecting national sovereignty against internal erosion" (Tumlir, as cited in Slobodian, 2018, p. 250). In this Orwellian formulation, "protecting national sovereignty" implies its opposite. It means protecting the national political establishment from the wishes of the masses: an empty form of sovereignty.

The World Bank subsequently drew attention to what it described similarly as the "inherent dangers" of greater public openness and participation. Expanded opportunities for popular participation increased the demands made on the state. This, the Bank wrote, can enhance the risk of gridlock, or of state capture by vocal interest groups (World Bank, 1997, p. 130). Reflecting analogous thinking to Tumlir, the Bank stressed the role for international institutions as a protective mechanism for national governments when undertaking internal, and potentially unpopular, changes (World Bank, 1997, p. 15). The external commitments given by governments to global bodies made it easier for them not to backtrack on agreed reforms in the face of domestic opposition.

Like the international law "excuse" we discussed in Chapter 1, with an extensive institutionalised order national politicians are able to defer to the established rules to validate their actions or inactions (Slobodian, 2018, p. 283). It is convenient for national leaders to have a supranational master such as the WTO or the EU they can point their electorate to, and shrug: "We had to do this, there wasn't an alternative".

For instance, recall from Chapter 2 the rejection of democracy during the eurozone debt crisis in 2015 when a majority of Greek voters opposed the terms of the bailout agreement drawn up in Brussels and Berlin. In response, the German finance minister Schäuble succinctly summed up the globalist outlook that elections change nothing: "There are rules" he said (Hewitt, 2015). The elected Greek government succumbed.

It is not coincidental that Hayek's rejection of "minimal statism" mentioned earlier was in a volume that also critiqued democracy. He spelt out there the accordance for neoliberals like him between legalism and disdain for democracy. Specifically Hayek criticised what he called the "unlimited, unrestrained" representative democracy that led to stupid and damaging economic policies. This conclusion rested on his denial of the possibility of economic control, which led to another denial: people cannot be masters of their own fate.

Hayek was representative of the neoliberal input to globalism in openly arguing that restricting political freedoms, including democratic rights, was sometimes necessary to preserve economic freedom (Slobodian, 2018, p. 151). While Hayek thought that "democracy needs the broom of strong governments", he thought democracies could allow governments "too much power". This is why he explained that he was always very careful to distinguish between "limited democracies" and "unlimited democracies". And his choice was the limited variety (Hayek, 1981).

This was consistent with the way Hayek, and other neoliberal globalists, put increasing faith in the law – both national and supranational – as the alternative to "unlimited" democratic government. One of the reasons he recoiled from the expansion of democracy around the world was because he thought it brought about economic intervention through legislation. This was corrosive to his preferred separation of economics from politics. Hayek was careful in distinguishing the positive role "law" should play compared to the dangers of a "legislative state" (Slobodian, 2018, p. 143).

This type of thinking confirms that the globalist scepticism of the nation state is to a great extent driven by anxieties over its democratic base, over its mass political aspects. Globalism's concern about the nation state is primarily because it is a space for exerting democratic power. The attack on nationalism and sovereignty is really an attack on the "unlimited" power of the people. Complementing their earlier fears of a return of international conflict and of economic breakdown, what today worries globalists most on a day-to-day level is popular democracy. They baulk at the notion of people intruding into their technocratic practices and procedures.

Conclusion: Neoliberalism's Biggest Influence is Anti-democratic Politics Rather Than Pro-liberal Economics

Motivated by those three concerns – international conflict, capitalist collapse and the distrust of people – globalists of all political stripes are pragmatic about using state institutions to maintain and stabilise capitalist economic relations. Globalists are comfortable running international and national institutions, as long as they can build in protection from democratic accountability. The synthesis of the three fears accounts for the core of globalism being anti-politics rather than anti-state.

The subjectively neoliberal of today's globalists still repeatedly recite their belief in the "free market" and in "free trade". But the *freedom* that really motivates them is not freedom from state intervention. It is freedom from the intrusion of politics. In the end, this comes down to freedom from being answerable to the people. Slobodian (2018) appropriately describes neoliberalism as less a theory of the market, or of economics, than of law and the state (p. 268).

Neoliberal-informed globalism is far more a political project than it is an economic one. Hayek's most important contribution to globalism was not his romantic attachment to the free market. It was his arguments about the dethronement of politics.

The neoliberal goal of "depoliticising the economy" is itself a *political* programme. It seeks to shield capitalism from democratic influences. As early as 1932, the father of German ordoliberalism Eucken had openly denounced what he called the "democratization of the world", referring to the masses coming into politics via "universal" (although, then, mostly male) suffrage (Slobodian, 2018, p. 124).

Almost exactly 50 years later, after visiting Pinochet's Chile Hayek was equally explicit about his contempt for democracy. In his 1981 Chilean newspaper interview, he said he was "totally against dictatorships" as long-term institutions, "but ... at times it is necessary for a country to have, for a time, some form ... of dictatorial power". "Personally", he continued, "I prefer a liberal dictator to democratic government lacking liberalism" (Hayek, 1981). This summed up the globalist philosophy that although you cannot have political freedom without economic freedom, economic freedom is tolerable without political freedom.

A quarter century later, Jean-Claude Juncker expressed the same authoritarian message in declaring "There can be no democratic choice against the European treaties" (translated from Mével, 2015). At least Juncker was consistent. A few years earlier when leading the Eurogroup of finance ministers he had explained, "Monetary policy is a serious issue. We should discuss this in secret". He went on to acknowledge, "I'm ready to be insulted as being insufficiently democratic but I want to be serious ... I am for secret, dark debates" (Pop, 2011). It is not such a long step from Hayek supporting General Pinochet's Chilean dictatorship in the 1980s, to the secretive anti-democratic impulses of the EU bureaucracy in the twenty-first century.

Chapter 4

From Post-war Order to Disorder

The institutions and rules that globalists defend today were set up in a very different era. They are out of sync with a world driven now by dissimilar dynamics and
dominated by other players. A sensible approach to an outdated international settlement is for independent sovereign nations to come together to create a replacement modus operandi. However, the dominant globalist perspective has been to
insist on adherence to the old rules-based international order. As a consequence,
instead of aiding international stability, these international arrangements have
become sources of friction.

The deficiencies of the post-war order are not only due to changes in the balance of economic power. The existing framework is also flawed because of the
tensions within its "double government" model. However, well intended the original motivation, in their existence *supra*national bodies encroach upon national
sovereignty. This has become a block on people acting to make the changes necessary for invigorating domestic prosperity and international progress.

Since the individuals running these supranational institutions are appointed
rather than popularly elected, the control ordinary people exert over their lives
is diminished. This intrinsic democratic deficit has precipitated further strains
within, as well as between countries. These stresses were mitigated for several
decades but have come sharper since the 2008–2009 financial crisis and especially
since the mid-2010s. This chapter draws out the ramifications of intensifying
international tensions, within the West and between the West and the East.

A Puzzle of US Hegemony

As the paramount world power in 1945, the United States oversaw the new
international arrangements. However, it is striking that the United States had
initially been the most hesitant of all the leading capitalist countries in promoting an alliance-based system. It is far too simplistic to assess the institutional
foundations of globalism as being the creation of American hegemony (Murphy,
2004, p. 2).

Immediately after the Second World War, other nations had steered the new
international order. European leaders, in the beginning particularly French politicians like Schuman and Jean Monnet, took the direct lead in writing the rules

Beyond Confrontation: Globalists, Nationalists and Their Discontents, 53–66
Copyright © 2020 by Phil Mullan
All rights of reproduction in any form reserved
doi:10.1108/978-1-83982-560-620200006

for the new economic and financial architecture. Thereafter, European nations have usually been the strongest proponents of international law and institutions (Murphy, 2004, p. 354).

By dint of geography, Europe's intimate connection with the wartime horrors propelled this approach. In addition, the waning twentieth century clout of even the biggest European countries encouraged them to compensate by acting through international institutions. Thus, European states were to the fore in promoting the IMF, the Organisation for Economic Co-operation and Development (OECD), as well as their own European Community.

Significantly, it was European politicians who sought to delegate to these bodies jurisdiction over *national* government policies (Abdelal, 2007, p. xi). Making everyone follow a system of external rules was a means for the declining power of France, and later of the European Community/Union, to retain some influence. The Europeans hoped that rule following could not just help manage global relations but specifically allow it to capitalise on, as well as contain US power (Abdelal, 2007, p. 220).

In contrast, the instinctive post-war vision of some leading Americans had been ad hoc and less formalised. Having secured victory in both Europe and the Pacific, a world run on US terms seemed viable. The United States' huge strength made it possible to pursue its interests abroad directly, rather than having to operate through collective mechanisms.

This initial American aspiration – the same that its Senate had expressed in 1919 in rejecting the League of Nations – followed the Founding Fathers' advice to avoid "foreign entanglements". Americans are brought up to assimilate George Washington's warning, in his farewell presidential address of 1796, against entangling alliances:

> The great rule of conduct for us in regard to foreign nations is in extending our commercial relations, to have with them as little political connection as possible. ... It is our true policy to steer clear of permanent alliances with any portion of the foreign world. (Washington, 1796)

In short: trade and invest abroad but avoid binding political associations.

Washington stressed both the risk of getting involved in unnecessary wars and the threat to its own democracy. Foreign political alliances could elevate the interests of other nations above the will of the American people. Until the post-1945 era, the US governments mostly heeded Washington's recommendation.

In the end, though, after the war, the United States fashioned the "more ordered world that would be less likely to fall victim to the disasters of the 1930s" (Mazarr, 2018). Ironically, America's independent foreign policy tradition encouraged its leadership to embrace a formalised collaborative order. Agreeing with the victorious European nations that something was needed to prevent a resumption of 1930s mayhem, the American government concluded it was better to go along with a structured rules-bound approach to international cooperation than one where the United States might be subject to arbitrary political decisions made by foreigners. An ordered framework helped make America's overseas engagement acceptable to a public suspicious of discretionary alliances (Mazower, 2013, p. xiv).

America's international economic interests also favoured it going along with the new structures. Without stability in the war-torn industrial countries, it was feared that political as well as economic crisis could soon return. US worldwide commercial interests would have been compromised. America had good economic self-interest in wanting a stable world.

A rules-based arrangement met another American objective: how to keep control over a decolonising world now that the direct domination of empire was discredited. America's vocal support for self-determination was not based on a principled rejection of colonial oppression *per se*, as some of its later military interventions reinforced. It derived mostly from the new hegemon's desire to scale back British and French global influence, as well as to curb destabilising inter-imperialist contests over the direct control of foreign territories (Tooze, 2015, p. 120).

America successfully used the new institutional rules to help accelerate decolonisation as well as to weaken the old powers. A decade later, it humiliated Britain and France over the 1956 Suez crisis. This included using an emergency UN General Assembly resolution, revealing how the new arrangements could serve *Pax Americana* well.

In fact, from 1945, the European political classes already knew who had taken charge. They recognised they were so reliant on American engagement in the stabilisation of European and wider world affairs that they had to tolerate American double standards. While the rules the European nations followed were usually fashioned to be consistent with core US interests, the Europeans often went along with exempting America from meeting any responsibilities that it did not want to be constrained by (Mazower, 2013, p. xiv).

For example, although the United States officially agreed to the "compulsory" jurisdiction of the new ICJ, as early as 1946 America was allowed by the others to limit the Court's jurisdiction over itself. The disabling "Connally Reservation" gave the United States, rather than the ICJ, the authority to determine whether a matter was essentially within the domestic jurisdiction of the United States and outside that of the international court (Murphy, 2004, p. 3). While all countries were "equally" sovereign, one was clearly more sovereign than all the others.

With the same effect the United States could never be *formally instructed* by the UN to do anything against its will; the United States had veto power on the UN Security Council, alongside the other four permanent members. The United States also secured the same effective hold on the IMF's highest decision-making body, the board of governors. Its votes on substantive issues needed 85% approval, which the United States can thwart with its carefully set quota of just over 16%.[1]

---

[1]When the IMF reformed in 2015 to extend the voice of emerging countries including China, the United States saw to it that its quota fell only by a token amount from 16.7% to 16.5% to protect its veto power.

Similarly, the United States remains the largest shareholder of the World Bank and is the only nation that retains a block over changes to the Bank's structure.

Why So Durable, for So Long

Ultimately, the United States went along with the formalised set-up after 1945 reassured by the belief that as the sole superpower the international law and institutions would develop and operate in line with its own national interests. However, it was far from clear at that time that the overall settlement would survive as long as it has (Kagan, 2018, p. 38).

In other circumstances than those actually experienced, the United States might have reverted to favouring its traditional "non-entangled" approach once economic reconstruction and decolonisation had stabilised international affairs. This inclination has sometimes expressed itself, not starting with the Trump White House but with every US president since the 1990s. However, before that, the America's go-it-alone tendency was much less evident. This was because the post-war arrangements were powerfully legitimised by two significant unanticipated developments: another type of war and a long boom.

The first was the start of the Cold War. The Soviet Union became America's, and the West's, foremost ideological and geopolitical adversary. In his famous 1947 article in *Foreign Affairs*, the American diplomat George Kennan advocated the policy of Soviet "containment". Presciently, he anticipated that the Soviet threat could even work out well for the world. The Cold War could put an end to America's lingering reticence for embroiling itself abroad. Successfully meeting the "implacable challenge" from the Soviets required American people "pulling themselves together and accepting the responsibilities of moral and political leadership that history plainly intended them to bear" (Kennan, 1947).

It was the outbreak of the Cold War that conclusively transformed the urgent post-war need for reconstruction and stability into a formidable Western-led world order. The United States' *first* permanent military alliance with foreign countries came with the 1949 treaty establishing NATO directed against the Soviets. From then, the United States had to accept some level of foreign engagement as the global policeman. The North Atlantic alliance's first Secretary-General, the British General, Lord Hastings Ismay (n.d.), pithily summed up the purpose of his organisation as "to keep the Russians out, the Americans in, and the Germans down". For almost a half-century, NATO acted as the linchpin for the entire liberal order.

The historical emergence of the "West" had in previous centuries been set against a racially defined Orient. The new West – now also including Japan – became better cohered through opposition to the ideological enemy of Soviet "communism". Cold War unity helped consolidate all the West's other institutional arrangements. It gave time for the IMF, the World Bank and GATT to become the bedrock of the post-war infrastructure, at least in the non-Soviet controlled part of the world.

The Cold War effect in embedding the liberal order was reinforced by the second equally unanticipated happening: the post-war boom. Buoyant economic conditions in most Western nations tempered international competition. This put off for many years the prospect of another conflict between the major capitalist nations and thereby bolstered geopolitical stability.

Even after the end of the economic boom in the early 1970s, for two further decades the Cold War influence endured. Entrenched institutions provided a durable political framework for containing the growing inter-capitalist, crisis-inflamed tensions. Prior to the 1989 fall of the Berlin Wall, the advanced capitalist nations appeared almost united.

In response to the economic crisis, the existence of formalised international structures encouraged further collaborative economic and financial rule-making. For example, the Basel-based Bank for International Settlements, known as the "central bankers' bank", became increasingly interventionist after each bout of financial turmoil. A rules-driven mindset means that every financial crisis is put down to a deficiency of rules. The lesson invariably drawn is that the rules and state decision-making procedures need to be tightened further. As the historian Mark Mazower (2013) poignantly concluded, "on such statist foundations rested the liberalization of global finance" (p. 359).

Despite these institutional efforts, following the end of Cold War, the glue holding the West together has been gradually dissolving. It became harder to cover up the crisis-driven amplification of economic differences. With no respite from the West's economic atrophy, tensions between capitalist nations have sharpened, especially since the 2008 crash. The questions became: how long could the existing institutional order keep a lid on these rivalries? And when would the formalised arrangements themselves become sources of bitter conflicts?

An Asset Becomes a Liability

There is no strong strategic desire to challenge the current international settlement, either from the declining or the rising nations. Unsurprisingly, it is usually the writers of the rules that appeal to them most strongly in defence of their interests. This applies especially to Western European nations as countries on the way down. They try to preserve the old arrangements that have them on top. Meanwhile, nations on the way up have little incentive to rush upsetting the status quo either; they perceive that time is on their side, so why unsettle matters prematurely?

Despite these shared peaceable intentions, eventually the rising nations find that pursuing their own interests hits the barriers of the prevailing international order. And the further the old powers try to sustain their outdated settlement, the more the ascending powers are frustrated. The post-war system itself becomes a source of international tension.

NATO exemplifies this. Established as we saw in a different era to coordinate Western military power during the Cold War, since the end of that war NATO has turned into a disruptive force. Pursuing an "open-ended and ill-conceived eastward expansion" rekindled inter-nation tensions, rather than assuage them (Walt, 2018). This illustrates the broader trend that conflicting attitudes to the entrenched institutional order generates dissension, triggered mostly by economic and strategic pressures. National differences are expressed and then often inflamed through opposing or supporting the existing systems and rules.

This highlights the most dangerous contradiction of today's international political institutions: *their founding objective of stability is now generating instability*. Their leaders are proud of maintaining the peace yet the repercussions of their actions today sound like the faint drumbeats of a coming war. Nostalgia for a past that never existed wouldn't help to contain these strains.

A renowned "neorealist" international relations scholar Stephen Walt reminds us that the "so-called liberal order" wasn't quite the nirvana that is often imagined (Walt, 2018). It was never a fully *global* order comprising every nation. There was also an "awful lot of illiberal behavior" going on, even by countries and leaders who constantly proclaimed "liberal values". The United States propped up plenty of authoritarian illiberal rulers throughout the Cold War (and has continued to do so since).

Despite this history, globalist leaders will emphasise how their international organisations have helped preserve the peace since 1945. For example Romano Prodi, president of the European Commission in the 2000s, talked up the European project as having successfully overcome both the classic power politics of the nineteenth century and the armed truce of the Cold War (Tooze, 2018, p. 122). As a bastion of stability, prosperity and the rule of law, Prodi claimed the EU was realising Kant's vision of perpetual peace (European Commission, 2004).

Yet globalist practices have increasingly sparked new antagonisms. The rules become weapons in this struggle, especially by those who want to *preserve* the old order. They are used as a stick to beat those acting in objectively unsettling ways. When Britain, for instance, voted to leave the EU the European Commission response during exit negotiations was driven by its attachment to the existing EU rulebook. It dismissed as unworkable proposals for maintaining a simple close *economic* relationship post-Brexit. Although an open trading and investing relationship would be mutually beneficial in economic terms, the Commission rejected it because it did not fulfil the Single Market's primary *rule*: the indivisibility of the four "freedoms of movement", of goods, services, capital and people.[2]

On the face of it, the Brexit vote was a straightforward, if disruptive, decision by a country to withdraw from an international treaty. Implementing it though was a systemic affront to an institution that had defined how most European countries operated for over half a century. The EU was the pinnacle of a system where national political leaders could act with minimal popular accountability. This was why the political classes across Western Europe, including many in Britain, were so adamant that Brexit would be a disaster. With respect to maintaining their pan-European project Brexit was regarded as potentially catastrophic, because it sought to reverse something never imagined to be reversible.

---

[2]The "four freedoms" are sometimes presented as eternal to post-war European federation. Actually they were formally established only with the 1992 Maastricht Treaty, coming into force in late 1993 towards the end of the first year of the Single Market.

This official reaction to the Brexit vote illustrated that a significant threat to amicable international relations comes from those who are most invested in its current institutional structures. They feel compelled to fight for perpetuating an objectively indefensible status quo (Zammit-Lucia, 2017). As the world's most comprehensive rules-based institution – "the home of rules" – the process of European integration has been built around the idea that difficult issues are best bureaucratised and regimented (Abdelal, 2007, p. 21). However, this backfires when its technocratic forms of governance lack democratic accountability, making them a compelling target for anti-establishment populist movements (McNamara, 2019).

Today, EU peoples and nations are at loggerheads with each other over a variety of topics. Alongside Brexit, responses to the eurozone crisis, to migration flows, and to what is meant by the "rule of law" have also become sources of friction. Tensions have heightened between EU countries of the west and the east, as well as between the north and the south.

These conflicts are rarely the result of intentional provocation. But even with the best of motives international institutions impose decisions on constituent countries that can clash with national interests. A system where all countries must closely follow a set of common rules (including their future evolution) and apply them in a particular manner inherently curtails the sovereignty of members.

It is ironic, but dissension can occur even when the explicit aim is harmony. The EU's enthusiasm for the "harmonisation" of regulation across its region sounds like a sensible route to level the playing field. But in addition to being protectionist by discriminating against the different regimes adopted by nations outside the EU, these exercises often interfere with how particular member states are or want to operate. For instance, EU proposals to harmonise corporate tax rates have triggered strong opposition from low tax countries like Ireland and Hungary whose economies depend on attracting foreign investment.

Western Decline and the Rise of China

The national-*and*-international dual character of capitalism underlies the limitations of globalist organisations. This innate duality was manageable during the post-war boom but difficulties surfaced again after the 1970s with the West's return to persistent economic troubles. When economic conditions deteriorate at home, competitive tensions tend to magnify between nations over their access to and use of the world market. The 1930s slump illustrated how such rivalry can morph into military conflict.

When Cold War unity evaporated in the 1990s the maintenance of international cooperation became even tougher. Exuding both frustration and nostalgia, Kagan (2018) has drawn attention to how "the liberal world order began to erode at the very moment of its widely heralded triumph at the end of the Cold War" (p. 89).

This process didn't complete overnight. After the collapse of the Soviet Union a window of triumphalism, especially felt in the United States, initially extended the international order and helped mute economic rivalries. For example, the UN as the supreme international political organisation endorsed the US-led joint invasion of Iraq in 1990 that succeeded in forcing Iraq's withdrawal from Kuwait.

Nevertheless, by the end of the century, economic-based tensions were less easily contained. The order was noticeably fraying expressed in increasingly frequent geopolitical and economic clashes. Only a few years after the expulsion of Iraq from Kuwait, another UN-backed intervention in the Balkans exposed divisions between Western allies. Meanwhile, protectionist skirmishes between Western countries became more common, as we describe in Chapter 8.

Well before Trump made his impulsive political mark, the United States has responded to its declining authority by acting increasingly unilaterally in international affairs. Before the new millennium began "on issue after issue", the United States found itself "increasingly alone, with one of a few partners, opposing most of the world's states and peoples" (Huntington, 1999, p. 41). The United States was frequently sidestepping the "rule of law" in international affairs (Murphy, 2004, p. 4). Nor was this a peculiarity of US exceptionalism. It reflected an unravelling world order that saw all Western countries look to their own interests to a sharper extent.

Into this fraught intra-Western mix came an economically surging China. The unusual geopolitical conditions immediately after 1945 produced a world order reflecting the economic dominance of the advanced Western nations. That world is no more. Now the combined West accounts for the declining half of world output, dependent on the other faster-growing parts of the world for most of the West's remaining hints of dynamism.

The global predicament is that the composition of the world economy has changed, but the international political order has yet to follow. Meanwhile, those countries in notional global authority are themselves in discord. It is difficult to deny the assessment that to "believe that we have permanently overcome great power rivalry is overly optimistic, potentially dangerous, and, frankly, absurd" (Walt, 2015). Accomplishing a peaceable shift to new international arrangements appropriate to today's economic positions is an extremely demanding geopolitical challenge.

Initially, Western leaders' fanciful hope was that China would meekly accept its subordinate position as its economic development helped "modernise" it. Gradually but inexorably the overriding United States and wider Western approach shifted to containing China and curbing both its economic development and its extending international political influence. President Obama's "pivot to Asia" expressed a necessary America reorientation to the Pacific since the focus of the world economy had tilted decisively in that direction. Under Obama's leadership, the primary US intention with the Trans-Pacific Partnership (TPP) "trade liberalisation" project was not to free up trade but to exclude and restrain China.

The intra-Western and West-East tensions collided together in the subsequent transatlantic falling out over China. Two years before the Trump presidency the United States openly diverged with many of its Western allies over the China-initiated Asian Infrastructure Investment Bank (AIIB). This was a clear indication of China beginning to establish parallel arrangements to those of the US-led liberal international order (Stuenkel, 2016). Yet it was America's supposedly closest ally, Britain – not Germany or France – that led the West's AIIB membership drive in the face of strong US criticism.

When former British chancellor George Osborne announced his country's application to join in early 2015, a US government official was exasperated: "We are wary about a trend toward constant accommodation of China, which is not the best way to engage a rising power". The official rubbed in how far relations had cooled in claiming that the British decision was taken "without any consultation" with the United States (Parker, Chassany, & Dyer, 2015). Political commentator Janan Ganesh (2018a) later pondered the absence of an appropriate term in the English language to describe ongoing tensions Europe and America, sitting somewhere between "allies" and "rivals".

With the United States less in control of the world order and, in particular, under technological and economic challenge from China, it has both abused and used world rules to seek to bolster its position. Simply more openly than his predecessors, President Trump challenged WTO rules as inhibiting the United States' freedom of action. He frequently suggested leaving the organisation because of its alleged unfairness to the United States. To the outrage of the EU and some other WTO members, his opposition included refusing to sanction the appointments of judges, thereby threatening to gridlock its disputes system.

At the same time, though, Trump *appealed to* WTO rules to justify evicting China from the organisation in an attempt to halt or slow down China's economic ascent. Although the White House identified both the WTO and China as strategic targets, it has sometimes applied the rules of the former against the aspirations of the latter. Claiming that China was stealing technology from foreign investors, the United States turned to the WTO's intellectual property (IP) rules to seek China's expulsion. With this stance, the United States found itself in common cause with the EU who also filed WTO complaints about China's alleged IP breaches.

Sometimes, the rising powers also make use of the rules of the old order. For instance, when the United States escalated protectionist measures against China to try to impede its emergence as a high-technology economy, it was China that appealed for support to the existing international rules. Hence, the bizarre spectacle at the Davos World Economic Forum in early 2017 of President Xi Jinping from "communist" China berating the "free market" Americans for breaching free trade rules. When the United States subsequently continued its outbursts against the WTO, the Chinese were outspoken in denouncing America's "law of the jungle" approach to trade.

In this topsy-turvy world, the challenger China, alongside the old world EU, has sometimes been championing the merits of the WTO's "rules-based multilateral trading system" against the declining US hegemon, branded as the disruptor. Meanwhile, the EU agrees with the United States in regarding China as a "systemic rival" that needs to be contained. This peculiar fusion of a United States tending towards unilateralism, an EU that says it wants to defend multilateralism, and a China that seeks a bigger say in global affairs, is bound to bring clashes, intended and accidental.

Any action by a state that affects international economic activity contains the potential for friction with another – and often embroils other countries too.

In particular, when businesses become subject to the commands of two masters, their home and their host governments, not only does this cause problems for the companies involved – as many US firms have found in their Chinese operations in trying to avoid offending either Beijing or Washington – but also international rows often follow.

Transatlantic clashes included Obama's Department of Justice fining both Britain's pharmaceutical giant GlaxoSmithKline and its engineering leader Rolls Royce for what it deemed to be corrupt practices. On another occasion, the US Justice Department subpoenaed Glencore, the Anglo-Swiss multinational commodity trading and mining company, demanding that the company hand over records related to its compliance with US laws against foreign corrupt practices and money laundering concerning its business in Congo, Nigeria and Venezuela.

America also imposed multi-billion dollar fines on a number of European-based banks for breaking its sanctions against Iran. When Trump pulled out of the Iran nuclear deal in 2018, he not only prohibited American companies from doing business in Iran. He also threatened to go after companies from other countries whose governments still supported the deal.

On the other side of the Atlantic EU commissioners have been just as active in pursuit of US companies – especially information technology companies, a sector where EU-based companies lag far behind. The EU has issued anti-monopoly fines against Microsoft, Intel and Google on several occasions. The EU also ordered Apple and Amazon to pay back "illegal" tax deductions even though these were granted by its own member states.

Subsequently the European Commission has had Google and Facebook in its sights over internet privacy. The EU has been a proud pioneer of data protection rules with its GDPR coming into force in May 2018. Even though this has nothing explicitly to do with trade, these rules have potentially damaging effects on foreign commercial interests (Cross, 2018). Notably, the data protection regulations have *global reach* to regulate and police non-EU businesses, as well as EU ones. In practice, this mostly applies to the big Silicon Valley ones that operate within the EU. Even though Europe has few local competitors to "protect" in this area, the GDPR operates as a protectionist law penalising foreign companies that follow different data privacy standards.

Meanwhile, Western government attempts to contain the ascent of Chinese companies raises not only the East-West temperature but also sometimes exacerbate intra-West tensions. When the White House banned the Chinese telecommunications equipment maker Huawei from bidding for contracts in the United States, ostensibly on national security grounds, this was not just an affront to China. Demanding that other countries followed suit fostered friction within the West too.

State interventions that regulate and sometimes ban foreign investment are also becoming increasingly contentious internationally. It has become common for national and EU regulatory bodies to investigate and sanction, regulate or block cross-border mergers often involving businesses from other territories.

Controlling inbound foreign investment is not new. It was in 1975 that President Gerald Ford created the Committee on Foreign Investment in the United States (CFIUS). The purpose was explicitly protectionist to target mergers that could result in control of an American business by a foreign individual or company. By the 1980s, and initially directed at Japan, CFIUS was given a legal policing role in judging whether deals could threaten national interests. In 2018, the Foreign Investment Risk Review Modernization Act extended the mandate of CFIUS to review smaller, non-controlling investments in a wider range of 27 industries.

Now China has become the United States' main target. For example, the US government blocked a proposal by Ant Financial, a Chinese electronic payments company that is an affiliate company of the tech giant Alibaba, to purchase MoneyGram, a money transfer company based in Dallas. It cited concerns about Chinese access to US know-how. However, the battle is not all about the United States versus China. About four-fifths of CFIUS investigations cover non-Chinese deals, including a lot with supposed US allies.

Other Western countries have been adopting or extending similar controls over foreign firms' inward investment, both at the United States' request – as with Huawei – and at their own initiative. In late 2018, the German government tightened its rules on foreign takeovers by lowering the ownership threshold from 25% to 10%, and extending the coverage of what are regarded as "critical" sectors. The Japanese government has proposed an even tighter review threshold, down from 10% to 1%. The British government, too, is planning new powers to allow it to intervene in or block hundreds of foreign takeovers of British firms, also based on a wider interpretation of "national security".

The EU competition authorities regularly make judgements on cross-border acquisitions even when no EU companies are directly involved. They argue that mergers between companies even when based outside the EU can affect markets inside it. The European Commission has been especially active when US companies seek to merge. In 2012, it cleared Google's purchase of Motorola and in 2014 approved the acquisition of WhatsApp by Facebook. Assuming authority over companies from outside its territory both undermines national sovereign rights and whips up inter-nation tensions.

Controversially, the EU earlier blocked a proposed merger of the US companies General Electric and Honeywell, even though US regulators approved the merger as improving competition and reducing prices. The US Treasury Secretary at the time, Paul O'Neill, called the rejection of the merger "off the wall". He complained of EU regulators as the "closest thing you can find to an autocratic organization that can successfully impose their will on things that one would think are outside their scope of attention" (BBC News, 2001).

Now although such extraterritorial regulatory intervention has become almost normal, it remains highly provocative to other countries. For instance, in 2019, the ECJ ruled that member states could demand that foreign social media companies like Facebook take down content on a global basis. In addition to further intruding on free speech, this is likely to spark conflicts over jurisdiction.

The ruling means that the courts of one country can control what internet users in another country see, even when that content breaches no local laws.

Western Responses to the Shifting Tectonic Plates

When incumbents use their privileged positions to try to preserve the status quo at the expense of frustrating their challengers, this is bound to generate a potentially explosive international environment. Ultimately, it was tensions between the established and the rising countries that played out during the two world wars of the last century. The international system and institutions developed after 1945 were driven by a genuine aspiration to prevent war recurring. The tragic irony is that this same system is now a battlefield for the conflicts that could bring about the next one.

The challenge for maintaining peace today is not simply in the limitations of particular politicians – globalist or mercantilist – who might launch rash and arbitrary initiatives. Fundamentally, it lies in the international system they are bound up with, a system that is simultaneously resilient and fragile. The resilience is evidenced by the quarter century that has already passed since end of the Cold War without a serious breakdown. The fragility arises from how the liberal international order that was established after the Second World War reflects a world that has passed away.

The history of the past 150 years tells us that the geopolitical framework always finds it difficult to adjust to the emergence of industrial "latecomers" who want to play a role on a par with the dominant nations of the day (Findlay & O'Rourke, 2007, p. 545). However, although China is objectively the challenger nation – the Athens equivalent to America as Sparta – it is still essentially a status quo power. China's material interests remain best served by the maintenance of an open global economy where the superior competitiveness of its goods wins out, similar to Britain in the late nineteenth century or to the United States after the Second World War.

On the other side, by cracking down on Chinese goods, companies and capital flows, the United States and EU protectionist practices are inflaming geopolitical tensions. It is the United States and the EU that in practice are forsaking the liberal tenets of the post-1945 order. So far, it is not the rising Asian countries but the declining Western ones whose actions are undermining the old order and threatening peace. Adherents to the globalist order are not only failing to refresh the international settlement: their devotion to how things have been represents a huge obstacle to a peaceful transformation.

All this indicates that when declining powers rely on preserving the existing rules it can be more dangerous for the world than the actions of aspirant countries that seek to evade being restricted by them. This is also why the globalists, who most strongly profess their allegiance to the rules-based order, are as much a threat to world peace, as those they condemn as old-fashioned economic nationalists.

Mercantilists like Trump are certainly a danger to international peace, aggravated in his case by his reactive and impulsive unpredictability. Despite this, his foreign policy – until the time of writing at least – has been quite ordinary and conservative (Herbert, McCrisken, & Wroe, 2019). His "trade wars" have had less impact than his critics claimed. In actuality, this is true of all trade conflicts, as we describe in Part 2. We also have the advantage of history to warn us of the potential dangers of mercantilist practices. Eighty years ago, this approach was tried and found wanting. As a consequence, a direct re-run of the 1930s and 1940s is unlikely.

Globalist leaders, though, are just as hazardous as mercantilists because of their similar attachment to an anachronistic international arrangement. When globalists block substantive change to the international order, this bottles up pressures that could provoke major disruption.

The astute socialist journalist Henry Brailsford, introduced earlier, described something similar even as the First World War continued to rage. War can result from a static social order helpless to make the dynamic changes necessary to prevent it. He suggested military conflict often arises because of the "inertia, the impotence, the suspicion, the lack of social sense which [stand] in the way of these necessary changes" (Brailsford, 2012, pp. 324–326). To these perilous attributes that still well characterise twenty-first century international politicians, we can add today's prevalent fatalism.

There are three factors that reinforce the prime threat as coming from globalist ideas and practices. First, the globalists are in charge in most Western states. And even where globalists are not in official control of government, such as in the Trumpian US, there America's famous checks-and-balances have muted the excesses of old-fashioned mercantilism.

Meanwhile, within the big Western European countries, globalist politicians do mostly preside. There the potential for disruption is amplifying as the EU leaders work to build their military capabilities by developing a common "security and defence" policy. Taking advantage of the timing of Britain's referendum vote in 2016, the EU quickly adopted an explicit "global strategy" to strengthen its autonomous standing in the world.

Responding to the growing pressures from what were described as the other two members of the world's economic "G3" – the United States and China – the European Commission High Representative for Foreign Affairs and Security Policy argued that a "fragile world calls for a more confident and responsible European Union, it calls for an outward- and forward-looking European foreign and security policy" (European Commission, 2016, pp. 3–5). Since then, the EU has been establishing a range of what it calls "Permanent Structured Cooperation" projects, as well as a European Defence Fund to extend pan-European military capacities (Mills, 2019, pp. 4–6).

While tangible progress with this objective has been slow, the new European Commission President Leyen immediately indicated an enhanced ambition by pledging to lead a "geopolitical" executive. Her foreign policy chief Joseph Borrell has also been upfront in arguing that the EU must "learn to use the language of power", indicating a tougher-minded approach to pursuing its global political interests (*Financial Times* editorial, 2020). The militarisation of globalism is rolling on.

Second, globalism retains a moral authority and influence by speaking in the language of liberalism, peace and democracy. And third, the longer the globalist-controlled old system is perpetuated, the more fragile and hazardous it will become.

The coming breakdown of order is most likely to pit not mercantilist-versus-globalist but globalist-versus-globalist. This is because – like the market system over which they officiate – globalist politicians remain both national and international. Hence, the paradox of our "global times" that the main powerbase of globalism is not supranational but *national*, especially located in the leading Western nations. As Rosenboim (2017a) explained, "the idea that globalism is fundamentally at odds with national sovereignty is a false and misleading narrative".

It is nations that retain the potential for exerting real power, based on the tax revenues that fund their conventional and unconventional war-making capabilities. In contrast, supranational institutions only have membership fees and lawyers. With no disrespect to lawyers, the drone missile and the cyberattack is mightier than a judge's ruling. Despite the globalist claim that the age of the nation state is over, when events force action on politicians, the nation state remains their dominant instrument for effect. And this includes the globalist-inspired policies that are proving to be so divisive at home and abroad.

Part 2

Myths about Trade

Chapter 5

The Obsession with Trade

Contrary to conventional opinion, trade does *not* make the world go round. Yes, the visibility of cross-border trade makes it the most tangible expression of internationalisation. Pictures of ports stacked high with containers are among the most commonly used images of our global times. Likewise, scholarly discussions of globalisation also often elevate the importance of trade.

The belief that "increased trade always and necessarily results in increased wealth" is taken as a modern truth (Conner, 2004, p. 21). Similarly "deglobalisation" anxieties begin with trade too. The slowdown in world trade growth relative to output following the 2008–2009 financial crisis became emblematic of a supposed retreat from globalisation and rewinding the clock to needier times (Hoekman, 2015).

Complementing the privileged status of trade is the globalist idea that striking trade agreements is economically progressive. The converse assumption is that anything that undermines trade and trading arrangements is necessarily bad for the economy and a threat to global prosperity.

This, and the next three chapters, examines this significance attached to trade – and to trade agreements – and explains that it is not deserved. The relationship between trade and economic growth has confusingly been turned upside down. Trade is secondary for the economy and for society compared to the conditions prevailing in producing whatever is or might be traded. We don't trade thin air, so we need to start with a *thing*. Efficient, well-produced goods and services will be attractive anywhere in the world and generate trading activity. Meanwhile, inefficiently and shoddily made things are likely to go unsold and thus won't appear as trade.

The value of official trade pacts is also overstated. Trading agreements between governments are declarations of intent. On their own they don't make any trade happen. That depends on businesses and their productive capabilities. A trade agreement, however favourably written, is economically meaningless if a country's goods and services are not good enough to be wanted by people and businesses elsewhere.

Appreciating the derivative nature of trade is important for both economic and political reasons. The mistaken prominence attached to trade mystifies the real productive drivers of economic wealth and distracts from fixing the West's

Beyond Confrontation: Globalists, Nationalists and Their Discontents, 69–84
Copyright © 2020 by Phil Mullan
All rights of reproduction in any form reserved
doi:10.1108/978-1-83982-560-620200008

core economic malfunction: a broken engine of production. In these circumstances, government policies that boost trade are counterproductive: a palliative that covers up the further atrophy within domestic production.

Politically, trade determinism is equally diversionary. It has distorted many recent debates, from the significance of Brexit to the dangers of Trump's trade wars. Focussing on the wrong targets creates deceptive narratives that are proving to be divisive and dangerous.

Production problems are instead perceived as problems in exchange. Solutions are sought in this same sphere of supply and demand, ranging from protectionist restraints on imports introduced by mercantilists, to the "free trade" agreements recommended by globalists that discriminate against non-members. Far from ensuring a world of peace and prosperity a fixation on trade measures is turning into their nemesis.

This is why Part 2 of this book is devoted to putting the kernel of the global economy back on its feet. It explains that production, not trade, is the decisive force for social improvement. On this foundation, we examine in the final chapter of this part the *genuine* harm exacted on productivity and prosperity by all forms of protectionism, tariff and non-tariff.

The Miscasting of Trade

Trade and productivity growth – the amount produced by each person – do tend to be correlated. This correlation is widely interpreted, we argue misinterpreted, as meaning that trade is a substantial driver of economic growth and development. For instance, Richard Baldwin (2016), one of today's most eminent writers on trade and globalisation, claimed that without foreign trade, Britain's industrial revolution would not have been possible (p. 125).

Multiple channels are suggested for how trade boosts productivity: improving resource allocation, increasing scale and specialisation, encouraging innovation activities, facilitating knowledge transfer and fostering the expansion of higher productivity firms and the exit of the least productive ones (Acharya & Keller, 2008; Coe & Helpman, 1995; Grossman & Helpman, 1991; IMF, 2016; OECD, 2017a, p. 80). It is frequently asserted that post-1945 trade liberalisation brought about the subsequent expansion of global wealth. We often hear that trade has taken hundreds of millions of people out of poverty in China and other developing countries. Meanwhile, trade agreements are invariably justified by forecasts of so many billions of extra growth they will bring.

Just as increased trade is seen as a boon for growth, anything that might undermine a country's trade is regarded as a handicap. Mercantilists denounce "unfair trade" by other countries as the source of their domestic troubles. Globalists worry that any disruptions to smooth flowing trade, such as Britain leaving the EU, or Trump's trade wars, are bound to set back economic performance.

But trade's starring role in today's dominant narratives misrepresents how economies work. The genuine correlation of trade with productivity and growth is consistent with a straightforward Occam's Razor explanation, which is the other way round. Faster growth derives from higher productivity, and it is higher productivity enterprises that are likely to be successful exporters rather than low-productivity ones, because they will be stronger competitors in foreign as well as domestic markets. This explains the research showing that attaining high productivity *precedes* firms' entry into export markets (Bernard, Jensen, Redding, & Schott, 2012, p. 288). It is telling too that there are no successful exporting businesses that are domestic failures. Thus, better domestic productivity, and increased growth, propels trade volumes, not the reverse.

Despite his sympathy for "free trade", Douglas Irwin, a specialist on its intellectual history, recognised that causation flows *from* being efficient with healthier productivity *to* being a successful exporter, rather than the other way round (Irwin, 2015, p. 53). He suggested that the "fundamental problem" with much analysis on this issue is that "trade affects income and income affects trade". Perhaps, all that is shown by these studies is that countries with higher incomes and higher productivity are bigger traders (Irwin, 2015, p. 56, footnote 44). Foreign trade often accompanies a business's and an economy's productive strength, but it is not its precondition.

Privileging trade over production reverses economic dynamics. The process of production creates value. Trade – at home or abroad – only realises this wealth, converting value into money. Both chronologically and logically, actual trade comes *after* things are produced. Without production, there would be nothing to trade. You need to have produced something – even if it is extracting a "raw" material – to be able to engage with buyers. Production rather than trading is the real source of wealth and sustains all social life. A country that does not produce the means of life will soon face destitution and risk collapse.

Trading though *is* vital in a market economy. It turns things into money for sellers and enables buyers to obtain the useful things needed to consume and produce. The sales process is crucial for businesses to survive and thrive. Value that is stuck in the commodity form doesn't pay any bills, wages, interest charges or share dividends. Because trading is what brings in cash – the recognised, usable form of value – generating value *appears* to derive from exchange. This fuels the misleading presumption that trading is productive of value and economic growth. In fact, the flows, needs and challenges of production drive trade, not vice versa.

For instance, the expansion of production requires a greater mass of raw materials and intermediate products as its means. Productivity improvements only continue on a durable basis as a result of business investments in innovation mostly embodied in technologically advanced capital goods. When any of these goods are sourced abroad, imports expand. And because the final goods and services produced can fulfil social needs in other countries too, exports also increase.

Hence, capitalism as an advanced mode of production propelled a huge expansion in foreign trade. The globalist elevation of the economic importance of trade is not a fiction. It corresponds to how capitalist operations really appear, as a social system geared to production *for the market*. And since production is now undertaken for exchange, the preceding act of production falls from view in a society dominated by market relations. Production gets simply taken for granted as an ever-present technical process.

As a result, trade in a capitalist society appears to dominate everything. Capitalism is appropriately rendered as a "market economy", and as a "commercial society" centred on buying and selling things. Trading relations, and how people engage with the exchange process, attract the most attention in assessing the workings of the modern economy.

A fixation on trade seems even further justified under later capitalism, classically characterised as the stage of imperialism, when world trade assumes greater economic significance. As mature capitalist production confronted intrinsic barriers to its further expansion, the world market evolved into a vital mechanism for offsetting productive decay at home.[1] The scholar Robert Wade (2017) noted how British imperial activities encouraged the economic paradigm that economic prosperity was based on trade and overseas ventures, rather than domestic production.

In the late 1920s, the Marxist economist Henryk Grossmann described how foreign trade plays its counteracting role, drawing on the experience of the first wave of "globalisation" leading up to the First World War. Exporting helps to overcome the limitations of the national market. By expanding the size of the overall market for goods and services, it enables an increase in the multiplicity of products and extends product diversification.

Fixed costs can be spread over a larger output so that the average cost of production is reduced. An increased variety of products facilitate investment in the domestic production process and helps offset capitalism's drift into crisis (Grossmann, 1992, p. 166). On the side of imports, cheaper imported machinery, raw materials and supplies also ease the profitability constraints that are holding back struggling producers.

Of greater importance than the export of products in this later stage of capitalism is the *export of capital*, normally discussed today as foreign direct investment (FDI).[2] Capital exporting was common by the end of the nineteenth century because relocating some production abroad offered businesses lucrative opportunities for additional surpluses to offset profitability challenges at home. When decay within the advanced industrial countries took hold, the faltering domestic dynamic forced a greater business orientation to foreign arenas. This became a "typical and indispensible move in all the advanced capitalist countries" as a means of prolonging periods of crisis-free capitalism (Grossmann, 1992, pp. 194–195).

---

[1]In *Creative Destruction* (Mullan, 2017) I explained the causes and consequences of productive decay; that is the decay in mature capitalism's capacity to create new industries and new sectors, and enough decent jobs.

[2]The usual definition of foreign *direct investment* is investment that brings a significant voice in the management of an enterprise operating outside the investor's own country. The statistics generally include investments entailing ownership of 10% or greater of equity. FDI may involve either creating an entirely new enterprise – a "greenfield" investment – or changing the ownership of existing enterprises, via mergers and acquisitions. Reinvesting the earnings of the enterprise abroad is also included in FDI figures.

FDI illustrates again how a change in the structure of production has implications for trade volumes. The usual outcome of shifting productive activity abroad is increased trade, due to extra cross-border supplies and sales. Overseas production arising from a business's outward FDI often increases demand for intermediate outputs of its domestic facilities or for those of its domestic suppliers when they supply the overseas subsidiaries too. Also, at least some output from the FDI enterprise is usually exported back home or to third countries. Overall, capital exports provide a significant uplift to cross-border trading.

Half a century after Grossmann wrote, Raymond Vernon, a renowned scholar of globalisation and multinational businesses, adopted a similar appreciation of the part played by foreign production. The main business motivations for venturing into production abroad lay in the mutually reinforcing pursuit of profits, of market share and of hedging against business uncertainty (Vernon, 1971, p. 114). In particular, he noted that the domestic decline in profit margins enhanced the corporate search for lower cost locations for production abroad (Vernon, 1971, p. 74).

While expanded production propels trade, it is specifically the *internationalisation* of production that acts as a sizable driver of trading patterns and volumes. When capitalist nations mature economically, a bigger share of the cross-border trade they undertake becomes ancillary to the international production that helps compensate for sluggish conditions at home.

This explains why the economic slowdown that hit all the advanced countries at the start of the 1970s did not see a parallel decline in trade levels but instead brought their uplift. This tendency has continued ever since. Western businesses seek to boost their shaky profitability by doing more both to cut the cost of their inputs and to increase sales.[3] Much of this effort goes abroad, thereby stimulating trade volumes.

Fig. 5.1 illustrates how trade grew in importance again during the crisis years of the 1970s long *before* the supposed dawn of our era of globalisation in the late 1980s. Globally, exports rose from around 10% to 12% of world output during the post-war boom, to almost double that by the start of the 1980s, reaching 30% on the eve of the 2008–2009 financial crisis (World Bank World Development Indicators, 2020: exports of goods and services as % of GDP).

Significantly, the new wave of internationalisation coincided with the end of the post-war boom, rather than with the end of the Cold War when globalisation theories started to take off. This suggests that while internationalisation processes and globalisation theories are linked, the former was prior, arising out of the renewed problems in domestic production within the developed industrial countries. Meanwhile, globalist theories became attractive later in the new political circumstances after Cold War certainties receded.

Although trade has been helping toiling businesses cope with depressed conditions since the 1970s, it does not provide a *solution* for production's structural

---

[3]See Part 2 of *Creative Destruction* (Mullan, 2017) on the problem of falling profitability.

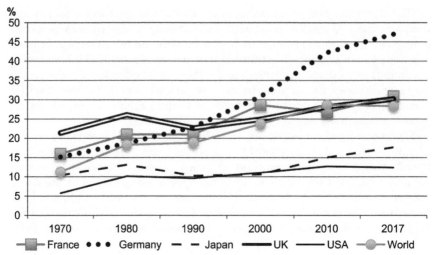

Fig. 5.1.   Rising Prominence of World Trade: Exports of Goods and Services as % of GDP, 1970–2017 (UNCTADstat, 2019: Economic Trends, National Accounts, GDP by Type of Expenditure).

stupor. Over time, the trade benefits diminish relative to worsening atrophy. This explains the so-called openness-productivity paradox. By most measures, cross-border flows of goods and services, as well as money, people and information, have risen to their highest levels ever. Yet at the same time, productivity growth across advanced economies has slowed, in some countries to a halt. So while external openness has switched up a gear, technological innovation and productivity advance simultaneously seem to have gone into "reverse gear" (Bank of England, 2018, p. 9). The principal explanation for this incongruity is that the additional surpluses gleaned from greater internationalisation have become inadequate to offset deepening economic malaise at home.

Despite these limitations, the appearance of trade's predominant part in economic affairs continues. With economic activity substantially internationalised, a larger proportion of wealth does derive from production abroad, and a lot of it enters domestic life through its material manifestations, most visibly through trade. The importance of trade thus continues to *appear* self-evident.

A Contrary View from Economists

An equally revealing paradox is that today's attachment to trade determinism seems undaunted by the absence of evidence. A large number of established economists have found themselves unable to establish the importance of trade for economic growth, both theoretically and empirically.

The IMF (2016) itself cautioned: "Identifying the causal effect of trade on growth is challenging due to potentially severe reverse causality and measurement issues" (p. 88). This explains why the IMF's former head Christine Lagarde admitted in April 2018 that the "actual impact on growth" of Trump's tariffs on Chinese imports "is not very substantial when measured in terms of GDP" (IMF, 2018, as cited in Frankopan, 2019, p. 160). A pair of economists, Jeffrey Frankel and David Romer (1999), introduced their own tentative attempts to establish a positive trade-to-growth relationship with the admission that "despite the great effort devoted to studying this issue, there is little persuasive evidence concerning the effect of trade on income" (p. 379).

Models and analyses can be found that suggest every type of causation, often in conflict with each other. Paul Krugman (1995), the celebrated Nobel economics laureate, summarised that the causes and consequences of world trade growth "are surprisingly disputed issues" (p. 328). In another much-cited work modelling international economic growth, Gene Grossman and Elhanan Helpman (1991) asked themselves: does trade promote innovation in a small economy? Their answer was a cryptic: "It depends" (p. 152).

Broadening their theoretical study to incorporate larger economies was no more definitive. They assumed that these countries' global interactions generate forces that accelerate growth, but immediately continued, "several suggest reasons why international integration might impede growth" (Grossman & Helpman, 1991, p. 336). This illustrates the classic evasive answer of professional economists: on the one hand, this and, on the other hand, perhaps the opposite.

In general, assessments of the direct impact of trade restrictions for growth are ambiguous. A decade later, the economic historian Kevin O'Rourke assessed the burgeoning literature on trade and growth. He also found conflicting opinions, and "an impressive array of models" that reveal protection can either increase or reduce long-run growth rates (O'Rourke, 2000). Another study found that the "new" growth theories of the 1990s, that distinguished themselves by prioritising the role of knowledge, were also equivocal about trade's impact on economic growth (Harrison, 1995, p. 1).

Empirical studies about trade and growth have also been inconclusive. It is easy to show a positive correlation between trade levels and productivity growth, but studies cannot establish the *direction* of causation. One recent analysis concluded that while "trade integration is often regarded as a principal determinant of economic growth, the empirical evidence for a causal linkage between trade and growth is ambiguous" (Busse & Königer, 2012, p. 1. See also Harrison, 1995, pp. 5–6, 24–25; Rodríguez & Rodrik, 2001; Vamvakidis, 1997).

Even the avowedly pro-trade World Bank (1993) noted in a celebrated report on the "East Asian Miracle" that it can be very difficult to "establish statistical links between growth and a specific intervention and even more difficult to establish causality" (p. 6). When the Bank surveyed the economic reforms implemented by many countries during the 1990s, it reiterated this difficulty. It conceded that the results of trade measures had varied and had sometimes "fallen short of expectations".

Historian Knick Harley similarly assessed that the economic effects of nineteenth century "trade" are difficult to discern. He found that Britain's rise to global economic leadership did not depend on foreign trade and that it is equally hard to blame Britain's relative decline after 1870 on foreign trade (Harley, 1994, p. 301).

Irwin (2015) concluded on the trade-growth relationship that despite the ubiquitous conviction that "trade raises productivity through a variety of mechanisms", it is "deceptively difficult" to empirically verify (p. 55). Nevertheless, trade determinism has proven to be a stubborn presumption over the ages.

The Rise, Fall and Rise Again of Trade Determinism

Trade plays a justifiable role in socio-economic histories. For the many centuries, when there was little progress in the techniques of production, novelties in life derived mostly from the discovery of things in other climes. The objective of trade was primarily about importing: securing access to commodities and goods unavailable, or too costly, to make at home.

With the emergence of capitalism, the emphasis changed to the active promotion of exports. Capitalism's distinction from all previous societies was generalised commodity production for exchange rather than for immediate use. Trade's function for the acquisition of things was overtaken by the dynamic of production specifically *for* the market, leading to the consolidation of a genuinely *world market*.

Mercantilist thinking had its roots in the early merchant phase of capitalism. Reflecting a vast expansion in overseas trade from the late fifteenth century, mercantilists identified exports as wealth generating. This enabled countries to build up riches in gold and silver. Imports in contrast were seen as wasteful, mostly frittering away wealth for unproductive luxury consumption.

With productivity still effectively flat, mercantilist writers could exaggerate the importance of trade to national economic well-being (Irwin, 1996, p. 29). Economic strength was expressed in a large positive balance of trade. The modern slowdown in Western productivity growth since the 1970s, and particularly since 2000, encouraged restatements of this outlook from today's mercantilists.

Historically, protectionist practices eventually brought the demise of mercantilist influence because of the fetters they placed on industrial development. The taxation of imports favoured by mercantilists protected inefficient production and held back domestic economic progress. In particular, it inhibited the development of new industries and sectors. This is why it wasn't only the landowners who benefitted from the protection of their corn cultivation in the late eighteenth century. Custom duties also protected early British textile manufacturers from Irish linen and Indian cotton, and its iron masters from cheap Swedish iron (Harley, 1994, p. 310).

Mercantilism was the scourge of classical political economy not because Adam Smith, David Ricardo and their fellow thinkers were obsessed with trade. Their great insight was in seeing *production* as the real source of a society's wealth. The original profundity of their thinking arose precisely because they resisted being swayed by how their emerging societies functioned on the surface in exchange. They were scientific enough to go beneath the generalised market to which all production was geared and instead paid greatest attention to the production process itself.

Appreciating the universalising potential of the advance of the productive forces, these classical writers wanted to remove the barrier of mercantilist protectionism. From their productivist perspective, the main shortcoming of import restraints was that it created or sustained inefficient monopoly industries by shielding them from competition. Resources that could be better deployed elsewhere, might be stuck in, or attracted to, economically backward areas of production (Smith, 2012, Book 4, Chapter 2, paragraph 2, p. 442). The result of such state regulation would be a less advantageous use of capital and reduced economic output (Smith, 2012, Book 4, Chapter 2, paragraph 11, p. 447).

The classical writers were not "economists" in the modern sense. They were Enlightenment figures motivated by the liberalising possibilities of economic development. Their writings articulated the interests of the rising industrial bourgeoisie, even though some were often highly critical of particular business practices. In their era, promoting "economic freedom" was about giving greater scope to market relations that were restricted by the shackles of previous economic ways. Their desire for a "free market" – significantly a phrase they barely used, and never with its modern connotations – was for an economy freed from feudal and early capitalist constraints.

Classical economy's reflections on trade derived from what best served wealth-producing efficiency. Andrew Skinner explained the transformative role of Smith as doing what none of his predecessors had: he presented a *systemic* framework for political economy. He gave analytical *shape* to thinking about the economy (Skinner, 1990, p. 157). This methodology saw Smith (2012) assess trade policy principally from the consequences for increasing the value of a country's annual production (Book 4, Chapter 1, paragraphs 35, 45, pp. 440–441).

Smith (2012) started the *Wealth of Nations* with how the *division of labour* improved society's productive powers (Book 1, Chapter 1, paragraph 1, p. 9). From his celebrated example of the multiple tasks involved in pin manufacture, he pointed out three benefits of specialisation: first, the greater dexterity of specialised workers; second, eliminating the time people could waste in shifting from one task to another; and third, facilitating the development of specialised machinery.

In addition to detailing the *technical* division of labour within a single enterprise, Smith also embraced the progressive consequences of a wider *social* division of labour between different commodity producers. This is where trade came in, by enabling the extension of this social specialisation. He explained that since it is the "power of exchanging that gives occasion to the division of labour, so the extent of this division must always be limited by ... the extent of the market" (Smith, 2012, Book 1, Chapter 3, paragraph 1, p. 22). An expanded market, including selling abroad, facilitated the benefits of larger scale production. He envisaged opening up "the whole world for a market to the produce of every sort of labour", seeing trade as mutually beneficial between countries by encouraging each other's industry (Smith, 2012, Book 1, Chapter 3, paragraphs 3–4, p. 24).

Smith, we should recall, wrote *before* the productive influences of technologies such as steam power and machines could be fully appreciated. His particular focus on scale and specialisation as drivers of productivity reflected a phase of capitalism prior to the innovation-based dynamic industrialisation during the nineteenth century. By then, after Smith's death, technological change became the predominant driver of productivity growth.

While the scale benefits from specialisation remain relevant today, they are relatively less important than when Smith lived. As size has now already expanded so much, additional economies from even bigger operations tend to be insubstantial. Irwin recognised that the benefits of larger scale can now be "overstated" because most plants have already attained the scale required for efficient specialisation (Irwin, 2015, p. 47). Businesses can be large in the home territory without capturing extra markets overseas, so the extra production scale from trade no longer leads to significantly lower costs.

In Smith's time though, trade's role in enabling specialisation from a wider division of labour was a lot more pertinent. Nevertheless, he was astuter than many writers today in denying that trade was an *independent* driver of higher efficiencies. What mattered was the change to production. The specialisation of productive labour is what made the goods cheaper and helped drive trade.

Unlike the mercantilists he criticised, Smith did not exaggerate the role of foreign trade for the domestic economy. Since for him the "great object of the political economy of every country" is to increase the riches and power of that country, it should give "no preference nor superior encouragement" to foreign trade over trade at home (Smith, 2012, Book 2, Chapter 5, paragraph 31, p. 366). In the light of modern trade determinism, it is no surprise that some globalist international trade zealots, such as Chicago school leader George Stigler (1976), described this view as a "proper failure" of Smith.

From Smith's productivist framework, it made sense that countries should produce and exchange goods where they had an *absolute* productive advantage over foreign companies. It was the other great classical economist Ricardo, writing in the early nineteenth century who, using the same framework of production, extended absolute advantage into the principle of *comparative advantage*.

Probably influenced by Britain's relatively higher productivity and higher cost competitiveness across many areas of production at the time, Ricardo's idea explained that trade remained advantageous *even* for a country that was superior in the production of *all* goods. The "comparative" adjective refers to countries playing to their *relative* productive strengths, even if all their industries were absolutely more, or less, productive than those in other countries.

Ricardo provided a famous hypothetical illustration based on England and Portugal exchanging wine and cloth. He showed that if Portugal were *more efficient at producing both items*, it would still be mutually beneficial for both countries to specialise in goods with the lowest opportunity cost (though that was not a term Ricardo used himself). "Comparative advantage" refers to what a country can make most efficiently while giving up the least efficient areas of production. A country should reject making a product that offers it less gain in favour of the product in which it is more efficient, even if it is the most (or least) efficient producer of both these products.

On the assumption that Portugal would be *relatively* more efficient internally in producing wine rather than cloth, and vice versa for England, then both countries would benefit by specialising in their comparative areas of strength. Wine making is Portugal's comparative advantage, and cloth production is England's. Portugal could then exchange excess wine for excess English cloth. She could obtain a greater amount of cloth through this trade than she could produce by allocating part of the capital engaged in wine cultivation to the manufacture of cloth (Ricardo, 1973, p. 82).

Ricardo thought that relative efficiency was of greater importance for driving business specialisation than Smith's discussion of absolute efficiency. In fact, it wasn't that big an intellectual leap. It had already been implied by Smith (2012):

> If a foreign country can supply us with a commodity cheaper than we ourselves can make it, better buy it off them with some part of the produce of our own industry, employed in a way in which we have some advantage. (Book 4, Chapter 2, paragraph 12, p. 446).

As Smith had done, Ricardo discussed trade as an outcome of the conditions of production, rather than the other way round. Retaining Smith's attention to production, Ricardo had simply extended his predecessor's thinking on specialisation. Thus, it is ironic today that trade-fixated writers often draw on Ricardo and this thesis to authorise the economic case for trade as a major source of prosperity. He is frequently acclaimed as the "grandfather" of international trade, and it is commonplace to assert that this principle "identified a new source of efficiency gains from international trade" (Evenett, 2017, p. vii). In fact, Ricardo's famed association with this theory is tribute to the influence of succeeding trade determinists rather than to the writer himself.

They gave greater importance to this argument than Ricardo himself did. Indeed, he never even used the term "comparative advantage". Irwin appropriately drew attention to the minor role comparative advantage played in Ricardo's overall work. He suggested that "Ricardo's mere three paragraph discussion was poorly expressed, awkwardly placed in [Chapter 7], and failed to bring out the essence of the theory" (Irwin, 1996, p. 91).

John Chipman (1965), the author of another survey of the intellectual history of international trade thought that Ricardo's statement of the idea was "quite wanting, so much so as to cast some doubt as to whether he truly understood it; at best, his version is carelessly worded" (p. 480). That so much importance is today assigned to a quite short and unclear statement written 200 years ago is not much of an endorsement for the intellectual depth of globalism's current arguments.

As hopefully our summary indicates, comparative advantage is a seductive idea, but its direct practical application is limited. Because it is based on so many rigid and static assumptions, it is especially appealing to those of a status quo disposition, including most present-day globalist thinkers.

The thesis assumes only two countries and two products, a single factor of production (labour), constant costs of production and no technological improvements. This forced abstractness has led some writers on economic development to criticise it as damaging for underdeveloped countries. It seems to imply these countries should eschew technological progress and instead rely primarily on producing raw materials or basic commodities (Chang, 2008).

Ironically, given that comparative advantage is today used to justify "free trade", it couldn't work as the outcome of *spontaneous* market forces. Ricardo (1973) claimed that under free commerce "each country naturally devotes its capital and labour to such employments as are most beneficial to each" (p. 81). But there is no inevitability that the attractions of efficiency (absolute advantage) at a business level translate into comparative advantage at a country level.

A company's executives make the decision what to produce. If successful, this illustrates absolute advantage. But for "comparative advantage" to apply at a countrywide level, states would need to intervene to prevent activity in sectors that are more productive *relative* to what is possible somewhere else in the world. In Ricardo's example, the Portuguese government would need to ban local cloth producers, and force them to make wine, because otherwise they would be market incentivised to undercut British cloth-makers. Not much of a "free market".

It is also anomalous that although the principle of comparative advantage features in many current discussions of the benefits of globalisation, it is inconsistent with an increasingly interconnected global economy. The Ricardian thesis presents comparative advantage as a *fixed* country attribute, with resources unable to flow *between* countries, from the lower productivity country to the higher productivity one (Ricardo, 1973, p. 82). Hence, the astute international business authorities John Dunning and Sarianna Lundan (2008) concluded that the principle of comparative advantage requires some "reassessment" now, given that cross-border factor mobility is the norm rather than the exception (p. 750).

Globalists who have ignored this suggestion should mull over the first sentence Ricardo wrote in the chapter "On Foreign Trade" where the principle is introduced: "No extension of foreign trade will immediately increase the amount of value in a country" (Ricardo, 1973, p. 77). Until they do this, the popularity of Ricardo's brief example is stronger evidence of the hold of trade determinism today, rather than the incisiveness of this particular idea.

For someone hailed as the theorist of *free* trade, it is worth noting that contrary to conventional wisdom, Ricardo didn't even campaign for *fully* free trade in corn, in the sense of zero tariffs for imports into Britain. Although he died in 1823, long before the 1846 repeal of the Corn Laws, the debate over their reform in the 1820s was mostly between Ricardo's particular proposal and a sliding scale duty, as proposed by the government's President of the Board of Trade William Huskisson.[4] Ricardo (1997) argued for a fixed duty that should be gradually reduced as domestic corn prices rose, down to a set level of 10 shillings per quarter of wheat. Actually, his reform suggestion did not prevail at the time: a sliding scale was adopted in both the 1828 and 1842 amendments to Corn Law legislation (Schonhardt-Bailey, 2006, p. 9).

---

[4]Huskisson may be better remembered as the Liverpool MP who was hit and killed by George Stephenson's Rocket on the occasion of the 1830 opening of the Liverpool to Manchester railway line.

The true intellectual insightfulness of Ricardo, which is of weightier relevance today, was in his explanation of the benefits of freer trade that drew on the *perspective of advancing production*. He compared the potential impact of cheaper imported corn to that of the introduction of new technologies, such as Arkwright's cotton machine. In both circumstances, capital can be moved from less to more productive uses, something that is hindered by prohibitions either on cheap imports or new technologies. Stopping cheap food imports, he wrote, is like stopping improvements in agricultural production. Economically, it would be as consistent, he argued, to "arrest improvement" as to "prohibit importation".

Writing mid-nineteenth century, the last of the great classical political economists J.S. Mill built upon the insights of Smith and Ricardo on the benefits of economic freedom. He shared the classical tradition's antipathy to protection as inimical to the efficiency of domestic production. What is striking in Mill's writings on trade was his claim that "the economical benefits of commerce are surpassed in importance by those of its effects which are intellectual and moral" (Mill, 1848, p. 119).

For Mill, trade brings people into contact with others of different experiences, cultures and outlooks. It helps break down prejudices that can come from insularity and spurs intellectual development (Irwin, 2015, p. 60). This is another indication of the superiority of classical political economy over today's narrow economicised attitude to trade. Expanding trade, and especially international trade, is socially and culturally progressive, regardless of any economic effects. The act of trade itself, interacting with non-familiar "others", undercuts parochialism.

Another earlier Enlightenment thinker, Montesquieu had argued similarly that trade encouraged individuals to see the world through the "positive-sum lens of mutual beneficial interaction" rather than through the "zero-sum lens of conflict". Trade spread ideas as well as technological know-how. These enlightened insights remain relevant today: there is good "intellectual and moral" reason to promote trade and international interconnectedness without pandering to misleading trade determinism.

The "Global Trade Slowdown" Demystified

A recent practical example of how the trade obsession can lead us astray is the post-financial crash slowdown in world trade growth. Instead of world trade growing at greater than double the rate of global GDP, in the aftermath of the crisis its growth – see Fig. 5.2 – has usually exceeded the global rate of economic growth by much less, if at all (Constantinescu, Mattoo, & Ruta, 2015). Note this discussion is not about a *contraction* in trade but only a *relative growth slowdown* compared to output. Nevertheless, this variation prompted much anxiety about "deglobalisation", a "retreat from globalisation" and, in particular, the dangers of protectionist trade policies.

The OECD reported that since "the financial crisis the contribution to world trade from … liberalisation has plateaued and with creeping protectionism from a myriad of small measures has gone into reverse" (Haugh et al., 2016, p. 7).

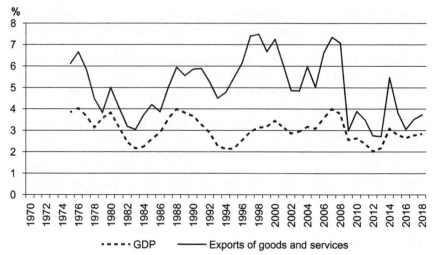

Fig. 5.2.   Global Annual Real Growth: GDP and Exports (Five-Year
Moving Average), 1976–2018 (World Bank World Development Indicators,
2020: GDP, Exports of Goods and Services (Constant 2010 US$)).

This tempering of trade has become blamed for undermining productivity growth and living standards. In reality, the trade slowdown was not driving changes in production but was a reflection of them.

The trade-focussed perspective again turned what was happening upside down. The downturn in business investment that was already ruining productivity was the main contributor to the deceleration of trade growth. In addition, a shift in the character of Chinese production provided a further dampener to global trade volumes.

Just as the earlier expansion of trade had been driven by the state of production in the mature countries, trade weakness is also rooted mostly in developments within production. Unfortunately, misdiagnosis invited the wrong remedies. Governments should have been devoting effort to addressing the underlying productive decay at home, not evade this responsibility by blaming trade wars and other frictions inhibiting trade flows.

The changing ratio between trade and output growths was principally driven by adjustments in the character of production. Three stand out: the investment slump in the mature economies, the changing Chinese/East Asian production model and a structural deceleration in global value chains.

For the first of these, IMF analysis attributed up to three-quarters of the decline in relative trade growth to weaker economic activity (IMF, 2016, pp. 85–86). The sluggishness across Western production led to smaller increases in trade volumes. The IMF report helpfully contested the conventional wisdom by admitting that the contribution of trade policies to the slowdown had been "limited, so far".

The IMF highlighted instead the particular impact of subdued private capital investment in the advanced industrial countries. Spending on investment – new equipment, buildings, infrastructure – has an above average trade intensity. This is partly because only a few countries specialise successfully in the heavy production of machinery and other investment goods. Machinery and transport equipment make up about 40% of merchandise trade. An investment slump in the advanced economies inevitably dampens the pace of trade growth (Freund, 2016). China's reorientation away from persistent heavy investment to build up domestic consumption has added to the global investment slump (*The Economist*, 2015).

This is only a small part of the Chinese influence. Complementing an investment-led slackening in trading, the second production-related shift has been China's transition since the 1980s through its different stages of economic development. The country's early phase of expansion was dependent on importing high volumes of intermediate goods and on exported finished goods. Its huge growth requirements fostered new supply chains, especially around East Asia, and faster trade than output growth – regionally and globally.

Then, since about the start of the millennium, after two decades of extensive economic growth, emerging countries led by China have started to build up their internal markets at home. In particular, exports became less important to China's national economy, dropping relative to the country's GDP in the decade between 2006 and 2016 from 37% to just below 20%. The country is likely to remain the leading exporter of industrial goods for a long time, but its share of global production of tradable goods is much less likely to grow as fast as previously.

In addition to selling relatively more end products at home to its thriving businesses and richer households, China has been building up its own internal production supplier networks, reducing its need to import so much. Thus, China's demand for imported intermediate goods has been increasing slower than previously. For instance, a larger share of intermediate products for its cars is now made within China (Timmer, Los, Stehrer, & de Vries, 2016, p. 23).

Overall, Asia's regional supply chain, which accounts for around 40% of world imports of intermediate goods, has been shrinking relative to its output, as China develops its local production capabilities and becomes increasingly self-sufficient. This is also consistent with China moving up the global value chain since 2011, with its advancing domestic intermediate production sector supporting its local manufacturing activities (Haugh et al., 2016, p. 19).

As a result, East Asia's earlier boost to faster global trade growth has tailed off, reversing its impact on the global trade-output relationship. The sectoral shift in developing Asian economies from manufacturing to services, which are mostly less trade intensive, has reinforced this narrowing effect on the global trade-output gap.

Change within Asia's regional supplier relationships is one part of the third main production effect on global trade levels: a *structural decline* in the *growth rate* of global value chains (IMF, 2016, p. 85). Trade grew so much faster than GDP since the late 1980s chiefly because of the expansion of international production away from the advanced economies. When a bigger quantity of the goods that advanced countries consume are produced in other parts of the world – in East Asia and especially China – then cross-border trade *had to increase* relative to the scale of production.

A statistical distortion, that traditionally measured trade on a *gross value* rather than a GDP *value-added* basis, exaggerated the impact of internationalised production for changes in the trade-to-GDP ratio, both upwards and downwards. Because the value of exports *includes* the value of imported intermediate goods, the total revenues of a country's exports tend to be much higher than the value added to them by production domestically. The changing sources of components within traded goods exaggerate trade measures further when parts cross borders multiple times in the process of producing final goods (Maurer & Degain, 2010).

Even without this exaggerated measurement, increased country specialisation in the production of components and intermediate goods ensures world trade structurally grows more rapidly than output. It is estimated that about one third of the increase in world trade volumes since the 1970s is the result of this greater fragmentation of production across borders (Irwin, 2015, p. 18). The extension of this method of production accounted for much of the widening gap between world trade and GDP growth. This shift in the structure of global production is unlikely to reverse absolutely – this side of a major disruption such as another world war – but is now so well established that it is harder to maintain its previous *pace of expansion*.

The structural expansion in cross-border supply networks is now likely to have passed its peak rate of growth. This is why integration along global value chains appears to have slowed or even reversed in recent years (Timmer et al., 2016, pp. 3, 30). Adjusting for business cycle effects, global value chains expanded at an average 4% per annum from 1991 to 2011 but contracted by an average of 1.7% per annum between 2011 and 2015 (Haugh et al., 2016, p. 17).

The second and third developments within global production mean that the rapid growth of trade *before* 2008 was the exception, not the subsequent relative slowdown. Recent weaker trade growth represents a "great normalisation" of global trade (Al-Haschimi, Gächter, Lodge, & Steingress, 2016). The structural stalling of the previous sharp rise in global value chains has removed an important source of global trade growth. Thus, the trade "slowdown" really reflects a return to the customary trading levels before the 1980s due to the moderation of the unusually rapid expansion of internationalised production in the two decades after the end of the Cold War.

In conclusion, the "global trade slowdown" is the *trade expression* of the relative exhaustion of the internationalisation of production as a means of counteracting Western economies' domestic decay. In particular, China's re-integration into the world economy from the 1980s – a beneficial consequence of expanded internationalised production – had a juggernaut effect on the volume and structure of world trade. This period has now passed its peak and is unlikely to be replicated (Gaulier, Santoni, Taglioni, & Zignago, 2015, pp. 105–106). Whatever happens to future trade levels, the key point is that changes within production relations have been and will continue to be its decisive drivers.

Chapter 6

Trade Becomes Weaponised

In Chapter 2, we described how when a subject matter is *economicised* politicians evade arguing with the public over substantive political and moral questions. As illustration we drew on the official debate over the UK leaving the EU that was dominated by claims about the economic and financial damage or benefits that would ensue. Actually in large part, this discussion was narrower still. Much of it focussed on the implications for Britain's *trading* relationships.

Most official Remain campaigners asserted that it was the height of stupidity for Britain to cut itself off from easy access to its biggest market. Following the assumption that trade is a crucial driver for productivity growth, inviting trade barriers between Britain and its closest trading partners seemed the craziest instance of shooting oneself in the foot. Meanwhile, the official Leave campaign claimed that the possibility of new trade deals with faster growing parts of the world like India and China, as well as America, would make up for leaving the sluggish Single Market.

Yet for the prior four decades of European Community/EU membership few British politicians, and not many members of the public, had shown much interest in trade levels, nor in how the Customs Union or, later, the Single Market operated. Until 2016, and probably beyond, the vast majority of people would have been unable even to explain what these arrangements were. Brexit, a decision of supreme political importance to do with democracy, sovereignty and control, was instead diverted into a bland and often technically mystifying contest between two opposing views on the future of trade. Somehow the matter of trade attained apparently huge significance.

The channelling of political arguments into the implications for trade is not peculiar to Brexit. It was paralleled on the western side of the Atlantic by the deployment of trade-related arguments for and against the Trump presidency. During the 2016 election campaign, Trump's team reiterated his support for protectionism as making him the "change" candidate (even though his Democratic Party opponent Hillary Clinton came from the political tradition better known for trade protectionism).

Beyond Confrontation: Globalists, Nationalists and Their Discontents, 85–98
Copyright © 2020 by Phil Mullan
doi:10.1108/978-1-83982-560-620200009

Meanwhile, concerns about electing a "rude" and "self-centred" dealmaker to the White House[1] were given some substance by claiming that harm could come from his trade plans.[2] Critics frequently denounced him as an economic nationalist and a trade isolationist[3] – descriptions Trump has relished.[4]

Subsequently, many complained that President Trump set back the United States and global economy with his protectionist threats and actions.[5] People bemoaned the economic damage caused by withdrawing the United States from the TPP. They also forewarned the potential economic dangers from his renegotiation of the North American Free Trade Agreement (NAFTA).[6] Unphased, Trump asserted that tariffs helped the US economy,[7] backing up his earlier statement that trade wars were good and easy to win.[8]

Such political prominence of trade is a relatively recent phenomenon. It contrasts with an almost opposite trait dominant throughout most of industrial capitalism: the *politicising of economic interests*. While differences over economic matters, including trade controversies, have always usually expressed wider social or political clashes, in earlier times – unlike today – these subjects were usually debated on their political implications. It was the converse of how trade projections now hold sway over some major political clashes.

For instance, Britain's nineteenth century repeal of the Corn Laws was a focal point for antagonistic political views that reflected divergent class interests. The Corn Laws had limited and effectively banned the importation of cheaper corn. This pushed up food prices and wages, benefitting the aristocratic landowners at the expense of the rising class of industrialists. The Anti-Corn Law League succeeded by helping turn the narrow economic concerns of manufacturers into a broader political objective shared by other sections of society. Cheryl Schonhardt-Bailey, a world expert on this period, described the success of the League as depending greatly on the wider politicisation of a trade issue. Particular economic objectives were rationalised as being for the wider social and public good.

Interests defined by economic outcomes will be more successful in obtaining their political objectives when they are able to "nationalize the interest" (Schonhardt-Bailey, 2006, p. 76). This political technique was often posed in the explicitly non-economic terms of "societal welfare", on what would be positive for the "natural environment", "family values" or "national security".

Schonhardt-Bailey provided the striking counter-example when the League at first unsuccessfully sought to appeal to workers' direct economic interests. The League argued repeal of the laws would reduce food prices and increase real

---

[1]McAdams (2016).
[2]Noland, Hufbauer, Robinson, and Moran (2016).
[3]Brinkley (2018).
[4]Cummings (2018).
[5]Farley (2019).
[6]Baker (2017).
[7]Farley (2019).
[8]Franck (2018).

wages. However, when this economic case failed to gain much traction with workers who had bigger social concerns, the League turned with greater success to
political appeals using pro-democracy, anti-aristocracy arguments.

Over the past couple of decades, we have increasingly seen the opposite
approach. Instead of pursuing economic objectives, such as trade reform, through
political claims, political concerns are framed through economic arguments. Political objectives, from what to do about Britain's membership of a pan-national
organisation, or the foreign policy direction of the United States, are economicised through the medium of trade.

The writer Rebecca Harding appropriately described such arguments as
the *weaponisation* of trade (Harding & Harding, 2017). At a Brexit discussion
attended by French, German and British politicians, academics and business
leaders late in 2017, she recounted someone asking:

> why are we all suddenly so interested in trade? It used to be in the
> backwaters of economics and politics and now it is the only thing
> we think about.

She answered that the reason is simple: trade has been extraordinarily
weaponised.

The recent elevation of trade as an instrument in political argument is not
the result of any qualitative shifts in the real significance of trade to modern
economic developments or to economic growth. Trade has now acquired an exaggerated importance because of the malaise in mainstream politics rather than
anything being different in the fundamentals of trade.

The Intellectual Roots of the Weaponisation of Trade

We noted in the previous chapter how in discussions of economic affairs, trade
has usually assumed precedence over the conditions of production. This perspective underpins the mainstream consensus that "trade liberalisation" is a
valuable economic reform. Globalists are conspicuous in their vocal attachment
to "free trade".

In parallel, they castigate their opponents as "trade protectionists". To disparage them further, they often brand them as mercantilists, summoning up the sense
of serious antiquation evidenced by their revival of pre-nineteenth century thinking. Globalists seek the moral high ground by alluding to an association with the
anti-mercantilist critique made by classical political economy. In the firing line are
China's export promotion tactics and its support for advanced technology industries, as well as Trump's tariff measures. Trump has, bizarrely, also been vocal in
accusing China of mercantilist practices.

An incongruity from all this is that despite the globalists' professed classical political economy heritage, they have much in common with the mercantilist assumptions that the classicists critiqued. Both mercantilists and globalists
elevate the economic importance of trade over that of production. Similar to the
original mercantilists, today's globalists attribute substantial economic powers to

exporting as a bearer of wealth and prosperity. Both also share a penchant for the state regulation of trade, the latter simply preferring non-tariff to tariff controls. Deploying trade as a way to attack each other draws on their mutual exaggerations of the economic impact of trade.

Nevertheless, globalists still profess they are following the classical economists in the prominence they attach to international trade (Gilpin, 1987, p. 173; Goddard, Cronin, & Dash, 2003, p. 33). In practice, their overlaps with mercantilist trade obsessiveness mean that they share a lot with the *neoclassical* schools that have dominated economics since late in the nineteenth century. The essential difference of neoclassical with classical economics is the intellectual return to *exchange* taking pride of place over *production*.

Notably, the classical political economists' labour theory of value had sought to establish value as the objective result of the process of *productive* labouring. It is true that they were inconsistent in making this case, a defect pointed out later both by Karl Marx and also by their neoclassical critics. Nevertheless, despite its limitations, the classical analysis of the workings of *production* distinguished their school both from its mercantilist predecessors and from its post-classical successors. In contrast, before and after them, the beneficence of nature and the exchange of things took centre stage, not the social labour process.

The neoclassical outlook that took off in the 1870s rejected that labour created value. It instead formulated a *subjective* marginal utility-based theory of value. The "marginalist revolution" of that decade is associated primarily with Carl Menger – who inspired what became the Austrian free market school of economics – Léon Walras and William Stanley Jevons. Their methodology once again looked to exchange rather than production to explain the workings of the market economy.

This was the origin of the fixation on scarcity and the supply-and-demand analysis that became the staple of economics through to the present. By the 1880s, elite thinking had aligned itself with these marginalist theories of value and of utility. For example, the intellectual elevation of exchange and trade informed the proceedings of the Berlin Conference of 1884–1885 that regulated European colonisation and trade in Africa. The leading European powers there – Britain, France and an ascending Germany – sought to manage their colonial "Scramble for Africa" and minimise inter-imperialist tensions.

They also tried to articulate a refined moral justification for colonialism, based on a European "civilising mission". Trade was no longer just what it had been earlier: a means of making profit. Rather it became a part of the civilising mission itself. As the character Charles Marlow says in Joseph Conrad's *Heart of Darkness*, the thing that redeems the profit and plunder of colonialism is the "idea only. An idea at the back of it; not a sentimental pretence but an idea; and an unselfish belief in the idea" (Conrad, 1995, p. 20). The expansion of trade and commerce was the realisation of the "idea" that the backward natives could be civilised.

Moral and material well-being were presented as the twin objectives of colonialism. Because in that worldview trade was seen as the mechanism for advance and progress, it seemed justified that trade should be extended as far as possible into the interior of these colonial possessions (Anghie, 2004, pp. 96–97). This early instance of the weaponisation of trade helped promote a broader Western belief in the progressive effects of trade.

Trade War Confusions

Today, in line with our fearful times, the weaponisation of trade operates chiefly as an intellectual warning, in reiterating the possible regressive effects of interferences with trade. We see this in the way *anxieties about trade* were weapons deployed to argue against Britain leaving the Single Market and against US-led tariff "trade wars".

In practice, winning the argument against all protectionism is undermined by today's narrow fixation on tariffs alone. While tariffs are damaging, of greater long-term detriment to the world economy has been the escalation of the *nontariff* barriers that most tariff-critics subscribe to. Yet these accepted policies of discriminatory regulation and state subsidy are far more widespread and persistent than tariff hikes and are an even bigger protectionist threat to economic growth.

The common association between trade feuds and military combat is another misleading meme. Donald Tusk, former President of the European Council, summed up this presumption when he responded to additional US tariffs in 2018 by warning that trade wars "turned into hot conflicts so often in history" (Hornby, 2018). Not only is this assertion hard to substantiate, it oversimplifies the reasons countries fight. Governments declaring war is the weightiest of all political decisions. The suggestion that trade wars turn into shooting wars obfuscates the deeper risks of big power combat.

It is true that economic competition often exacerbates tensions between big countries that can erupt in "hot conflicts". Developed countries mostly go to war over vital contested advantages, including over their economic interests. Unevenness in the pace of economic and technological progress between countries is a perennial underlying source of inter-country strain. As all the mature countries expand abroad for economic respite, their foreign interests tend to collide. History tells us that this expansion goes hand in hand with countries taking steps to protect these stakes (Frankopan, 2019, p. 139).

But it does not follow that "wars" over trade – better described as "skirmishes" – are necessarily precursors of fighting wars. While unevenness between economies is often manifested through trading positions, a focus on trade confuses an effect with one of the underlying drivers of friction. Moreover what goes on in trade is never the reason for a nation's economic troubles that expand national imbalances. Fighting between countries is a much bigger cause of trade disruption than disrupted trade is a cause of war. Trade skirmishes are an *expression* of geopolitical fragmentation rather than an *explanation* for it. They can appear and then fade away, yet the underlying sources of potential combat can remain.

Ultimately, armed conflict is about deciding who rules. By the start of the twentieth century, the whole world had been divided up into spheres of interest between the leading capitalist countries. Jostling for political influence has been a fluctuating feature of international relations ever since. In some circumstances, economic cooperation crumbled, and rows over trade became common. But of greater consequence was how intensifying geopolitical rivalry eventually descended into the armed encounters of last century's world conflagrations.

As we described in Chapter 1, the roots of the Second World War lay in the failure to resolve the mismatches that led to the first one. The imbalances between economic weight and political influence remained up in the air in 1918. A rebalancing between the declining and rising nations was still to come, especially between receding Britain and France relative to the United States, Germany and Japan. Underlying the unsettled geopolitics, the international economic system never properly recovered from its disintegration during the First World War.

Far from the folklore of Germany and Japan being the constant disrupters, the inter-war years saw constant infighting among Britain, France and the United States, not least over economic policy and over how to treat defeated Germany. Disagreements between them over war debts, reparations and exchange rates were sharper than the later tensions over tariffs and trade. The historian Robert Boyce astutely remarked that by 1934, economic relations between these three powers had "declined to a state of virtual war". The three each thought the "gravest threats" came not from fascism or militarist powers but from the "other democratic powers themselves" (Boyce, 1989, pp. 88–89).

However, since the 1940s, a trade-causing-war story has dominated Western accounts of the two big global conflicts. For instance, some historians still argue that a build-up of protectionism was a driving force behind the First World War. The "ultranationalism, militarism and tariff wars" of the late nineteenth century spilled over into the twentieth century and ended in global warfare. From this perspective, restricting trade doesn't just hurt the economy. It "threatens peace and stability across the globe" (Palen, 2017). But trade fixation overshadows that the real sources of fighting then derived from sharpening economic unevenness and political imbalances. Geopolitical strains in the world order had long been bubbling, especially as Britain lost the relative economic strength to justify its hegemonic position.

The trade-becoming-military war narrative is especially typical with respect to the Second World War. Commentators point to the "1930s trade war" as a key driver in the outbreak of fighting in 1939 and in the Pacific in 1941. For instance, the think tank head Amin Rajan wrote that the "trade wars of the 1930s gave rise to fascism" (Rajan, 2018). This ignores that fascism in European countries was developing throughout the 1920s, preceding the United States initiation of tit-for-tat tariff increases in 1930. It was specific national political conditions in the unresolved aftermath of the first war, not trade squabbles that had brought the rise of fascism in Italy, Spain and Germany.

Many other modern writers go along with the idea that trade wars in the 1930s catalysed the actual war. They say the initial collapse in trade relations was triggered in the aftermath of the 1929 stock market crash. The history unfolds how the following June, the United States responded to the economic downturn by passing the Smoot–Hawley Act that substantially increased American tariffs on over 20,000 imported goods. Other countries followed, illustrating the retaliatory beggar-thy-neighbour pattern that Smith had warned about 150 years earlier. Some say this was what directly led to, others that it aggravated, the Great Depression.

This narrative implies that the momentum behind the tariff conflict built steadily throughout the 1930s, eventually culminating in the world war. Substantiating this view, it is claimed that tariffs restricted "almost half of the world's trade" by the end of the 1930s (Jones, 2005, p. 28). Baldwin concludes that the breakdown of the trading system "surely hastened the world down the path towards World War II" (Baldwin, 2016, p. 66). It is still said that the legacy of pre-war protectionism was so strong that it took huge effort and time to untangle after 1945. Smoot–Hawley supposedly produced "economic knots" that took "decades to unravel" (Bremmer, 2018, p. 102).

This is a false reading of history. It exaggerates the effect of the tariff impositions on trade, never mind on the broader economic and political deterioration in relationships. Trade levels fell in the 1930s primarily because of *falling incomes*, not because of rising tariffs. World trade had begun to drop after 1928 as a result of the collapse in production in the industrial economies. This was reinforced by the deflationary effect of many nations adhering to the gold standard (Eichengreen, 1992; Findlay & O'Rourke, 2007, pp. 448–449; Krugman, 2016).

Significantly, a decline in trade *preceded* the subsequent jump in tariffs. Smoot–Hawley was itself relatively unimportant in reducing trade (O'Rourke, 2017, p. 20). Krugman (2009) too, who won his Nobel Prize for his work on international trade, explained that "Like the spectacular trade contraction in the current crisis, the decline in trade in the early 30s was overwhelmingly the result of the overall economic implosion". Krugman goes further in concluding that protectionism was a result of the depression, far from being its cause.

A detailed study of the rise and fall of world trade flows from the late eighteenth century to the outbreak of the Second World War substantiated this alternative perspective. It found that the steady enlargement of world output was throughout the main driver of rising world trade. Analysing the specific inter-war collapse of trade before 1939 they found that rising transport costs, on top of currency payments difficulties, were of weightier significance than the "frequently blamed culprit" of tariff protectionism (Estevadeordal, Frantz, & Taylor, 2003).

Economic historian Barry Eichengreen has also disputed the conventional interpretation of the inter-war years. He explains that rather than leading to a dramatic across-the-board decline in the volume of US imports, the Smoot–Hawley tariffs imposed in 1930 had very different effects across sectors. Rejecting the belief that tariffs worsened the Great Depression by reducing foreign demand for US exports, Eichengreen argued that the direct macroeconomic effect of the tariff was probably slightly *expansionary*. In any case, relative to the production-based drivers of the depression, the direct effects of the tariff were small (Eichengreen, 1986).

Irwin also summarised that today most economists "both liberal and conservative, doubt that Smoot–Hawley played much of a role in the subsequent contraction" (Irwin, 2011). Nevertheless other, mostly non-specialist, pundits continue to link a 1930s protectionist tariff war directly to the Great Depression and to the subsequent global bloodshed.

It is also misleading to think we are now so much more enlightened about, and critical of, tariffs' deleterious economic effects than people were in the 1930s. In fact, the economic arguments against the use of tariffs had been well known by policy-makers *since the early nineteenth century*. For developed countries, tariffs were recognised to be a blunt and self-harming instrument. They damaged some domestic producers as well as pushing up some prices for consumers. Meanwhile, retaliation by other countries could hit exports. Business organisations already had a critical view of these beggar-thy-neighbour policies well before the 1930s slump. The International Chamber of Commerce, for instance, had previously made clear most Western businesses' opposition to tariffs and their wish for a "world without walls" (Slobodian, 2018, pp. 36–37).

The Rise *and Fall* of 1930s Tariffs

Throughout the twentieth century, tariffs were not usually introduced as an actual weapon to punish or damage others. Instead, governments imposed them in the hope of offsetting economic difficulties at home, by keeping out imports. Additionally, until the mid-1930s, they were one of the few anti-crisis tools governments adopted. Still under the influence of traditional economic orthodoxies, other ways of coping with economic slowdowns were thought to be worse than tariffs.

The commitment to "sound" currencies exercised through the attachment to the gold standard monetary system narrowed the room for manoeuvre in dealing with domestic economic troubles (Eichengreen, 1992). Keeping currencies linked to gold ruled out for these countries both reflationary devaluations and activist monetary policies cutting interest rates. Meanwhile, the standard commitment to balancing government budgets also limited the use of expansionary fiscal policies. Governments were not able to cope with the Great Depression using the monetary, fiscal or exchange rate mechanisms that became prevalent in the post-war era. They resorted instead to the remaining levers at their disposal, chiefly tariffs and quotas.

Only when the old economic orthodoxies were discredited by the disruptive impact of the depression were governments freer to experiment with other types of state intervention. Notably in 1931, the "gold fetters" were abandoned by Britain and, two years later, by the United States and Germany. Immediately, countries gained the flexibility to depreciate their currencies to provide some domestic relief, removing so much dependence on tariffs.

This transition towards greater state activism explains Keynes' famed flip-flop on protectionism in the early 1930s. Keynes was better versed than most in the economic dangers of import tariffs. But before Britain left the policy constraints of the gold standard, he surmised there was no alternative other than tariffs when unemployment became so entrenched. In a famous newspaper article in September 1931, Keynes reluctantly, and to many surprisingly, endorsed tariffs as the necessary response to economic depression. He explained,

> Neither free trade nor protection can present a theoretical case which entitled it to claim superiority in practice. Protection is a dangerous and expensive method of redressing a want of balance

and security in a nation's economic life. But there are times when we cannot safely trust ourselves to the blindness of economic forces; and when no alternative weapons as efficacious as tariffs lie ready to hand. (Keynes, 2012, p. 117)

Keynes did not have much opportunity to respond to his critics because the tariff debate was cut short by events. He had endorsed tariffs under the assumption that the option of devaluation had been ruled out. As it happened, just days after his September 1931 article, the government abandoned the gold standard. Sterling depreciated sharply on foreign exchange markets. In a letter to the *Times* shortly after, Keynes promptly dropped his call for tariffs and proposed moving on to discuss other supportive state policies (Irwin, 1996, p. 198). Keynes changed his mind because circumstances changed. Similarly on the other side of the Atlantic, the pioneering FDR government's introduction of New Deal policies from 1933 allowed it soon after to rescind the Smoot–Hawley tariffs.

This sequence points to one of the distortions we've already alluded to: the belief that there was a continued augmentation of tariff increases throughout the 1930s. It is even a bit misleading to regard tariffs as especially high in most developed countries in the early part of that decade. Tariff revenues as a share of total imports of around 18% in 1931 would have been a low tariff by nineteenth century standards and was below the level of 1900 in many countries (DeLong, 1998, p. 358). It is also not even true that all major countries scrambled to raise trade barriers; there was substantial cross-country variation in the movement to protectionism. As we've noted, countries that had remained on the gold standard had fewer options than those that had previously left the gold link (Eichengreen & Irwin, 2009).

Besides, in most of countries where tariff levels increased in response to the depression, they declined again from the mid-1930s. Using data from 35 countries, Michael Clemens and Jeffrey Williamson estimated a *world* tariff level that rose steadily from 8% at the end of the First World War to peak at almost 25% in 1933. It then fell again just as precipitately to below 20% on the eve of the world war (Clemens & Williamson, 2001, p. 32). As the decade progressed, most advanced industrial countries were increasingly deploying other state tools to protect national capital. As a result, they were able to avoid or limit the cruder instrument of tariffs.

The peak *US* trade-weighted tariff between the 1929 crash and the signing of General Agreement on Tariffs and Trade (GATT) in 1947 occurred as early as 1932. It reached just over 24%, then before falling pretty steadily to about 8% at the end of this period (Bown & Irwin, 2015, pp. 7, 8, 21). In France, Britain, Canada, Italy and the Netherlands, tariff rates fell a little between the mid-1930s and the outbreak of war. Even in the few countries – notably Germany and Japan – where they didn't decrease, tariffs rose only marginally (Eichengreen & Irwin, 2009).

By 1934, trade and tariff liberalisation was underway, with the United States passing the Reciprocal Trade Agreements Act and effectively repealing Smoot–Hawley. It is telling too that this Act also incorporated the non-discriminatory

MFN concept. As noted in Chapter 3, under this principle any tariff cut offered to another "favoured" country had to be extended to all countries. This non-discriminatory version of an original nineteenth century principle had already been promoted at the 1927 World Economic Conference. It went on to become the cornerstone of global trade rules after the Second World War – though as we'll see in the next chapter, this is not as liberalising as it is usually presented (Slobodian, 2018, p. 42).

Baldwin, who usually presents a globalist narrative, broke from the "escalating trade wars" convention in describing how the 1934 Act,

> flipped the United States from a unilateral tariff setter to a reciprocal tariff cutter … from the mid-1930s right up to the end of the Second World War, US tariffs fell as did world tariffs – a fact that many modern accounts of globalisation miss. (Baldwin, 2016, p. 67)

Backed by the many business leaders who knew that tariff protectionism was hurting them, by mid-decade, the political elites in most advanced capitalist countries were able to de-emphasise this policy instrument.

Significantly, the US-led reduction of tariffs after 1934 didn't stop the drive towards global war. There were then, and are today, much deeper drivers of international rivalries than tariff tensions.

The Post-1945 Trade War Narrative

Thus, today's powerful trade war narrative does not correspond to the real sequence of events in the run up to the First and Second World Wars. It emerged mainly *after* the 1930s and was conditioned by the horrific experience of the world wars themselves.

It is striking, for instance, that Alvin Hansen's famous "secular stagnation" thesis that he developed in late 1938 didn't mention protectionism, trade war or economic nationalism. He focussed instead, and appropriately, on insufficient business investment and the risk of too little technological progress, phenomena with strong resonances to today's actual circumstances too. His approach displayed refreshing attention to the fundamentals of production, contrasting with the surface-level exchange preference of much post-war economic discussion (Hansen, 1939).

The barbarism of the Second World War provided the backdrop to a reassessment of the dangers of protectionism and to the negative connotations trade wars hold today. As we've explained the brutal wartime events arose from the endemic tendencies towards bitter rivalry between developed capitalist countries. The elites' reaction to these horrors triggered a search for explanations of what had happened but without delving too far into the nature of capitalism. The notion that trade war led to military war appealed because it gave stress to policy mistakes rather than *systemic* factors. It appeared that a misguided, unnecessary trade war had spiralled out of control.

While it was known by anyone who read Adam Smith that protectionism might throw grit into the wheels of market capitalism, it now became regarded as something far graver. Protectionist policies pushed by reactionary politicians in Germany and Japan supposedly helped bring about the global fighting war. Douglas Irwin described how for officials at the end of the war, the lesson of the 1930s was absolutely clear. Like appeasement in the realm of diplomacy, protectionism was a serious economic policy mistake that made the decade a disaster.

Quite early in the war, the free market economist Lionel Robbins had already pinpointed the national protectionist policies that imposed restrictions on trade and migration as crucial, if sometimes unintentional, motivations for war (Robbins, 1941, as cited in Rosenboim, 2017b, p. 137). At the outbreak of war, Robbins had previously argued for pan-national mechanisms to prevent the dangerous influence of nationalistic sectional interests. He wanted a centralised federal authority in Europe to take away the national state powers to wage war and to set economic policies for trade, migration and money. His thinking was, of course, eventually realised in the post-war European political project and in today's EU (Robbins, 1939, p. 106).

Before that, at the immediate end of the war, world leaders agreed that cooperative actions should be taken to reduce barriers to international trade (Irwin, 2015, p. 242). Symptomatic of this perspective in 1945 Cordell Hull, the Secretary of State under FDR, was awarded the Nobel Peace Prize for his services trying to end trade disputes and establish friendly commercial relations between nations. Hull had been the architect of the 1934 Reciprocal Trade Agreements Act that reversed Smoot–Hawley. Although his peaceable efforts were soon overtaken by other confrontational events, this was forgotten in elevating the significance of trade war within post-war thinking.

As we explained in Chapter 3, the post-war institutional regime was partly instigated as preventing similar antagonistic conflicts in the future. The trade war/ shooting war link became embedded in thought through the push towards multilateral trading agreements. Although a proposed International Trade Organization never came to pass, negotiations on the GATT moved quickly to agreement in October 1947, spurred by the impending Cold War.

The national protectionism account of the war was consistent too with the dominant warfare narrative that centred on the madness of Hitler and his aggressive nationalism. In his discussion of today's culture wars, sociologist Frank Furedi showed how nationalism became blamed for the catastrophe of the Second World War (Furedi, 2017, p. 52). He explained that the perception of nationalism as inherently a threat to global security only gained momentum during the 1930s, but had become an incontrovertible truth by the 1940s. The post-war story of trade war became part of this demonisation of nationalism. The evil of protectionist policies went along with the contemporary emphasis that nationalist programmes lead inevitably to war.

By the 1960s, it had become common to treat nationalism as an irrational pathology. Particularly voices on the political right blamed nationalism and national competition for inter-country hostilities. While "nationality" was regarded simply as an historical natural characteristic, "nationalism" was seen as a dangerous political ideology. Critics castigated nationalist thinking for promoting exclusive and protectionist policies implemented by autarkic nation states. Right-wing intellectuals like David Mitrany summed up how these measures generated the international antagonisms that culminated in world war (Rosenboim, 2017b, pp. 34–35).

Globalist Complacencies

Considering the epochal power contests that brought about the two world wars, stopping another such war is a tough challenge. Thus, it would be naive to believe that putting an end to tariff skirmishes and maintaining the current relatively low tariff levels will themselves preserve peace. Moreover, exaggerating the role of "trade war" to serve as a polemical weapon is unintentionally diverting focus from the deeper roots of political rivalries.

Identifying *trade* disputes as a significant driver of international conflict can act as a false comfort: "easing trade" maintains "peace". The trade-war-to-real-war narrative not only muddies the past but also dodges the genuine challenges of the present. And when globalists are themselves the architects of today's pervasive non-tariff protectionism, it is disingenuous too.

Globalists use the conventional trade war story to warn that, as happened in the inter-war years, demagogues are inflaming protectionist thinking. They caution that this could again spiral uncontrollably with disastrous consequences. Their attacks on mercantilist rhetoric from the likes of Trump gain moral authority by associating today's populists with the fascist nationalists of earlier in the twentieth century. It also allows them to reject the tariff protectionism of the past while endorsing the predominantly non-tariff protectionism of the present.

Prioritising the de-escalation of trade wars bypasses more serious economic and political challenges that will continue to fester. This is a triple evasion: first, of geopolitical tensions; second, of the conflicts engendered by other measures, including non-tariff protectionism; and third, of domestic production problems. All three are overshadowed by the fascination with tariff trade wars.

Geopolitical factors are the crucial channels of global ferment. These ebb, flow and transform. This is why in different circumstances, the responses to very similar economic developments will vary. For example, the United States broadly welcomed the industrial and technological advances of Japan, South Korea and Taiwan in the 1960s, because this strengthened allies in Asia against the Soviet Union. Today, in contrast, an anxious and less confident United States is opposing the industrial and technological rise of China.

It is in the realm of politics, specifically geopolitics, not directly in economics or technology, and certainly not in trading relations, that we find the trigger for the unravelling of an existing international order (O'Rourke, 2017, p. 1). Politics becomes particularly disruptive when the leading capitalist powers face both domestic and international challenges. This characterised the first half of the twentieth century, and it is happening again now.

Second, the spotlight on tariff trade wars takes attention away from rivalry pursued through other measures. It is true that occasionally politicians have used trade policy as a weapon in pursuing national interests against rivals. In these circumstances, trade policies both reflect and contribute to geopolitical divisions (O'Rourke, 2017, p. 24). A classic instance of an aggressive trade policy was when the United States placed restrictions on oil supplies to Japan in the 1930s, an act which helped precipitate the Pearl Harbor attack.

However, even these exceptional uses of trade policy against rivals operate alongside other economic policies and in parallel with diplomacy, spy craft and overt militarism. Giving excessive attention to trade policies distracts from these other developments including, today, extensive non-tariff forms of protectionism. This risks leaving national societies insufficiently alert to the momentum building towards a conflict that only they can resist.

For instance, in today's heightening of economic frictions, production interests dominate. Major developed countries have implemented controls on inwards and outward investment: in 2018, the US government sent a significant message in blocking a planned takeover of American chipmaker Qualcomm by its former compatriot but, by then, Singapore-based rival Broadcom.

Third, warning about trade wars takes attention away from the domestic sources of economic depression. This is the mirror image of blaming trade for domestic decline. Governments of depressed nations often seek to internationalise their domestic economic malaise. Problems at home are blamed on unfair external competition. Irwin, who wrote the authoritative account of the politics behind Smoot–Hawley, described how its origins were in *domestic* US politics, not in international rivalry. It started as a Republican ploy to win the farm vote in the 1928 election by increasing duties on agricultural imports. These tariffs quickly grew into a "pork barrel" free-for-all in which duties were increased all around (Irwin, 2011).

Just as Trump and others scapegoat other nations for job losses and factory closures at home, the globalist fixation on trade wars sidesteps the substantive sources of productive decay. Focussing on market relationships with other countries covers up the domestic constraints on business investment that need to be resolved. This applies both to those who warn that other countries are trading unfairly as well as to those who talk up the dangers of trade skirmishes.

Fretting over trade diverts from doing what is under a country's and its businesses' control. The managing director of the University of Michigan's Automotive Futures Group alluded to this during NAFTA renegotiations when he claimed that US businesses "could be doing R&D on electric vehicles if they didn't have to worry about what to do with their supply chains" (Donnan, 2018b). Addressing domestic economic renewal is too often avoided by dramatising external circumstances.

Sluggish economic conditions at home are important not just for domestic prosperity. They aggravate fiercer competition between countries. While protectionism does not itself originate geopolitical discord, trade squabbles certainly tend to flare up in periods of economic depression. We saw this after the 1870s, in the 1930s and again today. This is because depressions invite national state intervention while tending to exacerbate the unevenness of global capitalism. Countries facing hard times become fiercer in seeking to protect their national economies.

Behind Today's Trade Skirmishes

And today the resulting tensions *between* the advanced industrial nations are compounding the larger geopolitical pressures from the great power contest between America and China. Tariff disputes are mostly a sideshow to intensifying strife over economic and political influence in the world. Trade wars can always get out of control, but simply calming them down will not stem competition. Other "economic wars" over technology and cross-border investment flows have deeper roots because they pertain to the productive base. The mercantilist tariffs imposed by Trump on China in 2018 reflected the wider anxieties over China winning the innovation and technology war with the West.

President Xi's "Made in China 2025" industrial strategy openly seeks to establish Chinese leadership in the next generation of technologies, notably AI, advanced robotics, batteries and genomics. In response, the White House denounced China's so-called economic aggression and its "theft" of American companies' IP. Peter Navarro, when US director of trade and industrial policy, explained that the underlying motivation for the anti-Chinese tariffs was to combat China's growing technological prowess. China, he said, had targeted "America's industries of the future". Trump understood, he continued, that if China successfully captured leadership in these industries, "America will have no economic future" (Donnan, 2018a).

The US attack on Chinese trading success turns things upside down. Trade balances express relative levels of economic prowess. Pressuring China with mercantilist tactics to reduce its trade surplus with America won't change these differential levels of productive expansion. A country can "win" a trade war by getting the other side to make trade-related concessions, but this doesn't translate into an economic fix. It doesn't resolve the economic sources of friction in the first place.

The US trade actions against China, paralleled by European ones, are symptomatic of the changing economic balance that is unsettling the Western-created international order. Today's trade tensions could dissipate, just as they did in the late 1930s, but the underlying imbalances will remain. Until the advanced industrial nations effectively restructure their productive capabilities, they won't be able to keep up with Asian development.

The faster momentum of technological progress in China and other parts of Asia should be a wake-up call to the Western nations to sort out their own zombie economies. Instead, their home-grown problems of productive atrophy are almost ignored. Worse than that, they prompt protectionist China-bashing.

China is not averse to weaponising trade too. Its expanding global dominance in one industrial sector after another allows it to voice support for multilateralism and "free trade". This follows the historic pattern that economically stronger countries are able to compete successfully with less need for protectionist support. China's rhetorical defence of globalisation in recent years is an echo of how previous British and American hegemons were earlier the respective pre-eminent proponents of "free trade". But has free trade ever really existed? This is what is explored, and refuted, in the next chapter.

Chapter 7

Free Trade Illusions

"Free trade" is the clarion call of present-day liberalism. It is often said that from the end of the Second World War, "free trade" enjoyed a resurgence culminating in the 1995 establishment of the WTO. "Free trade agreements" (FTAs) such as NAFTA and the EU have proliferated (Bagwell, Bown, & Staiger, 2016; Herghelegiu, 2017). However, just as classical liberalism has lost its way since the nineteenth century, free trade has also become a misleading term, a symbol rather than a genuine description. While heralded as on the side of the liberal virtues, in practice it has co-existed with some very illiberal policies and procedures.

The literal interpretation of free trade as trade's *freedom from state controls* – such as tariffs or regulatory constraints – has always been illusory. In particular, the conventional notion that the post-Second World War victors built an open, liberal, free international economic order is misplaced (Ruggie, 1982). The negotiators at Bretton Woods in 1944 never sought to establish free market conditions. Instead, they constructed a "decidedly *non*liberal order" in which, for instance, the use of national capital controls was strongly endorsed (Helleiner, 1994, p. 4).

Although the phrases "a rules-based international order" and "free trade" are often used in the same breath, they are mutually exclusive. What does "free" mean if not freedom from having to follow rules? The reality is that the WTO has always been much more engaged in managing trade, than in "freeing" it. Meanwhile, the expansion of *regional* "free trade" agreements over the past three decades has been intrinsically protectionist by discriminating against countries outside the specified region.

The Illiberalisation of Western Economies

Far from the post-war years being a long process of liberalisation in the sense of lessening economic regulation and state restriction, the direction of change has been to the contrary. Despite the common conviction of a "free market" or "neoliberal revolution" being ushered in by Thatcher and Reagan in the 1980s, national state apparatuses have been taking increasing *illiberal* control of their economies over the past half-century.

It is true that particular forms of state intervention have been discredited for periods of time as was the fate of Keynesianism in the 1970s. But other types have

Beyond Confrontation: Globalists, Nationalists and Their Discontents, 99–113
Copyright © 2020 by Phil Mullan
All rights of reproduction in any form reserved
doi:10.1108/978-1-83982-560-620200010

replaced these, continuing to extend state influence on how the market economy operates. For instance, privatisations of state-owned industries have resulted in expanded regulation of private businesses with a host of new regulatory bodies established. Despite "deregulation", there are now longer government rulebooks, greater regulatory spending and higher numbers of regulatory personnel than ever before (see Dudley & Warren, 2016).

The introduction of "market mechanisms" into public activities, such as health care, means that additional public services are outsourced to private businesses. Cuts in public sector employment often result in extra state procurement of services and goods from the private sector. Public spending, and in most places public debt, have continued to move upwards.

Businesses, especially big incumbent ones, have become increasingly reliant on public subsidies and procurement policies.[1] And when efforts have been made to limit public debt creation, this has often meant new public–private financial partnerships. The overall consequence is that greater numbers of companies, especially the large ones, earn a relatively bigger part of their revenues and income from the public budget. This has been appropriately described as "corporate welfare" (Farnsworth, 2015).

Changing forms of state intervention have accompanied an evolution of goals into *preserving* rather than *transforming* the economic order. State activities have morphed, mostly unintentionally, into "conservator" state functions. They have gone beyond compensating for the impact of the depression into multifarious attempts to stabilise economic life and conserve things as they are (Poynter, 2020). This has bolstered a zombie economy at the expense of the creative destructive processes necessary to bring about economic renewal.

At least since the late 1980s, national central banks have led these stabilising actions on behalf of politicians. Favouring ever easier monetary policies they have helped sustain and stabilise economic activity. For example, in the 2007–2008 period, the US Federal Reserve used a series of bilateral swap arrangements to lend almost US$600 billion to other central banks to sustain troubled firms and markets in their jurisdictions. This level of *national* state intervention was far higher than *international* IMF lending during the crisis (Helleiner, 2014, p. 6).

The nation states of the advanced industrial countries have been on a roll with economic meddling, rather than being "rolled back". Notionally, free market international institutions have sanctioned this approach. Since the Asian and Russian financial crises of 1997–1998, the IMF and OECD have become fainter in their advocacy of liberalisation. The priority in their advice has shifted from "public austerity measures" to "prudence" and "gradualism" instead (Abdelal, 2007, pp. 197–202).

Self-described supporters of free markets are mistaken in branding state intervention in the economy as "anti-market", never mind as "socialist". Its predominant effects, whatever the motivations for specific measures, have been to *sustain*

---

[1]See *Creative Destruction* (Mullan, 2017, pp. 169–179, 228–236).

market relations. As Susan Strange explained, it is too easily forgotten that markets exist "under the authority and by permission of the state" and are conducted on whatever terms the "state may choose to dictate, or allow" (Strange, 1986, p. 29). State intervention serves to help out an ailing private sector. It has spread regardless of the governing political ideology because the market is no longer able to function without backing from the collective resources of the state. The state and market are steadily fused together.

The Myth of Free Trade

Illiberalising trends within Western economies are well matched in the arena of trade. The movement away from the use of the traditional policy tools of tariffs and quotas over the past half-century is also a story of illiberalisation: the growth of other state controls interfering with trade. Lower tariffs have been talked up to perpetuate the pretence of an era of trade liberalisation while murkier non-tariff forms of protectionism have spread (Aggarwal & Evenett, 2013).

Throughout its history, "free trade" has never meant international trade being fully *free* from state intrusion. Originally, economic freedom became an important tenet of early capitalist thinking because it marked freedom from the constraints of feudalism achieved by the actions of the young capitalist state. It meant the freedom for the new enterprising capitalist class to produce goods and services, sell them and employ people, free from the previous control of the nobility and feudal mores. When that anti-feudal battle was won, "freedom" had become well established as a legitimising principle for the market system. While retaining its ideological centrality, the form "freedom" has taken has not been fixed through the evolving stages of capitalism.

"Free trade" has itself meant different things at different times. For instance, at the start of the 1600s, the natural law thinker Hugo Grotius wrote that under the "law of nations", all men should be privileged to "trade freely with one another" (Irwin, 1996, p. 23). Grotius was not then using "free trade" in the sense of no government restrictions on one's own trade. Rather he was denouncing Portuguese attempts to exclude the Dutch from East Indies trade. This "free trade" opposed specifically a foreign state acting to deny the opportunities of others to engage in trade.

This evolved into the concept of "neutral rights". This was the idea that during a conflict, no belligerent could interfere with the trade of a neutral country even if they were trading with an enemy nation. (It is telling for today that this "free trade" principle no longer applies as otherwise it would deny the US practice of penalising foreign firms and governments for not following its sanctions regime against Iran.) Subsequently, in response to mercantilist policies, "free trade" entered the economic vocabulary as part of a broader movement against monopolies and state control.

The term then referred to *freeing* trade from medieval controls and government restraints on either domestic or foreign commerce (Irwin, 1996, p. 46). It meant primarily that governments did not *discriminate* between domestic and foreign goods in their tax and regulatory policies. In these earlier times, import tariffs were consistent with "free trade" if they were the equivalent of taxes imposed on domestic production (Irwin, 1996, p. 5).

Adam Smith followed this particular interpretation in acknowledging that it was legitimate to use tariffs to compensate for local excise duties, as this would equalise the treatment of foreign with domestic goods (Smith, 2012, Book 4, Chapter 2, paragraph 31, pp. 454–455). Classical and early neoclassical economists held this version of "free trade" as "axiomatic" (Irwin, 1996, p. 225). It is clear from the writings of Smith, Ricardo and J. S. Mill that this was not anything like a laissez-faire doctrine, nor even implied the abolition of all import tariffs or export subsidies. They used the term to promote the historic process of freeing the economic system not only from feudal, pre-modern but also contemporary measures that were constraining the rise of industrial capitalism (Irwin, 1996, p. 46).

This is why Smith's support for freedom of trade was never absolute. He maintained that although it was a positive ideal, in practice, completely free trade was an absurd utopia:

> To expect, indeed, that the freedom of trade should ever be entirely restored in Great Britain, is as absurd as to expect that an Oceana or Utopia should ever be established in it. (Smith, 2012, Book 4, Chapter 2, paragraph 42, p. 460)

Smith recognised that import controls can be disruptive to reverse, wishing instead that they had not been introduced in the first place. However, once implemented, he recommended that moves towards *freer* trade should be slow, gradual and "after a very long warning" (Smith, 2012, Book 4, Chapter 2, paragraph 43, p. 461).

Paralleling the ambiguous intellectual connotations of "free trade", in practice, trade has never been fully free from state regulation. Even at the high point of classical capitalism in the mid-nineteenth century, Britain denied complete freedom of trade. The 1846 repeal of the Corn Laws is conventionally seen as the victory of free trade, but as we noted earlier, it was of greater significance as a political rather than economic milestone. Repeal marked the era-defining defeat of the political influence of the declining landowning class (Schonhardt-Bailey, 2006, pp. 25–30).

As the historian Anthony Howe put it, the Anti-Corn Law League successfully turned free trade into a popular moral crusade. It became "a symbol of new community of interest and a new understanding of the nation itself. Free trade replaced the Corn Laws as a symbol of Britishness" (Howe, 1998, p. 36). Repeal was beyond a technical measure; it had become "elevated in the public mind into a test of governmental integrity" (Gash, 1986, p. 714).

Furthermore, repeal was not the dawn of truly "free" trade, never mind of a "free market" era untrammelled by government intervention. At home, the British state was already becoming increasingly active in a range of domestic economic matters. In fact, the 1840s was a period of intense domestic legislative activity, particularly in the spheres of transport, public health and working conditions.

Meanwhile after repeal, foreign trade protections continued in many areas. Protective duties of 10% remained on a number of manufactured goods, while duties on some foods (butter, cheese, hops and fish) were retained at a reduced level. Overall, British tariffs were lowered only slightly (Harley, 1994, p. 310). In fact, the ratio of tariff revenue to the value of imports in Britain remained higher than in France until the 1870s (Nye, 1991). Even after Gladstone's 1860 budget that eliminated other protectionist duties, including on all manufactured goods, import tariffs continued in areas where there was no existing domestic production or to balance excise duties on domestic producers (Irwin, 1993).

Thus, the biggest victory of free trade policies in British history was very far from being an ideological rejection of protectionist impulses. In fact, some Conservative MPs presented a "protectionist" case for repeal. Offering other countries freer trade in agriculture was motivated as discouraging them from industrialising and thereby helping protect Britain's dominance in world trade in manufacturers (Schonhardt-Bailey, 2006, p. 225).

It is no coincidence that around the same time, the protectionist British state was also extremely active in other overseas commercial interventions. Notoriously, it fought two wars against China in support of the British opium trade, forcing China to tolerate widespread drug addiction so that the British could obtain fine Chinese porcelain in exchange (Encyclopaedia Britannica, n.d.). Anticipating today's illiberal FTAs, the 1842 Treaty of Nanking (Nanjing) that Britain imposed on China at the end of the first Opium War has been described as the world's first "free trade agreement". China was made to open five of its ports, including Hong Kong and Shanghai, to overseas trade. Not only was there no freedom for China here, it was also a rather one-sided affair – Britain had no obligations in return.

During the late nineteenth century heyday of British capitalism, the dominance of many of its businesses on world markets saw it champion "free trade" in the sense of opposing foreign restrictions on Britain's freedom to exercise its hegemony. With Britain's subsequent economic decline, this free trade rhetoric became a lot quieter.

Today's intellectual attachment to free trade is partly a legacy of the United States taking on that hegemonic role during the course of the twentieth century. The revered status of the term has also been fuelled by the peculiar arrangements of the post-Second World War international order: the ever-malleable "free trade" tag underwent another transfiguration that remains influential to the present.

The Post-war Management of International Trade

Despite the present-day appeal to defend free trade and the post-war order, the immediate consideration of trade after 1945 rarely promoted the goal of freedom. Instead, it was mostly driven by the narrative described in the previous chapter, of the 1930s trade war escalating wildly into a shooting war. Discussion focused on how to stop tariffs getting out of control again, rather than about the idealistic merits of free trade.

Writing just after the war Jacob Viner, one of America's leading mid-twentieth century economists, described how there were few "free traders" in the world then: "no one pays any attention to their views, and no person in authority any-where advocates free trade" (Viner, 1947, p. 613). Decades later, one respected political scientist endorsed this assessment when he emphasised how "orthodox liberalism has not governed international economic relations at any time in the postwar period" (Ruggie, 1982, p. 405).

Instead of "free trade", it was "international economic cooperation" that first attained totemic significance as a safeguard against another unruly breakdown in international relations. As we've described earlier, the emphasis was on rules that could police trading relations between countries. The intention of the victorious post-war leaders was primarily about managing trade, not freeing it. "Free trade" was reinterpreted again, now as the multilateral governance of trade.

Just as national economies fell increasingly under the sway of state control, on the international level too, countries were expected to respect interstate mecha-nisms. This meant *reduced* trade freedom, not its expansion. Although several rounds of GATT negotiations brought reductions in tariffs, this did not amount to the liberalisation of trade. For a start, trading arrangements remained cir-cumscribed by the extension of national non-tariff state economic policies. The greater importance of regulation and other aspects of state intervention for national capitals necessarily had repercussions on cross-border trade in goods and services. Meanwhile, each further GATT agreement added another layer of international regulatory controls.

It is also illusory to interpret GATT's encouragement of tariff reductions as a revolutionary approach. With the main exception of the elevated levels of the early years of the Great Depression, the long-term direction in import tariffs had been downwards since the latter half of the nineteenth century. The illustration in Fig. 7.1 of historic US tariff levels is indicative of the declining trend among all the advanced industrial countries.

In most developed countries, industrial tariffs had *already* fallen a long way from the early 1930s when these lower levels were codified *before* GATT came into effect at the start of 1948. By 1947, the import-weighted[2] average tariffs for more than two-dozen major economies were mostly under 10%. With the exception of a handful of countries – including New Zealand, Peru, Spain and Britain[3] – even before the first GATT tariff reductions had been imple-mented, post-war levels were lower than they had been in 1939 (Bown & Irwin, 2015, p. 7).

Subsequent absolute tariff declines under the auspices of GATT were also less significant than is commonly presented. Two leading trade specialists calculated that on an unweighted basis average tariffs for the major future GATT partici-pants – the United States, Western Europe and Japan – were only about 22% in

---

[2]Defined as the value of a country's total customs revenue divided by the value of its total imports. *Unweighted* measures tend to be higher because they ignore the effect of tariffs in reducing imported volumes of the affected goods.
[3]Substantially higher tariffs set by Britain were mostly for fiscal reasons: fighting the war had been bleeding it dry.

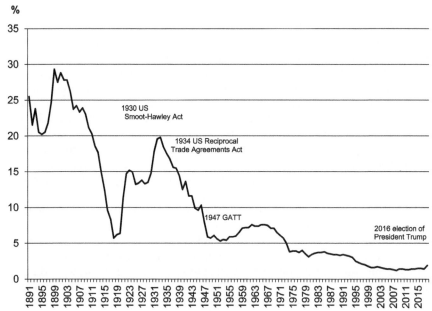

Fig. 7.1.   US Tariff Ratio to Total Value of Imports, 1891–2018
(US International Trade Commission, 2019).

1947, much lower than the oft-cited figure of 40%.[4] From this lower base, the tariff reductions negotiated in the initial GATT rounds had only a "modest" impact (Bown & Irwin, 2015, p. 2). Other trade experts have assessed similarly that the GATT reductions themselves "hardly affected levels of protection". Many rates contained "extra margins" that could easily be cut without changing effective protection levels (Brusse, 1997).

Post-war tariff cuts had mostly run their course by the end of the 1970s when the Tokyo round of GATT negotiations concluded. This was described as the "coup de grace" on any meaningful post-war tariff abatement (Ruggie, 1982, p. 404). Although this round reduced industrial tariffs by a headline 34%, this big percentage fall was from an already low tariff base. The only other completed trade talks since, the 1986–1994 Uruguay round, was mainly concerned with what turned out to be fairly hollow pledges regarding trade in textiles, agriculture, services, investment and IP (Crowley, 2003). That round's most concrete decision was the institutional one to set up GATT's successor body, the WTO.

The official post-war commitment to lowering industrial tariffs was less significant than often claimed. With other forms of national protection for industrial goods spreading – we'll examine the ascent of NTBs in Chapter 8 – headline

---

[4]Cited, for example, in the World Bank's *World Development Report* for 1987, pp. 134–135.

agreed tariff reductions cannot be interpreted as bringing about free, or even, more liberalised trade. Two other trade specialists summarised that by 1980, 35 years after the end of the war, the overall picture as regards world trade liberalisation was "disappointing" (Findlay & O'Rourke, 2007, p. 496).

GATT explicitly avoided getting involved in most "behind-the-border", nontariff trade restrictions. Instead, it adopted the so-called shallow-integration approach of rules, dealing mainly with tariff and quota measures. GATT officials were aware that trade flows could be affected by domestic state policies introduced, at least notionally, for non-trade reasons. However, when the organisation was created "governments would never have agreed to circumscribe their freedom in all these other areas for the sake of a mere trade agreement" (Hudec, 1990, p. 24). Sovereign rights of the leading countries got in the way of further substantial trade liberalisation since 1948.

The WTO mostly retained its predecessor's "shallow-integration" approach. Although it formally extended GATT's focus on goods to trade also in services, it has, in practice, been just as ineffective in making trade freer. A recent assessment found that its General Agreement on Trade in Services (GATS) has "yet to produce meaningful liberalization" (Bagwell et al., 2016, p. 1126). Likewise, during its quarter century of existence, the WTO has been unable to implement even one new multilateral liberalisation agreement. The fashionable notion that Trump is rendering the WTO impotent – by blocking senior judicial appointments – covers up its overall barren history.

Partly, this unproductive record reflects the increased political clout of large developing countries, not least China, India and Brazil. Not being in the WTO's driving seat, they are understandably resistant to having new rules imposed on them. Actually, much of recent genuine trade liberalisation has come not from multilateral agreement but from less developed countries making sovereign policy changes, such as China in 1979 and India in 1991. According to the World Bank, two-thirds of the tariff reductions by developing countries between 1983 and 2003 were due to unilateral reforms, with just a quarter due to the Uruguay round (World Bank, 2005, p. 42).

But the absence of additional WTO accords also reveals the post-Cold War fracturing of the Western alliance. Sharpening tensions between the advanced industrial countries have made it harder to reach new agreements. At its Ministerial Conference in 2017, WTO members hit a new low in cooperation when they were unable to even produce a shared Ministerial Declaration. It is telling too, that a significant share of the disputes initiated by the United States and the EU – the two most frequent litigants under the WTO's disputes procedure – has been directed at each other (Bagwell et al., 2016, p. 1135).

In addition to the liberalising steps they have failed to agree on, the GATT/WTO have also acted to facilitate *reduced* trade freedom by sanctioning provisions that tolerate protectionist measures. For example, the system of "bound" tariffs – that is the maximum permissible tariffs a country can apply – contains plenty of flexibility to raise actual tariff levels. Also the richer countries have been allowed to resist opening up their domestic markets in areas that are of particular interest to less developed countries. These include textiles and agriculture, which have been mostly exempt from tariff reductions (Findlay & O'Rourke, 2007, pp. 491, 536). By some measures, developed countries today maintain far *higher levels of protection* in agricultural products to support their landowners and farmers than before the First World War (Jones, 2005, p. 32).

In a similar fashion, the richer countries established the Multifibre Arrangement in 1974 to manage world trade in textiles and garments to their advantage. Quotas were imposed on the amount developing countries could export in order to protect the textile industries in the advanced countries from cheaper competition. The textiles trade does now fall under WTO rules but without much liberalising benefit.

The result of this advanced country illiberalism is that developing country exporters mostly face higher restrictions than developed country exporters. This is despite how many benefit from non-reciprocal market access schemes for *tariffs*, such as the Generalized System of Preferences. The explanation is because their exports are relatively more concentrated in the agricultural sector where NTBs are frequently used (Ederington & Ruta, 2016, p. 29).

Compounding this factor, the WTO has gone along with a range of national state policies that impede trade freedom. These measures mostly avoid openly discriminating against foreign producers, but they certainly favour and protect producers operating within national borders, whether domestically or foreign owned. Policies that are usually allowed by the WTO include state aid and bailouts, currency devaluations, investment incentives, export taxes, trade finance and actions taken by subnational local governments and state-owned enterprises (Aggarwal & Evenett, 2012, p. 278). Nation states are generally able to engage in most industrial policies even when the formal rules claim to be anti-protectionist (Young, 2014).

The GATT/WTO's core MFN principle is also far from a free trade mechanism. Recall from earlier that this principle applies the lowest tariff levels imposed on a "favoured" country to all other countries (in the absence of an overriding regional trade agreement). MFN is often praised as outlawing the uneven discriminatory tariff practices of the 1930s. However, what it does not do is prevent discrimination *in favour of* domestic and *against* foreign producers. It only manages measures to be *equally discriminatory* against all foreign goods and services.

The WTO is explicit in waiving the MFN principle and allowing import protection in certain circumstances. Tariffs can be applied unequally to discriminate against particular countries in three situations. Action against dumping, defined as selling at an unfairly low price; action against other "unfair" trade practices involving subsidies and special "countervailing" duties to offset the subsidies; and emergency measures to limit imports temporarily, designed to "safeguard" domestic industries (Amsden & Hikino, 2000, p. 108). Especially since the early 1990s, an increasing number of member countries have invoked these exceptions to their negotiated tariff bindings.

Simply claiming that *other* countries are protectionist enables WTO members to impose protectionist retaliation, even when the targeted countries reject the charges (Bagwell et al., 2016, p. 1133). For instance, the official definition of dumping is when a foreign exporter sells at below "fair value". But "fair value" is not an objective assessment: offering lower prices is not necessarily evidence of some underhand practice but is a normal feature of market competition. One person's "competitive" pricing is another's "unfair" pricing. Anti-dumping rules "are intentionally stacked in favour of the domestic petitioner, both in reaching a conclusion that dumping has occurred and in the size of the dumping margin". Unsurprisingly, 98% of US dumping claims between 2000 and 2014 were confirmed by the US Commerce Department (Irwin, 2015, pp. 168, 178).

While leading nations are creative in getting around the international rules to pursue their own state economic policies, even countries that fully comply with provisions of the WTO still have many options to be protectionist in practice (DiCaprio & Gallagher, 2006, p. 784). Under its rules, they are allowed, for instance, to develop innovation clusters, promote research and development (R&D) and support the integration of their firms into world markets (Aggarwal & Evenett, 2014, pp. 489, 491). These are all measures that have been taken to protect local businesses.

Especially in the aftermath of the financial crisis, Western governments were able to employ a range of policy instruments while escaping WTO sanction. Post-2008 many regimes supported their car industries with effectively protectionist measures such as bailouts, public procurement and quantitative restrictions on imports. Partly because just about every major advanced producer was at it, there was little "legitimate motivation" for a member to challenge other national subsidy programmes at the WTO. At the time, some did criticise the huge US bailouts for General Motors (GM) and Chrysler as discriminating against foreign automakers, but in practice, they served as a precedent upon which other countries justified their own interventions.

After the crash, the European Commission effectively suspended its state aid controls, as member countries provided subsidies to weakened industries. For instance, the French government supplied bailouts of €3 billion to both Peugeot and Renault. It was indicative of their protectionist effect that these funds were not to help these businesses restructure but in exchange for *not* restructuring. The aim was to stop layoffs, halt plans to move production abroad and suspend factory closures specifically in France for the duration of the bailouts (Oh, 2014). These were not so much policies to support "infant industries" as to sustain senile ones. In general, European state aid increased massively to help stabilise national economies, reaching 3.5% of EU GDP in 2009 against an annual average of below 1% in the previous decade (Naess-Schmidt, Harhoff, & Hansen, 2011, pp. 10–18).

Extensive government intervention to save national banking industries during the financial crisis was also not challenged by the WTO. Using the argument that intervention was necessary to restore financial stability, some governments undertook both sector-specific and firm-specific favouritism. Financial protectionism practised in the banking industry included market entry restrictions, asymmetric treatment of domestic and foreign firms as well as government subsidies and bailouts.

Overall, the two international "free trade" institutions have been engaged in *ordering* the operations of trade, rather than in freeing it from restraints.

The WTO's own explanation of its purpose admits that its rules can support the maintenance of trade barriers, "to protect consumers, prevent the spread of disease, or protect the environment" (WTO, 2015, p. 7). The WTO has endorsed a lot of protection for a supposedly anti-protectionist body.

We've noted earlier that the main difference between the WTO compared to GATT is the extent of active intervention in the internal affairs of its members. This is further illustration that the direction of change has been away from freedom. Formally, the WTO has not much additional power than its predecessor to force countries to negotiate or obey agreements reached or even comply with the findings of its dispute settlement cases. It has no policy-making authority independent from what its members decide between themselves. However, in practice, the WTO has assumed greater authority to intervene in countries' domestic affairs. Leading members have mostly tolerated this because they have invited it upon themselves. It has been convenient for them to outsource some of their own national power to the WTO, mainly because this allows decisions made to avoid democratic accountability.

The Tokyo round of GATT (1973–1979) had already begun this shift in scope. Although only voluntary, and with no enforcing mechanism, this round of negotiations between governments had agreed codes of practice in several non-tariff areas such as subsidies and technical standards. This established a precedent for being able to extend the remit of trade agreements into the area of NTBs.

In addition to formally establishing GATS, GATT's final Uruguay round also ventured into trade-related investment measures (TRIMs). The cross-border investment measures agreed were modest but, as a result, national governments had agreed to a further extension of international institutional interference in non-tariff matters. A third major new initiative agreed to by members under this round in addition to services and investment was trade-related intellectual property rules, known as TRIPs.

National governments were now sanctioning that, in principle, global trade organisations could stray beyond traditional tariff matters into areas not previously regarded as having much to do with trade: into the realm known as "deep integration". The WTO institutionalised the harmonisation of rules in many "areas of what had previously been considered domestic policy" (Goodhart, 2017, p. 88). In the same direction, the WTO's now failed Doha round was able to produce one measure: a Trade Facilitation Agreement. This dealt with simplifying technical trade bureaucracy at the border, such as procedures for clearing customs.

One problem with nation states authorising international bodies to intervene in their affairs is that these bodies' functionaries can sometimes stretch their authority. They begin to interfere in a seemingly autonomous manner. For example, there are signs that the WTO has started to undertake judicial legislation that exceeds its mandate and is trying to impose new obligations on members. This has been evident in criticisms the WTO has made of some countries use of trade "remedies".

Even the generally WTO-sympathetic Irwin described how the WTO Appellate Body has "sometimes offered up questionable, sometimes contradictory, often idiosyncratic, legal reasoning and final decisions that bring into doubt the credibility of the dispute settlement system" (Irwin, 2015, p. 269). It is perhaps not surprising that a body that has never genuinely promoted freedom in trade has become a source of broader illiberal tendencies.

The Take-off of Regional Agreements

The misrepresentation of the word "free" with regard to trade reaches new heights with regional trading agreements (RTAs). With the inability of governments to agree any full global trade pacts since the early 1990s, localised preferential accords have proliferated instead. Their expansion is often offered as evidence of a continued liberalising of trade despite this deadlock in multilateral talks at the WTO. These narrower substitutes for global trade arrangements are, however, usually described as FTAs.

But to paraphrase Voltaire's assessment of the Holy Roman Empire, these "free trade agreements" are neither free, nor exclusively about trade, nor a product of universal agreement. They are not usually even evidence of trade "freedom" to their members, in that rarely is all the trade between them tariff-free (Bagwell et al., 2016, p. 1136). Indeed, their alternative description as "preferential" discloses that they are inherently *unfree* for non-members by discriminating against them (Dunning & Lundan, 2008, p. 721). Given that barriers remain in trading with the rest of the world, RTAs institutionalise illiberal protectionist trade practices.

Meanwhile, these labelled "trade" agreements are now as much about non-trade, non-tariff matters as they are about trade, covering areas such as investment, IP and regulation. Finally, they are "agreements" only between their exclusive members. In fact, RTAs arise due to the antithesis of agreement, from a failure of worldwide agreement to secure multilateral deals that cover every country.

With the notable exception of Europe, RTAs are a quite recent development and were not much in evidence between the Second World War and the late 1980s (Aggarwal & Evenett, 2013, p. 551). This began to change from the mid-1980s when the United States initiated a series of bilateral trade agreements, starting with one of its closest allies, Israel. Among the first regional agreements, the APEC was set up in 1989 to promote free trade among an initial 12, now 21, Pacific Rim economies. The original 1994 NAFTA between the United States, Canada and Mexico began life in 1988, as a bilateral United States–Canada trade agreement.

The number of RTAs in force has since rocketed from 22 in 1990 to more than 300 by early 2020 (Fig. 7.2). The initial surge followed the break-up of the Soviet Union and the Eastern Bloc. But the momentum has grown since then. They now cover about one half of world trade, up from less than a third in 1990 (Bagwell et al., 2016, p. 1136). Every single WTO member has now signed at least one preferential trade agreement.

The EU in its various institutional formats has been distinctive in going much further than other RTAs and much earlier. This happened not for narrow trade reasons but derived from the politics of European alignment in response to Europe's tumultuous early twentieth century experiences. Going far beyond the standard RTA, the EU launched its Single Market in goods, services, labour and capital at the start of 1993. This built upon preferential arrangements that go right back to the 1950s with the ECSC, that soon evolved into the original six-country European Economic Community and Customs Union.

The EU exemplifies to the extreme the illiberal characteristics of RTAs. Frequently described as the most developed "free trade area" in the world, the implication is that the EU is a global leader in promoting the benefits of free trade and opposing the dangers of protectionism. In practice, the EU operates as the world's most protectionist trade bloc. Paralleling the European Commission's policing of internal Single Market rules on its own members, these same rules present a robust barrier to the rest of the world's goods, services, people and capital.

It is true that the European Customs Union established in 1958 permits tariff-free trade between the member states. But even for tariffs, this represents a freedom to trade for only a small proportion of the world's countries. The Customs Union's "Common External Tariff" regulates and taxes imports from non-members resulting in 13,000 different taxes, including quotas, imposed by the EU on goods from outside. Its constraint on selected protectionist practices *between* member countries came at the expense of its *extending bloc protectionism* with respect to most of the rest of the world (Scharpf, 1988, p. 241).

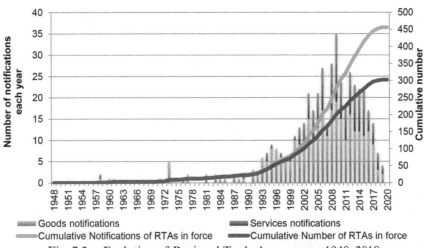

Fig. 7.2.   Evolution of Regional Trade Agreements, 1948–2018
(WTO, 2020).[5]

---

[5]Notifications of RTAs: goods, services and accessions to an RTA are counted separately. The cumulative *number* of RTAs combines these notifications.

When, for instance, the EU imposed its own tariffs on steel imports from China – which was before Trump did so – the language of the European Parliament's rapporteur was very similar to what we heard later from Trump's team. Tariffs were "vital legislation" to help "preserve the European industry" and "prevent the loss of hundreds of thousands of jobs in the EU": an explicitly "Europe First" initiative.

Significantly, the tariffs customarily enforced against non-EU members are among the highest in the developed world. According to the WTO, the *simple average* of the EU's standard MFN tariffs in 2016 was 5.1%, compared to the US average of 3.5%, Canada's 4.2%, New Zealand's 2% and Australia's 2.5%. On a *trade-weighted* basis, the EU's average applied tariffs in 2015 were 3%: higher than the United States' 2.3%.

Trump regularly attacks the EU's high tariffs on importing cars from the United States, with some reason: EU car tariffs are set at 10%. Elsewhere, they are 6.1% in Canada, 5% in Australia, 2.5% in the United States and 0% in New Zealand. (The US though has no moral superiority on transport tariffs, it has imposed a 25% import tariff on light trucks since 1964.) The EU car tax is so high not because of "WTO rules", as is commonly claimed. It comes from its own ministerial decisions to protect EU-based car manufacturers, not least those in Germany, France and Italy. The only WTO rule involved is the MFN one that the tariff has to be applied equally to third countries.

Fragmentation Sharpens

In the ideal of a multilateral free trading system, such regional agreements would not exist. By creating preferential markets, they undermine a level *global* playing field. Geographically, limited agreements represent stumbling blocks in the way of an integrated global economy, prompting some criticism of their restrictive consequences (see Bhagwati, Greenaway, & Panagariya, 1998; Karacaovali & Limão, 2008). Contradictory views have been voiced including within the WTO as to whether regional agreements help or hinder the pursuit of a multilateral trading system (WTO, 2019).

In fact, the many present-day RTAs agreements are not really that novel a departure. Right from its origins, the GATT/WTO regime accepted the principle and practice of preferential deals. In 1947, a blanket exemption was allowed for all existing preferential arrangements. Initially, the acceptance of such agreements reflected the reality that particular countries already had special political relationships with specific countries. In particular at the time, Britain, France, the Netherlands and Belgium all retained colonial holdings that they ensured were recognised within the GATT founding agreement.

Although setting up further regional trade blocks or customs unions would seem to violate the core MFN principle of non-discrimination, GATT's articles [6]

---

[6]Article 24 of GATT, Article 5 of GATS and the GATT Enabling Clause (Paragraph 2(c)) all allow WTO members to conclude RTAs.

permitted additional geographically limited agreements. The main stipulations were that these protocols should eliminate tariffs on "substantially all" trade among the exclusive members, and that the tariffs that member countries continue to apply to other countries' imports would not increase as a result.

The legitimation of such arrangements reflected the broader political and economic divisions in the world, not just those due to the contracting colonial empires. The advanced industrial countries saw no inconsistency in being able to sign localised trade agreements alongside other creative ways to protect their own interests, often against poorer developing countries. GATT/WTO rules allowing these regional pacts illustrate again how globalist institutions were not designed to bring about genuinely *free* trade through outlawing all discriminatory and protectionist practices.

Even *relatively freer* trade within RTA member countries comes at the expense of consolidating the group's individual and collective barriers to trade with non-members. By systematising trade restraints, RTAs actually impede trade liberalisation. In the jargon of trade literature, these localised agreements are mostly "trade diverting" rather than "trade enhancing". Trade with non-members is diverted into trade between member countries. As a result they also do little to expand trade volumes (Bagwell et al., 2016, pp. 1192–1194).

Some attribute the recent growth in RTAs as a pragmatic response to the failure in 2008 of the Doha multilateral round of trade negotiations. But as we've seen, their rapid expansion long preceded this. Rather both developments share a common source. The stalemate in the Doha round is symptomatic that the world polity had already become fractured and regionalised. Cold War unity kept crisis-triggered divisions in check during the early years of the Long Depression, but since the fall of the Berlin Wall divisions have mounted. The spread of RTAs reflects the same trends. RTAs are not evidence of deeper globalisation but of the fragmentation of economic cooperation into narrower exclusive variants.

Many governments have been happy to outsource the management of their international economic relations to regional institutions. Some governments have even justified membership of proposed RTAs to provide themselves with an external pretext for undertaking tough domestic economic reforms. This informed the positive approach of Japan and Vietnam, and probably other nations, to the original TPP.

The current fragility of the post-1945 multilateral order is not an institutional failure of an insufficient commitment to "free trade". It derives ultimately from the objective process of the decay of productive vitality in the countries that had originally established that order. This has been driving greater state activism in trade and many other economic matters, providing the material wellspring for escalating international conflict.

The recent spread of divisive protectionism – to which we now turn – means that the pretence of cooperative liberalisation and of free trade is becoming harder to sustain. Clarification on this will be helped when people recognise that non-tariff protectionism is now much more pervasive than conventional tariffs.

Chapter 8

The Rise and Rise of Protectionism

Who said the following? The use of tariffs as retaliation is a good policy

> when there is a probability that they will procure the repeal of the
> high duties or prohibitions complained of. The recovery of a great
> foreign market will generally more than compensate the transitory
> inconveniency of paying dearer during a short time for some sorts
> of goods.

It could have been a modern mercantilist justifying trade wars.

In fact, it was the acclaimed father of "free market capitalism" Adam Smith in his *Wealth of Nations* (Smith, 2012, Book 4, Chapter 2, paragraph 39, p. 457). The language used by their favourite hero should give "free trade" critics of President Trump's use of tariffs cause for reflection. Smith's words show that protectionist policies are not restricted to mercantilists, old and new, but have been a perennial feature of capitalism since its earliest days.

Yet globalist politicians have been denouncing what they see as the recent dangerous return to economic nationalism and protectionism – atavistic forces that they think had successfully been kept at bay for over 70 years. They say they are fearful that the peace, prosperity and progress achieved by closer global economic integration since the end of the Second World War could be coming to an end. In this chapter, we show that this notion of a resurrection of protectionism is a fiction and explain that what accompanies this globalist perspective is just as dangerous for peace as Trump's antics.

The American presidential candidate had been clear on his intention to oppose unfair trade practices, telling the electorate that "NAFTA's shortcomings were evident when signed and we must now amend the agreement to fix them" (Carlsen, 2009). But these were not the words of candidate Trump during 2016. They were his predecessor's Obama on the campaign trail eight years earlier. Trump's protectionism is thus not that much of a departure from the self-described globalist who preceded him. Trump is simply franker about it.

In fact, many of Trump's predecessors, as well as the United States' liberal allies on the other side of the Atlantic, have upped tariffs, also usually directed at China.

Beyond Confrontation: Globalists, Nationalists and Their Discontents, 115–128
Copyright © 2020 by Phil Mullan
All rights of reproduction in any form reserved
doi:10.1108/978-1-83982-560-620200011

The Obama administration itself imposed a five-fold increase in import duties on Chinese steel, following the post-war tradition of measures protecting the US steel industry from George W. Bush, his father George H.W. Bush, Ronald Reagan, Jimmy Carter, Richard Nixon and Lyndon Johnson. The EU too has form in introducing anti-dumping duties on Chinese steel. Protectionism is certainly no recent phenomenon.

What is Protectionism?

Protectionism denotes the *protection of domestic interests*. Its common feature throughout the capitalist era has been government policies to protect local commercial interests from foreign competition. While they have never completely disappeared, protectionist procedures tend to spread when economic conditions deteriorate at home, such as since the end of the post-war boom. The expansion of state intervention to assist ailing economies is simultaneously the expansion of protectionism because the vast majority of state economic policies favour local businesses over foreign ones.

There is a political aspect to this discrimination too. When economic growth falters, international unevenness stretches and cross-border competition intensifies. The perception of other economies doing better recasts the domestic challenge into a foreign one as complaints about "unfair competition" escalate. Governments extend their protection of domestic businesses often justifying this by blaming foreigners for the malaise at home (Aggarwal & Evenett, 2013, p. 550).

Sometimes, as with import tariffs and quotas, the control on foreign competition is explicit. Other times – as with financial subsidies, or currency devaluations, or through restrictive product regulation – the discrimination is by default. These state actions are mostly presented as non-discriminating, because they apply to home-owned and foreign-owned businesses. However, they discriminate against any producers that don't adhere to them, which are going to be most foreign-situated ones that follow different regulations and standards (Ederington & Ruta, 2016, p. 21). Firms based at home, whatever the nationality of ownership are privileged in local markets by state actions that effectively disadvantage foreign-*located* ones.

Even when introduced for genuinely non-trade reasons, such as consumer health and safety, or the environment, these measures generally impact on trade. For instance, most industrialised countries have been competing in offering "green growth" subsidies for wind power industries (Aggarwal & Evenett, 2012, pp. 264–269). These often discriminate against suppliers from abroad, because they are neither eligible for subsidies nor allowed to compete for state contracts (Aggarwal & Evenett, 2012, p. 272).

The new measures taken are sometimes motivated as a legitimate and necessary response to foreign protectionism. In content though, this sort of interventionist "anti-protectionism" is still protectionist, since the effect is to discriminate in favour of local producers (Evenett & Fritz, 2018, p. 31). Formally, this is in violation of the GATT/WTO "national treatment" principle that prohibits discrimination between imported and domestically produced goods with respect to internal taxation or other government regulation. However, when introduced to "oppose protectionism" they are officially allowed. It is an Alice-Through-the-Looking-Glass world when rhetorical opposition to protectionist practices legitimises protectionist practices. Liberal-sounding defences of so-called free trade become excuses to impose trade sanctions against competitors.

Protectionist Fallacies

Critics of protectionism often disparage it as causing *external* damage to a country's economy. It is usually seen as impairing foreign trading relationships. For instance, trade experts Simon Evenett and Johannes Fritz explain their opposition to protectionism because anything that

> throws sand into the wheels of a nation's export machine can limit its economy's growth prospects and the potential to create employment, raise wages, and lift individuals and families out of poverty. (Evenett & Fritz, 2015, p. 267)

But the graver problem from protectionism arises from its *internal* consequences on the country applying it. Just as we've argued earlier that trade is not an external wealth creator, similarly protectionist infringements on trade are not *external* wealth detractors. Protectionism's drawbacks primarily impact on domestic production. As a policy, it is driven by home-grown difficulties, which, perversely, it aggravates. Import prices will likely increase hitting local firms' supply costs (as well as consumers). Protection often also invites retaliation abroad, thereby restricting export sales by indigenous producers.

But the greater domestic damage arises from its mollycoddling effects on local business. By cossetting companies, it relaxes pressure on them to undertake the investments needed to innovate and take productivity forward. Pampered firms can muddle through and are able to avoid, or at least postpone, making technological change. This is a fundamental barrier to productivity growth and to rising prosperity.

Smith's classic critique of protectionism made these core points a quarter millennium ago. He ridiculed the belief that a country could cure domestic depression and unemployment by "beggaring all their neighbours". Trying to shift demand away from imports onto home-produced goods doesn't do anything in itself to improve productivity. These measures, he argued, divert resources into or keep them in less productive uses (Smith, 2012, Book 4, Chapter 3, Part 2, paragraph 9, p. 484).

In periods of depression, protectionism thus helps to sustain, not end, economic entropy. As the late Paul Samuelson, America's first Nobel economics prize winner explained, protectionism breeds "economic arteriosclerosis" (Samuelson, 2004). Shielding existing businesses provides them with a cloak for outdated practices. Weaker, zombie firms are given a lifeline for survival, perpetuating congestion effects on the wider economy. Protectionism dulls the incentive for industries to transform and improve. At a countrywide level, it evades the need for whole-sale economic restructuring.

The big economic problem with protectionism should be clear from the etymology of the word: *measures that* **protect** *the status quo* (Krueger, 1996). Protectionist policies help perpetuate existing conditions, when economies really need a thorough shake-up.[1] They are also palpable expressions of Western countries' impulse to preserve a geopolitical order with them sitting pretty on top.

Protectionist acts also help to perpetuate uneven economic development in the world. When the OECD grouping of industrialised countries propose international agreements to create a "level playing field", they usually have the effect of protecting the developed against the less developed countries. "Global arrangements" are upheld as guarding against the risk of "a race to the bottom in terms of institutions and in terms of standards, in particular for labour and environmental protection standards." The fear of lower standards in poorer countries is used to justify the West's protectionist policies (OECD, 2017a, p. 67, 2017b).

A False Solution to Unemployment

Despite the classical political economy tradition explaining the economic dam-age of protectionism, the notion that it can preserve jobs remains attractive today. This idea also has pedigree. Trade historian Irwin claims that it was the mercantilist John Asgill who, in 1719, introduced the word "protection" to the trade discourse. Asgill wanted government policies for the "protection and encouragement" of industry and jobs at home. The employment argument for protection has been its most persistent and popular justification ever since. James Steuart, for example, writing in the mid-eighteenth century argued that government trade policies should be geared to encouraging the exportation of "work" – by which he meant, confusingly, processed goods, not jobs – while discouraging the importation of goods that could undermine domestic employ-ment (Irwin, 1996, pp. 40–41).

It seems self-evident that stopping imports protects the local employment engaged in producing the same goods. The flaw is that this appearance tells us nothing about the viability and profitability of the local producer. Job losses are always mediated through trade, through the process of exchange, in that the mar-ket for the things produced by a particular business will disappear if prices are excessive or if new products or services have replaced them. But trade is not the *cause* of jobs being lost. Changes in the production process (innovation), or the lack of changes (stagnation), are.

A country could stop the import of say robots, or lamb, but if it has no com-mercially successful producers, then one of two things happens. The demand goes

---

[1]See *Creative Destruction* (Mullan, 2017), especially Chapter 13.

unmet or a subsidised producer supplies it. Society suffers either from restricted choice, potentially impairing other businesses advancing, or by the heavier subsidising taxation draining the resources for productive economic activities.

Even when there is initially an efficient local producer, ongoing protection will hold back further technological progress, resulting eventually in the same wasteful production and insecure employment. In a fully protected economy, additional businesses and sectors will stagnate so that society will eventually lose the capacity to support decent paying jobs for all. In all possible protected scenarios, employment does not benefit over the medium term.

The widespread debate over whether trade or technology, or both, destroys jobs misses the point that permanent or long-term unemployment arises not because of jobs being destroyed but because *not enough new replacement jobs are being created.* Long-term social progress – and personal gain for employees and their families – can only happen through the disturbances of workers moving into better higher productivity jobs. Protectionist support for less productive incumbent enterprises reinforces economic congestion and gets in the way of creating the new businesses and sectors necessary to replace jobs that are no longer socially justified. By blunting the process of economic renewal, protectionism is a drain on good jobs, not their defender.

Nevertheless, the many interests in advanced countries that resist disruptive transformation mean that as the West's economic slowdown has dragged on, the employment argument for protectionism has persisted. It has appeared truer because of the evident rise of production in the rest of the world, especially in East Asia. As a result, the "rise of manufactured exports from newly industrialising economies" has become the most politically controversial aspect of trade (Krugman, 1995, p. 343).

The expansion of manufacturing activities in the emerging economies is seen as responsible for the decline in the quality of employment, for slower or no growth in wages and for rising income inequality in the advanced industrial countries. In particular, imported Chinese goods are highlighted as destroying jobs in the West. This again confuses effect with cause.

The rise of Chinese and East Asian industry was in part a response to the decay of Western production. The global shift of production eastwards was not just the result of other nation states and businesses taking advantage of the hollowing out of the West's industry. The export of capital from the slow-drifting advanced countries for investing in the dynamic parts of the world accelerated industrial development elsewhere. (We'll investigate this relationship further in Chapter 9.)

Internationalised production neither causes nor contributes to the atrophy of domestic economic life and the loss of employment in the advanced industrial countries. In better Western economic conditions, rising competitiveness from the East could have been an incentive to invest and innovate at home (see Ahn, Dabla-Norris, Duval, Hu, & Njie, 2016; Bernard, Jensen, & Schott, 2006).

It is the tougher, less profitable conditions in the homeland that both cause weaker employment conditions and drive companies to seek profitable opportunities elsewhere. Rather than undermining the internal base, the positive profit impact of these overseas operations temporarily helps compensate for financial shortfalls. In this way, the financial returns from the foreign investment help sustain, not destroy, indigenous jobs.

For example, the US net export performance was relatively favourable in the same product areas in which its overseas operators dominated. Overseas production has correlated with export strength, rather than with hollowing out production and jobs at home (Vernon, 1971, pp. 16–17). The OECD recently concluded a large review of studies with the assessment that there appeared to be *no determinate relationship* between offshoring and the loss of middle-skilled jobs back at home (OECD, 2017b, p. 83). Contrary to the conventional fears that multinational business activity is at the expense of domestic production, the opposite seems to have been the case.

However, two much-referenced papers by David Autor, David Dorn and Gordon Hanson suggested that about a fifth of the aggregate decline in US manufacturing employment between 1990 and 2007 could be attributed to Chinese import penetration (Autor, Dorn, & Hanson, 2013, p. 2140; 2016). These studies drew upon the correlation between the rising share of US spending on Chinese goods, and the falling fraction of the US working age population employed in manufacturing. The former increased from 0.6% in 1991 to 4.6% in 2007, while the latter fell from 12.6% to 8.4%.

Correlation, though, is no proof of a determinate link between the two developments. Although less cited than their headline claim about China and US joblessness, the authors ultimately admitted that the overall impact of Chinese competition on US innovation and productivity remains "unknown" (Autor et al., 2016, p. 229). Rising Chinese imports establishes with certainty only one thing: Americans are in total spending a greater amount on Chinese goods.

The growing US trade deficit with China since the 1990s does indicate that Americans are living beyond their means, a trend confirmed by rising US indebtedness. But a trade deficit can't establish *why* US manufacturing employment has been falling. The study's authors noted the possibility – though without emphasising it – that "increased imports from China could be a symptom of (the US manufacturing) decline rather than a cause" (Autor et al., 2013, p. 2135). They also recognised the "remarkably slow" adjustment of US local labour markets to the rise of Chinese manufacturing (Autor et al., 2016, p. 235). This limited "adjustment" to external changes points to a *domestic* source of America's economic difficulties. High joblessness in certain declining sectors resulted from the inability of American businesses to invest enough to stay competitive on world markets.

The timing of the decay of US manufacturing employment establishes too that it started much earlier than the big jump in Chinese exports of manufactured goods. The decline in employment *preceded* the post-1990 rise in Chinese imports. Likewise, the overall US trade deficit as a symptom of domestic industrial atrophy has been rising pretty consistently since the 1970s, long before China's economic take-off.

Trade is never the cause of sustained joblessness. The flip side is that restricting trade won't create or permanently safeguard jobs either. Protectionist measures, like all state economic support, can preserve some inefficient jobs temporarily, but they can't replace the need for these businesses to renovate themselves if they want to thrive and offer decent employment over the longer term. Looking beyond one's borders for answers to home-grown problems is bogus economics and divisive politics.

The Post-1970s Protectionist Surge

Protectionism has been expanding again since the start of the Long Depression. By the late 1970s, a surge in protectionism was already widely recognised (see e.g., *The Wall Street Journal* article "Surge in Protectionism Worries and Perplexes Leaders of Many Lands" (1978, April 14), as cited in Krauss, 1978, pp. xix–xx). Some critics at the time shrewdly identified this "new protectionism" as a reflection of the ascent of the interventionist state at home (Krauss, 1978, p. 36).

Since then, though, the discussion about protectionism has become politicised and distorted. Globalists have tended to concentrate narrowly on the dangers of *tariff* protectionism, drawing on the conventional narrative of the 1930s. This has not only clouded their own record of implementing tariffs but also camouflaged the other pervasive protectionist practices they have been responsible for.

For instance, when the G20, the leaders of 20 top economies, first met together in November 2008 in response to the financial crash, they stressed "the critical importance of rejecting protectionism and not turning inward" (Statement From G20 Summit, 2008). However, their commitment to refraining from imposing barriers to trade referred primarily to tariffs and other overt restrictions on imports. It is telling that the WTO – acting as the G20's trade monitor – has reported mostly on a limited traditional set of trade restrictions. These cover import tariffs and taxes, quotas and other quantitative restrictions, export taxes, duties and restrictions and local content requirements.

Yet, as we saw in Chapter 6, the post-1930s expansion of state economic intervention has greatly reduced reliance upon tariffs. Extensive activism by states, especially since the onset of economic crisis again in the 1970s, has made protection possible without resorting so much to that blunt instrument (O'Rourke, 2017, p. 17). Controls on trading arrangements are increasingly about regulatory standards and other aspects of state economic intervention as a result of these having become so much more important for the advanced industrial nations. Thus, the noted absence of a recent version of the Smoot–Hawley cannot be interpreted as an official rejection of protectionism.

Moreover, the much-cited Global Trade Alert (GTA) organisation – set up just after the financial crash – warned that those "fixated" with avoiding a modern-day Smoot–Hawley have "failed to see, or take action against, the widespread resort to other trade distortions". For far too long, the leading countries have "maintained a diplomatic fiction that crisis-era protectionism has been tamed. It wasn't – governments just tilted the commercial playing field in ways that differed from the 1930s" (Evenett & Fritz, 2017, pp. 6, 25).

In fact, the very existence of the GATT/WTO has encouraged the expansion of *non-tariff* measures. Because these trade bodies were originally set up to control traditional forms of protectionism, governments have tended to adopt other kinds. Discriminatory state policies veer to areas less covered by WTO rules (Aggarwal & Evenett, 2012, p. 278). Products facing foreign competition that have experienced reductions in tariff levels are the same ones with a higher probability of receiving protection by NTBs (Herghelegiu, 2017). The international trade organisations have impacted the *composition* of protectionism, rather than its amount (UNCTAD, 2014, p. 17).

Murky Protectionism

Tariffs today are only one of a larger collection of protective mechanisms that prop up anaemic economies (Ghodsi, Grübler, Reiter, & Stehrer, 2017). It is non-tariff controls that now restrict international trade flows to a far greater extent than tariffs (Hoekman, 2015, p. 14; Kee, Nicita, & Olarreaga, 2009). They are well characterised as "murky" or "dirty" protectionism, not least because their implementers often claim to be fans of free trade. When self-identified supporters of "free markets" approve even limited types of state intervention, they usually find themselves going along with protectionist practices. While rejecting "trade distorting" industrial subsidies, they still often welcome public subsidies for R&D, regional development and environmental compliance that are just as discriminatory (Irwin, 2015, p. 165).

Unsurprisingly, Western governments tend to deploy these restrictions most for industries that are weak, in decline or politically important (Lee & Swagel, 1997). The actions taken are what economists call "counter-cyclical", because they increase as economic conditions worsen (Bown & Crowley, 2013; Grundke & Moser, 2014). As a result, industrial countries compensating for the atrophy of their productive capabilities tend to be larger users of NTBs than developing countries. In fact, the EU is reputed to have the highest coverage ratio of all (Ederington & Ruta, 2016, p. 11).

These controls are so prolific that they have spawned a range of new monikers: not only "non-tariff barriers" but also "behind-the-border barriers" and "technical barriers to trade". The common telltale word "barrier" gives away their protectionist purport.[2] The GTA organisation has helpfully documented the huge expansion of non-tariff protectionism over the past decade. Its analysts astutely pointed out that the main protectionist activity is in "state financial support, not import restrictions". Governments have frequently used a blend of trade restrictions, state largesse and localisation requirements to discriminate in favour of local producers (Evenett & Fritz, 2017, p. 41).

The most common such actions are production, export and other financial subsidies, localised procurement rules, product standards, environmental, health and safety regulations, energy and other labelling requirements and trade "defence" duties. Sanitary and phytosanitary rules feature prominently, targeting

---

[2]In recent years, the official language has knowingly shifted from 'barriers' to the more neutral term 'measures' (Ghodsi et al., 2017).

the agri-food sector designed to control diseases, pests or contaminants (Ghodsi et al., 2017, p, 4). ("Sanitary" measures apply to humans and animals; "phytosanitary" are to do with plants.) Alongside increased procedures covering goods, many service industries have also seen tougher licencing requirements and restrictions on who is eligible to be authorised.

Meanwhile, other long-established economic policies have taken on a clearer protectionist hue. For instance, "trade finance" has evolved from its original rationale of providing covering finance for small- and medium-sized exporters that find it difficult to tap financial markets. Now, it has become a source of export incentives and is recognised as "a systemic trade concern" (Evenett & Fritz, 2018, p. 62).

The ramping up of trade finance as an export incentive is indicative of a wider shift of protectionism from defensive import restrictions to policy distortions that *promote exports*. The latter have been the most prolific of trade-impacting state measures since the financial crisis. They now cover a greater spread of world trade than import controls (Evenett & Fritz, 2018, p 62). Many governments have been trying to shift foreign market share towards their own nation's firms, instead of simply using blanket trade restrictions to increase their own firms' sales in their home markets (Evenett & Fritz, 2017, p. 25).

This reorientation is indicative of the expansive, and expensive, protectionist interventions these days. While import controls are often cost neutral or cash generative for governments, export incentives are generally tax-financed. These may involve lower taxes on inputs and rebates of other kinds for firms that export or provisions that ultimately reduce the taxes on profits earned from exporting.

The switch to more diverse types of protectionism means that the GTA estimates that about three-quarters of G20 exports face some type of trade distortion in foreign markets, far higher than official WTO figures of only about one tenth of that level (Ederington & Ruta, 2016, p. 18). It seems that only a small percentage of global trade in investment goods does not now face discrimination when competing in foreign markets (Hufbauer, Schott, Cimino, Vieiro, & Wada, 2013).

The diversity of regulations across different jurisdictions, especially with respect to product standards, itself impedes international trade. For instance, different vehicle emission policies in the United States and the EU led to drastically different adoption rates of diesel cars in the two regions (Miravete, Moral, & Thurk, 2015). Specifically, the US policy concentrated on combating acid rain. This imposed very stringent standards that were difficult for diesel cars to meet, leading many European manufacturers to stop selling diesel cars in the United States.

In contrast, the EU emissions policy primarily targeted global warming and carbon dioxide emissions. Its initially less stringent nitrogen oxide standards allowed for the proliferation of diesel models in the European market. It was estimated that this was the equivalent to a tariff of 20% in protecting the domestic market share of European diesel manufacturers[3] (Ederington & Ruta, 2016, p. 52).

---

[3]Now that sentiment has turned against diesel in Europe too, plants in the EU producing diesel cars have lost this protection and are contracting or closing.

Globalist Protectionism

Unlike old-fashioned tariffs, mainstream globalism often openly upholds NTBs as legitimate policies. For instance, the spread of "localisation" procurement requirements was spearheaded by Obama's 2009 "Buy America" policies. President Trump's sloganising about "putting America first" followed directly from his liberal predecessor. Globalists are caught as much as mercantilists in the contradiction of capital being both national and international at the same time. When they act to preserve their national economic interests in world markets, they are as protectionist as the outmoded tariff protectionists.

The G20 bureaucracy has itself sometimes recognised the proliferation of NTBs. In 2016, for instance, it set up a global forum on the steel sector. The secretariat sought information on public policies supporting domestic producers (Evenett & Fritz, 2018, p. 11). It is revealing that the WTO's follow-on study to report on them was abandoned due to the poor response rate to its request for government information on subsidies and general economic support measures (Evenett & Fritz, 2018, p. 20). No doubt the "poor response rate" reflected the reluctance by governments to see commonplace state policies labelled as protectionist.

Non-tariff protectionism is not only accepted by globalist bodies but is coordinated. For instance, the WTO agreements on sanitary and phytosanitary measures and on technical barriers to trade permit deviations from the WTO principles on non-discrimination on certain agreed "non-protectionist" and "scientifically-defensible" grounds (Aggarwal & Evenett, 2014, p. 507). WTO trade negotiations now specify the *inclusion* of behind-the-border regulations, product and process standards, not their proscription (Ederington & Ruta, 2016, pp. 2–3). We have moved to a world of deeper, prescriptive agreements involving the "coordination" of behind-the-border policies courtesy of international bodies (Ederington & Ruta, 2016, p. 55). Modern protectionism is managed, not outlawed.

Consumer safety has become a prominent justification for murky protectionism (Herghelegiu, 2017). Pascal Lamy, the former chief of staff to European Commission President Jacques Delor and then the Director-General of the WTO, motivated this in a lecture delivered in his old place of work, Brussels. He explained that because production has become "transnational", obstacles to trade have shifted from protecting domestic producers from foreign competition to *protecting the consumer* from risks.

> We are moving from the administration of protection – quotas, tariffs, and subsidies – to the administration of precaution – security, safety, health, and environmental sustainability. This is a new version of the old divide between tariffs and non-tariff measures. (European Centre for International Political Economy, 2015)

Old-fashioned protection of the producer has been replaced by the new protection of the consumer, under the fashionable risk-aware flag of "precaution".

The line between protecting consumers and protecting producers is invariably a blurred one, so appeal to "precaution" justifies measures even when recognised as protectionist. For example, the EU ban on importing US hormone-treated beef began in 1985. Because the EU ban was "non-discriminatory" between European and foreign production, it was claimed to be consistent with GATT rules.

Later though, an independent WTO panel of scientists found that there was no public health risk and that the ban violated WTO obligations. Flouting this ruling, the EU justified keeping the ban on the grounds of the "precautionary principle": science could not prove beyond any doubt that hormones were safe for people to consume. The EU applies the same principle to exclude genetically modified foods and crops imported from the United States. In turn, the United States similarly relies on public health arguments to ban some French cheeses on the grounds that they are made from unpasteurised milk.

Protectionist Divisions

Globalists correctly warn that Trump's tariffs are a threat to international cooperation and peace. However, simply maintaining today's historically low levels of tariffs will not preserve accord. On the contrary, the non-tariff policies long implemented by globalist politicians are themselves potent sources of inter-country tension.

Describing the particular build-up in discrimination against foreign commercial interests witnessed since the 2008 financial crash, Evenett and Fritz underscored that the "rot set in" well before the United States–China trade war intensified in 2019. They conclude that there is "little desire to liberalise on the part of many governments" not just mercantilist ones like Trump's (Evenett & Fritz, 2019, p. 7). Astutely, they forecast that confrontations arising from "subsidies" and other "brazen attempts" to steal export market share from foreign rivals are more likely than from the "squabbling over tariff increases and anti-dumping actions" (Evenett & Fritz, 2017, p. 6).

Judicial decisions over protectionist state aid subsidies, taxation levels, competition rules and foreign investment plans have already strained international relations. For instance, the EU has attacked America for illegal state subsidies to aircraft manufacturer Boeing, while justifying its own subsidies to competitor Airbus in response to the parallel US government attacks. In the end, both jurisdictions were found guilty at the WTO for illegal state subsidies. As a result, the WTO sanctioned the implementation of remedial trade measures directed at each other. Adding to the discord, EU member Italy consequently found some of its food exports – including Parmesan and Pecorino cheeses – penalised by the United States. This fed particular Italian resentment since the country was not part of the Airbus consortium of France, Germany, Britain and Spain.

This case illustrates how the post-Cold War expansion of RTAs described in the previous chapter has exacerbated the inherent divisiveness of modern-day protectionism. RTAs have helped to institutionalise the fragmentation of the world around three major centres: the United States, Europe and China. By providing vehicles for the spread of new protectionist regulation and controls, they are also prime sources for the division and tension inherent within protectionist practices.

The EU, for instance, does not disclose its protectionism only through its relatively high tariffs. It set the precedent for many subsequent RTAs to go beyond traditional trade matters to include wider economic relations. Standards and restrictions adopted by the EU impede imports to a greater extent than policies across the Atlantic (Ghodsi et al., 2017, p. 16). In addition to goods, the Single Market/Customs Union covers not only trade in some services but also the intrusive areas of product standards, investment rules, intellectual property rights (IPR), e-commerce and data regulation. This extension in scope exemplifies again the greater importance of behind-the-border barriers in the operation of modern economies. The EU has pioneered the use of various forms of subsidies – including bailouts, trade finance and investment incentives – that account for a large proportion of their protectionist actions (Aggarwal & Evenett, 2012, pp. 278–280).

Since the financial crisis, the EU has led the world in deploying explicitly discriminatory state policies and controls. Over the period from 2008 to 2011, more than 90% of the state measures implemented by the EU and by its member governments discriminated against foreign commercial interests. At the same time, more than 80% of these measures were not, or were only covered to a limited extent, by WTO rules (Evenett & Fritz, 2017, Fig. 6.1, p. 31). Thus, these EU protectionist measures were mostly permitted by the WTO regime and enabled by the absence of genuine anti-protectionist provisions.

With the policy shift to murkier forms of protection, these multiple support measures have turned into tools of competition between struggling mature economies. Not only can RTAs set region against region, they can also generate *intra-regional* conflicts too, setting nation against nation. This has been evident in tensions between the NAFTA members as well as within the EU over many issues.

For example, countries within regional agreements compete over levels of subsidies to protect or promote particular industries, such as steel production. Or they compete over corporate tax benefits to attract FDI. Several EU countries, including Ireland and Luxemburg, offer attractive tax deals to host big US technology companies, which as we noted earlier have now been found illegal by the European Commission and penalised.

RTA negotiations have become notoriously complex and sometimes extremely protracted partly because their scope now goes way beyond tariff levels and quotas venturing deeply into the domestic realm of economic policy. When differences between countries are no longer simply over quantitative matters like tariffs levels and quotas, nations bring their conflicting political interpretations of the debate to the negotiating table (Ederington & Ruta, 2016, p. 3). With the attempted inclusion of non-tariff matters, the potential grows for greater jurisdictional strife between nation states.

For instance, the significant troublesome provisions in the renegotiated NAFTA – renamed the United States–Mexico–Canada Agreement – were about investment rather than trade. The United States insisted on legal protections that encouraged and protected American corporate investment, while enshrining weak labour protections and environmental standards. The United States secured lengthy patent, licencing and copyright protections that supported its businesses not least in pharmaceuticals, entertainment and information technology.

RTAs are arduous to negotiate not only because of their extended coverage, nor because of the complexity of the schedules, nor even because of the sensitive sovereignty issues raised. In addition, the relevant regions usually encompass a mix of fluid economic and political power relations. As a result, the process of RTA negotiation has itself reinforced the fragmentation of the world trading system, both between different advanced countries and between richer and poorer countries.

The very same economic pressures driving advanced industrial governments to adopt national or regional protectionist measures are making it harder to achieve regional agreements. RTAs are, on the one hand, a means of pursuing sectional concerns and seeking to consolidate regional spheres of interest. On the other hand, they have become battlegrounds in which national differences are fought over. Agreements made are tools for international competitive advantage and rivalry, yet intra-regional conflicts obstruct their completion.

Fragmentary trends have got in the way of concluding some major proposed regional agreements, especially the so-called mega trade agreements, like the TPP and the Transatlantic Trade and Investment Partnership. National responses to domestic economic difficulties initially propelled support for these ambitious agreements. Some leading countries, especially the United States, were keen to promote them – not just for domestic economic objectives but also for wider geopolitical reasons.

President Obama famously defended the TPP as being about "competition over international rule setting"; it was aimed at containing China. But other transpacific tensions, not least over trade, led the United States to pull out of talks. Opposition to the TPP was articulated not only by Trump but also by several of his Democratic challengers in the 2015–2016 presidential campaign. In response to the United States' changed attitude, the remaining 11 members led by Japan agreed to go ahead without the United States, renaming it the Comprehensive and Progressive Agreement for Trans-Pacific Partnership.

Especially when proposed regional groupings include developed *and* developing countries, clashes often break out over the differential national interests of economies at disparate stages of economic development. In both bilateral and regional settings, it has proved easier to "coerce poor countries into accepting harsh terms" in a trade deal, such as through stringent environmental and labour standards, that they would "find virtually impossible" to meet (Narlikar, 2018). As a consequence, unevenness in the world is reinforced.

Economically mature nation states are usually most motivated to sign combined rich-and-poor country deals because their businesses want access to the faster growing areas of the world. Advanced countries are often keen to facilitate the export of their capital, including the protection of their firms' IPR. On the other hand, less developed countries often seek improved conditions for inward investment, as well as markets for their products, while avoiding their existing industries, including farming, from being hit. These different objectives are not easy to reconcile.

Take the proposed EU–India trade agreement that began over a decade ago in 2007. Since India starts with higher tariff barriers than the EU, an elimination or reduction of tariffs in both EU and India will provide EU businesses a greater market access gain in India than for Indian firms into the EU. Meanwhile, one of the biggest hurdles is the major disagreement between the two parties with respect to IPR protection. The EU is keen that India should adopt stringent IPR protection standards. These go beyond the WTO-specified standards that most countries have agreed to, including India and the EU. In turn, India is resistant to agree to the EU request as this could compromise its own industrial development, including its successful generic medicines industry.

Bigger Conflicts Loom

The tensions and divisions fostered by "murky" protectionism in both national and regional frameworks risk being even more dangerous than those from traditional tariffs. Tariffs are mostly transparent and consequently easier to manage. In addition, because the narrative about the destructiveness of inter-war tariffs – misleading as we've explained – is so accepted, the appetite for containing tariff conflicts is stronger than for those deriving from other protectionist measures.

There is no certainty that tariff skirmishes don't escalate into all-out economic wars. However, the general recognition of the futility of tariff measures, along with the existence of many alternative economic support mechanisms, does temper this possibility. Fearing an uncontrollable explosion due to tariff conflicts today is the trade version of the notorious generals who plan to fight the previous war rather than the next one.

In contrast, recent murkier protectionism has not been similarly tested and exposed. Additionally, its particular schemes often appeal for justification on morally fashionable claims about safety, risk management and the environment. As a result, challenging their protectionist effects and dangers is unpopular in some circles; opposition can be branded as heretical to conventional nostrums.

Although it is not the intention, the globalist promotion of non-tariff protectionism is unsettling geopolitics in a big way. Their "legitimate" protectionist policies are becoming weightier obstacles to economic progress and prosperity than mercantilist "illegitimate" tariffs. Their murky measures also threaten peace just as much.

The self-contradiction here is that the lesson the globalists took from the 1930s about the danger of tariff wars has brought about alternative channels for protection, which are now fuelling bitter inter-nation frictions. We have examined earlier how in their desire to avoid another global conflagration the post-war leaders promoted a "rules-based system" for the international trade and economic order. One expression of this attachment to rules is how post-war governments of all political stripes have extended regulation in their national and regional economic affairs. The result is today's murky and discordant protectionist environment.

Part 3

Internationalism Starts at Home

Chapter 9

Internationalisation: Sustaining Atrophy

The final part of this book makes the case for breathing new life into popular internationalism. We argue that this is only possible by invigorating democratic national politics. This priority is because effective worldwide collaboration between peoples calls for clear national borders to collaborate across. Autonomous nations sustained by dynamic economies give people the capacity to look outwards with courage rather than fear. Strong democratic nations are vital to withstand and reverse today's drift towards international conflict.

In this chapter, we examine how the past four decades of economic internationalisation has not been driven by an enlightened vision of one world but primarily has been the response to the economic crisis within the mature industrialised countries. This leads into the argument in the following chapter that energising genuine internationalism starts by overcoming economic atrophy at home.

Since the 1970s, larger companies based in the advanced industrial world have again become externally orientated with a growing share of sales and profits obtained outside their home territory. We explained in Chapter 5 that the take-off of *economic internationalisation* distinguished the capitalist era when businesses in the mature Western countries had to adopt consistently a foreign orientation. Business ventures abroad, especially investment overseas, became a "must do" for the survival of established firms, rather than a "nice to do" undertaken by a few adventurous businesses. With falling profitability at home, most big businesses were propelled to compensate through seeking surplus emanating beyond their national boundaries.[1]

When identified as "economic globalisation", globalist thinkers present internationalisation's features as something modern and progressive. Meanwhile, its mercantilist critics blame globalisation for their national economic problems. In reality, internationalisation neither heralds a new better world nor destroys an old one: it is a reaction to the return of the home-grown entropy of the production process.

Advanced capitalism experienced an earlier extended spurt of international activity in the period from the mid-nineteenth century until the outbreak of the

---

[1] I explore the source and consequence of the decline in profitability in *Creative Destruction* (Mullan, 2017, Chapter 5).

Beyond Confrontation: Globalists, Nationalists and Their Discontents, 131–149
Copyright © 2020 by Phil Mullan
All rights of reproduction in any form reserved
doi:10.1108/978-1-83982-560-620200013

First World War: Internationalisation 1.0 – now often called Globalisation 1.0. This marked the emergence of the era of *imperialism* as discussed at that time by the English liberal economist John Hobson (*Imperialism: A Study*, 2011), by the Austrian-born socialist Rudolf Hilferding (*Finance Capital*, 2007), and by the communist leader of the Russian Revolution Vladimir Lenin (*Imperialism: The Highest Stage of Capitalism*, 1996).

The world economy acquired an extra significance for the advanced countries indicating a new phase in the international division of labour. As Hobson (2011) put it, "It is not too much to say that the modern foreign policy of Great Britain is primarily a struggle for profitable markets of investment" (p. 53).

An interaction between the *national and the international* became indispensable for the survival and expansion of the businesses based in these countries. This draws out the essential feature of modern times that is neglected by mercantilists and globalists: that capital is both national and international at the same time. The international affects the national and vice versa (Almond, 1989). Thus, mercantilism and globalism are both flawed in their counterpositions of the national to the international as they, respectively, make judgements about what are good or bad economic trends.

The intimate interrelationship between the national and international became palpable again from the late 1960s as the post-war boom drew to its close. Serious profitability problems resumed across the developed industrial countries. This was initially expressed through the collapse of the Bretton Woods international financial regime between 1971 and 1973, and the subsequent synchronised Western recessions of 1973–1975. Productivity growth fell in the United States and in other advanced economies never again to attain its earlier dynamism. Thus began the Long Depression.[2]

Just like a century before, businesses in the advanced economies orientated themselves abroad as a means of coping with domestic decay. Western companies looked overseas for cheaper sources of materials and intermediate goods, for additional markets to expand sales in order to gain greater economies of scale and, most indicatively, for new locations to produce. While only about 0.5% of the seven largest advanced economies' GDP was invested overseas each year before the Long Depression, within 25 years, this had quadrupled to about 2%, peaking occasionally at over 3%. This means that in many years, the equivalent of about a quarter of corporate profits were being newly invested abroad.

Characteristically in response to economic depression, capital exporting, spearheaded by FDI, grew faster than the export of goods and services (Fig. 9.1). From the start of the Long Depression, global exports grew in real terms at an annual average of over 5%, almost double the gently waning 3% rate of economic growth. But the 11% annual average growth in FDI surpassed both by far. During the especially propitious conditions for cross-border business from the late 1980s until the 2008 crash, economic growth relied upon stellar levels of internationalisation. Trade grew at over 6% a year, while FDI rose by an annual average of 16%, more than five times faster than the world economy grew.

---

[2]See Chapters 6–8 in *Creative Destruction* (Mullan, 2017).

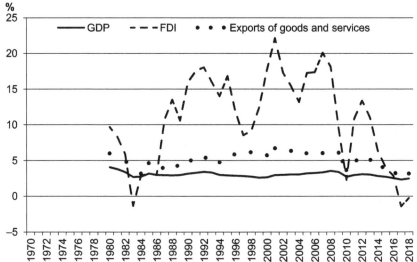

Fig. 9.1.   Global Annual Real Growth: GDP, Foreign Investment and
Exports (10-Year Moving Averages), 1981–2018 (World Bank World
Development Indicators, 2020: GDP; FDI, Net Outflows;
Exports of Goods and Services (Constant 2010 US$)).

Lots of Western companies have been successful in securing additional profit
from their internationalised activities. For example, overseas earnings accounted
for less than 10% of US business profits before 1970, but by 1990, this share had
doubled. It peaked at double this again in the year of the 2008 financial crash.
Since then United States-owned production in the rest of the world has continued
to provide about one-third of US corporate profits (Fig. 9.2).

However, since the 2008–2009 financial crisis, and even with the assistance of
extended central bank liquidity, cross-border capital flows have generally been
less buoyant compared to the pre-crash period. This indicates the limits of internationalisation in stabilising the crisis. These limits are manifest too in the FDI
trend towards *financialisation*, which has muted the beneficial consequences of
capital export for global economic development. Much FDI now is about shuf-
fling financial assets, rather than building new productive capacity.

The take-off of the post-1980s debt economy has encouraged mergers and
acquisitions (M&A) that involve the transfer of ownership of existing firms. FDI
too is a lot about M&A rather than "greenfield" investments in brand new production facilities. A relatively bigger share of FDI is now parasitic on what already
exists, by changing ownership of extant assets. The result is that the progressive
by-product of much capital export during Internationalisation 1.0 in developing
the world's productive forces has been narrower in its latest phase (though still
substantial for China and some other parts of Asia).

By the early 1990s, the M&A share was about one-third of FDI, and it has
exceeded a half in many years since. It is also striking that more than 80% of

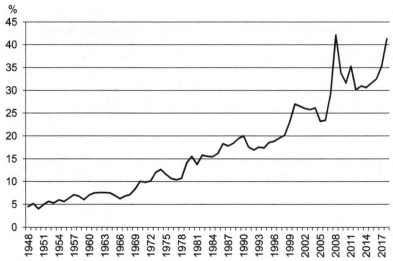

Fig. 9.2.   Overseas Earnings as Share of US Corporate Pre-tax Profits,
1948–2018 (US Bureau of Economic Analysis, 2019c: National Income and
Product Accounts, US Corporate Profits Pre-tax).

international M&A is the purchase of existing businesses in already *developed* countries (UNCTAD, 2018, Annex Tables 5 and 6). The consequence is that while FDI overall has grown, spending on new investment projects has been fairly static since the early 2000s, at around three-quarters of a trillion dollars each year. Most of this is still located into developing economies, accounting consistently for around a half of global greenfield projects. However, with the increased relative importance of financialised M&A, there are much fewer new production facilities than the headline FDI figures suggest. Nevertheless, in some developing countries, the impact has still been significant: notably, China's inward share alone peaked at about one fifth of all greenfield projects in 2004 (UNCTAD, 2018, Annex Table 14).

Novelties of Globalisation 2.0?

Modern literature about globalisation recognises that, despite commonalities, the two waves of internationalisation are not identical. Three supposedly distinctive features are often drawn attention to today. First, the greater prominence of trade taking place between firms, known as *inter-firm* or *intra-firm* trade; second, the related expansion of global supply chains (GSCs) or global value chains (GVCs) with trade growing in *intermediate goods*; and third, increased trade in *services*.

Actually, the attention given to these three traits is driven a lot by some important globalist presumptions, particularly the claim that multinational businesses are increasingly powerful actors in the world. This postulation represents the other side of the customary disposition that belittles democracy about the waning of national state power.

None of the three novelties offered as evidence of the supposedly unprecedented influence of Globalisation 2.0 are as original as suggested. They are exaggerated both in their freshness and in their scale. Instead, these genuine features are better understood as present-day expressions of some time-honoured measures taken by Western businesses to address their same old problem – the erosion of productive capacity at home.

Inter- and Intra-firm Trading

For example, the usual assumption behind the expansion of inter-firm and, especially, intra-firm trade is that "offshoring" and "outsourcing" by multinational enterprises have boosted the importance of trade flows between and within firms. But despite the use of these modish terms, increased trading between firms follows pretty automatically from the fusion of two *long-established* trends: the specialisation of production, combined with the depression era export of capital.

Ever since this combination first emerged in the late nineteenth century, production has become increasingly segmented into discrete activities *and* become geographically dispersed. As a result, much economic interaction between units of the same firm, or with partnering or outsourcing firms, will take place across national borders to dominate foreign trade flows (Grossman & Rossi-Hansberg, 2008).

Trade volumes within and between firms have grown with the extension of the international division of labour as firms spread production over a number of countries (see Baldwin, 2012; De Backer & Miroudot, 2013; Gereffi, 2011; Timmer, Erumban, Los, Stehrer, & de Vries, 2014; Wilson & Wood, 2016). One example: commercial airliners produced by Europe's Airbus are made up of four million parts from about 30 countries. The wings – at least pre-Brexit – are often assembled in Britain from parts made in Spain, which also produces the tailplane. The rear section of the fuselage and the tail fins are made in Germany, and the rest of the fuselage is produced in northern France. All these sections are transported by air, sea and road to a huge French factory in Toulouse for final assembly. All these movements necessarily boost intra- and inter-firm trading volumes.

Precise data on within-firm trade is limited, not helped by differing national definitions of what makes firms "related" (Lanz & Miroudot, 2011). Despite this, the UNCTAD suggests that interactions within the GVCs of transnational corporations account for some 80% of global trade. Breaking this down about one tenth of total trade is thought to be within business alliances, with a third being arm's-length trade *between* firms. Cross-border trade *within* related or affiliated firms make up the other third. The latter includes, for instance, a multinational company shipping intermediate goods to an affiliate abroad for assembly (UNCTAD, 2013).

This 80% is a high figure, but it is not peculiar to Globalisation 2.0. It reflects what international firms have always done: trade with each other and link together their own global operations. Inter-firm trading already dominated trade by the late nineteenth century (Findlay & O'Rourke, 2007, pp. 511–512). There is nothing qualitatively new about trade happening within and between firms (Cooper, 1968, p. 78). Even by the mid-1960s, before the return of economic crisis, it was authoritatively estimated that American multinational firms drove more than half of US trade, evenly divided between inter- and intra-firm transactions (Vernon, 1971, p. 16).

The UK's Department of Trade found that in the mid-1970s, nearly one-third of British exports were to overseas affiliates. In some industries, it was much higher: two-thirds of car exports were to related enterprises. Overall, it was thought that in the 1970s, about a half of American and British trade in manufactured goods was intra-company. This feature appeared to have been particularly widespread in chemicals and engineering (Panic & Joyce, 1980).

Intra-firm and inter-firm trade were thus already well established by the time the Long Depression got underway and have just expanded further since. In the words of one veteran international trade economist, the rapid growth of intra-firm trade in manufacturing, especially automobiles and machinery, has been a "striking manifestation" that the same internationalisation of production is now at a "deeper level than in the past" (Jones, 2005, p. 39).

The most detailed recent dataset of intra-firm trade covers American "related party trade" since the early 1990s, both trade by American companies with their subsidiaries abroad and trade by the US-located subsidiaries with their parent companies elsewhere (World Bank, 2017, p. 63, also see Fig. 9.3). Throughout the period covered, intra-firm exports have been flat at about one-third of total US exports, while the intra-firm share of US imports has been a little less than half. Neither shows any significant quantitative shift across a time usually regarded as the high point of Globalisation 2.0.

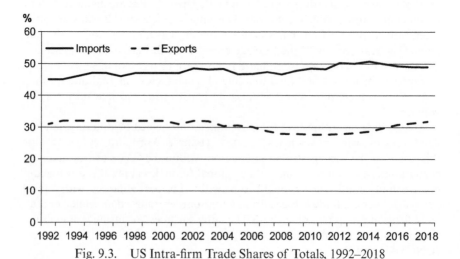

Fig. 9.3.   US Intra-firm Trade Shares of Totals, 1992–2018
(US Census Bureau, 2018).

Intermediate Goods Trading

Increasing trade by and within firms underpins the second frequently showcased feature of Globalisation 2.0: GSCs/GVCs and trade in *intermediate goods*, as opposed to goods for final use. Intermediate, also known as producer, goods are parts and components that are used as inputs towards the production of finished goods, either for individual consumption or for investment (Hayakawa, 2007; Hummels, Ishii, & Yi, 2001; Sanyal & Jones, 1982).

It is common to read that intermediate inputs now represent more than half of the goods imported by OECD economies and close to three-quarters of the imports of large developing economies, such as China and Brazil (Ali & Dadush, 2011; Haugh et al., 2016). Overall, the intermediate goods and services that go into the production of a final product are estimated to account for almost two-thirds of total global trade (Bank for International Settlements, 2017, p. 101).

But significant trade in intermediates is also not specific to the past couple of decades. By the late 1970s, the renewed internationalisation of production was already driving a rapid rise of trade in intermediate manufactured goods. At that time, pre-"Globalisation 2.0", trade specialists were explaining that this simply reflected "the growth in intra-branch specialization, foreign processing and sub-contracting" (Blackhurst, Marian, & Tumlir, 1977, pp. 15–16). Since then, the volumes of international trade in intermediates have grown in tandem with the spread of cross-country supply lines.

This trend is not only a function of technical possibilities; it also reflects the state of atrophy in domestic production. For instance, with the decline of Britain's manufacturing sector having gone further, its car manufacturers import a bigger proportion of their inputs than their German counterparts (Froud, Johal, Law, Leaver, & Williams, 2011, p. 32). The prolonged lack of investment in domestic supply industries has forced large British businesses to source most intermediate goods from abroad. This is another way that domestic production deficiencies spur higher levels of trade.

We should note too that the expansion of GSCs and GVCs also makes some trade statistics misleading. Today, a final good, such as a car or a laptop, is likely to be produced with inputs that go across national borders many more times than in the past, with each movement getting counted in the trade statistics. The increased trade in intermediate goods – commonly exported several times before becoming embodied in the final product – exaggerates trade volumes, and especially trade in parts, relative to final GDP. Indicative of this modern feature, sectors that have registered the largest export growth, such as electronics, are also the sectors where there has been a greater cross-border dispersion of supply chains (Nordås, 2003).

Consequently, this second idea that there is something qualitatively novel about trade in intermediates is also misplaced. Actually, there is no strong trend up or down. International sourcing strategies to grow profits can both increase and decrease trade in intermediate inputs (Miroudot, Lanz, & Ragoussis, 2009, pp. 33–34). Overall, the ratio of intermediate merchandise imports to all imported goods is reported to have been less than one quarter since the late 1980s, and to have *fallen* during the 1990s even as globalisation theories became prominent (Fig. 9.4).

Trading in Services

A third feature emphasised by globalist trade obsessives is the specific growth of trade in *services*. Services *have* been a fast-growing segment of global trade in the past two decades, but the performance of traded services has been remarkably similar to that of traded goods (see Fig. 9.5).

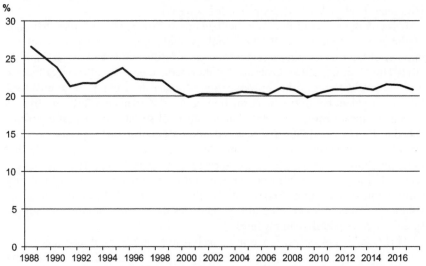

Fig. 9.4.   Intermediate Goods as Ratio of World Product Imports, 1988–2017 (World Bank World Integrated Trade Solution, 2020).

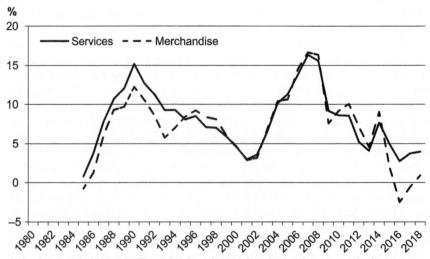

Fig. 9.5.   World Trade Growth: Goods and Services (Five-year Moving Averages), 1985–2018 (UNCTADstat, 2019: Trade Trends, Merchandise Exports Growth and Services Exports Growth).

As a result, the underlined rising importance of services in global trade is really quite modest. It has increased from just below 20% in the 1980s to the low 20s in percentages points since the mid-2000s. This moderately rising trend of services can be interpreted simply as the expression of the rising service intensity of Western economies generally.

The slight rise is also partly a reflection of the well-known blurring of the distinction between goods and services in modern production (Maurer & Degain, 2010, pp. 13, 16; Subramanian & Kessler, 2013). As the OECD reported, about

> three-quarters of the value of services traded consists of inter-mediate inputs that serve to coordinate value chains, support production processes and add value to products through quality differentiation and customisation. (OECD, 2017b, p. 78)

The derivative relationship of services trade to the needs of production is evident.

Again, the spotlight on services reveals nothing particularly new about Globalisation 2.0.

What *is* Distinctive Within Internationalisation 2.0?

Of greater pertinence than the three structural enhancements made much of by globalist writings, three other features help define the current wave of internationalisation. First, capital *importing* has complemented capital exporting for the most mature industrial countries. Second, internationalisation has been *state-led* to a greater degree than its predecessor a century before. Third has been the protracted *dampening of rivalries between nations*, at least before their post-2008 crash awakening.

Capital Importing

While the returns from capital exporting have been extremely valuable for particular Western companies, they have been insufficient to sustain their national economies as a whole. Relative economic decline in the most mature nations, especially America and Britain, has seen them also becoming increasingly indebted to the rest of the world: importing as well as exporting capital.

Less able to compete on world markets trade deficits have become the norm during the Long Depression and have been getting bigger. Contrary to the mercantilist narrative, these rising trade deficits did not arise because of "unfair" trade policies adopted by the industrialising parts of the world. Instead, they are the inevitable result of the enfeeblement of production within the already industrialised parts when people in these countries, and their governments, seek to maintain customary spending levels and buy goods from abroad instead.

The resulting trade deficits have to be funded from somewhere. For a few years, the returns from overseas investments helped compensate. However, with the depth of economic malaise, investment income soon became insufficient to cope with all the outgoing payments. Britain and America have been running pretty consistent current account deficits since the early 1980s.

In addition to selling off attractive domestic assets to foreigners, of which, of course, there is not an endless supply, the other main mechanism to fund domestic decay is to *borrow internationally*. Both these factors resulted in the odd feature of Internationalisation 2.0 of capital flowing "upwards". Instead of funds primarily moving out of the developed countries into the developing world, the direction has often been the reverse. The mature economies have been so needy of money that they have been getting spare capital from the less developed countries. As a consequence, the foreign debt of America and Britain has been rising steadily (Fig. 9.6). Thus, these countries are reliant, in the words of Mark Carney, the former Governor of the Bank of England, on "the kindness of strangers" (Bank of England, 2017, p. 6).

Taking into account all movement of funds between countries, it has been calculated that the flow of money from rich countries to poor countries now pales in comparison to the flow that runs in the other direction. In 2012, for instance, developing countries received a total of US$1.3 trillion, including aid, investment and income from abroad. But that same year, they sent some US$3.3 trillion abroad. In other words, a net US$2 trillion flowed out of developing countries. Taking all years since 1980, these net outflows are estimated to be greater than US$16 trillion (M. Roberts, 2018). The other side of these transactions is a more decrepit and dependent set of mature economies.

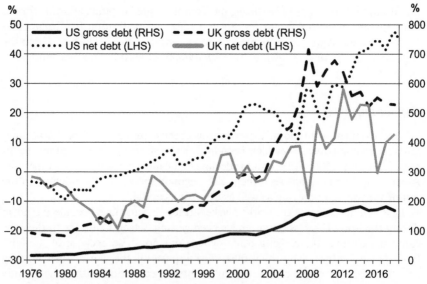

Fig. 9.6.   Foreign Debt Relative to GDP, United States and United Kingdom, 1976–2018 (US Bureau of Economic Analysis, 2019a, 2019b: International Investment Position, National Income and Product Accounts, GDP; Office for National Statistics, 2019a, 2019b: Economy, National Accounts, Balance of Payments, GDP).

State Internationalisation

Although, as we have described earlier, there has never been a market "free" from the state, much of the additional foreign orientation of business during Internationalisation 1.0 was driven by the private sector, rather than by government policy. In this respect, Internationalisation 2.0 is qualitatively different since it has been predominantly state-led internationalisation.

Governments in all advanced economies have been using their resources to support their local resident businesses, not just with the new protectionist mechanisms described in the previous chapter. The apparatus of state has been backing their businesses in setting up in overseas locations, as well as attracting inward investment from abroad.

For instance, the temporary economic stabilisation of Britain in the 1980s that is still inappropriately attributed to a small-state "neoliberal renaissance" reflected substantially the opposite phenomenon: it was predominantly state-led, directed to extending internationalised relationships. In particular, it owed much to the government's success in securing capital inflows. Thatcher opened Britain up to a wave of foreign inward investment, including signing deals that gave state support for setting up Japanese car factories by Nissan, Honda and Toyota.

Around the same time, the state was also behind the rebirth of the City of London as one of the world's top international financial centres. The government initiated Big Bang in 1986 to modernise the practices in the financial services sector and provide an attractive home for most of the world's biggest financial institutions. By the time of the 2008 financial crash, financial services centred on the City had expanded to contribute nearly one tenth of GDP.

All the bigger Western powers have similarly used the resources of their states to help their economies internationalise. Not least they deploy their diplomatic influence to ease the way in opening up foreign markets for sales and investment. When their national leaders undertake visits to other countries, scores of business people accompany them to try to secure new commercial deals. Meanwhile, the many new trade agreements set up to back domestic businesses since the 1990s are state-led acts negotiated between governments (Dunning & Lundan, 2008, p. 714).

Underlining the significance of the international–national relationship for capital, governments that have welcomed inward investment have, as noted earlier – and especially since the financial crisis – been extending control over foreign investment inflows as another protectionist mechanism. Mostly under the justification of "national security", the larger economies have been changing their rules on foreign takeovers of domestic firms (Pohl, 2019). New restrictions now go well beyond traditional defence sectors, such as military hardware, into information and communications technologies and public infrastructure. Western governments are now screening about half of all FDI flows (OECD, 2018, p. 2).

Western governments seem fearful of becoming dependent on advanced technologies in which Korean, Taiwanese and Chinese companies are becoming the global pacesetters. Technological competition has become pervasive. The OECD observed that preventing other countries from acquiring assets in one's territory was "then". The new state concern is also to prevent others acquiring "certain assets from anyone", including from one's own businesses investing in other countries. The American and Chinese governments are now to the fore in controlling outward foreign investment as well as inward. The perilous significance of state-led internationalisation is that it has the potential to escalate rapidly into geopolitical clashes between nation states.

Postponed Rivalries

The faster extension of state foreign investment controls since the 2008 crash is indicative of the third notable feature of Internationalisation 2.0 – the long mitigated heating up of rivalries. For most of the first four decades of the Long Depression, clashes between the leading industrial powers remained muted. International cooperation generally trumped confrontation, even when economic anxieties worsened during periods of recession. Occasionally, tensions would flare up, often over exchange rates, but they would soon subside. This was nothing like the conflicts of the decades leading up to the First and Second World Wars.

This benign, mostly cooperative situation in the years to 2008 is sometimes attributed to the subjective will of the West's enlightened leaders. The proponents of "democratic peace theory" claimed that liberal democracies do not fight each other – though this has been challenged empirically as well as theoretically (Kinsella, 2005). Others put the accent on the durable effects of the post-war institutionalisation of international cooperation.

Some complacently linked the absence of overt rivalries to globalisation *per se*: because of integrated global markets the "era of imperialist, inter-imperialist, and anti-imperialist wars is over" (Hardt & Negri, 2000). Here, the wish for stability is father to the thought. This brings to mind the calamitous pre-1914 reaction to Angell's *The Great Illusion*.

Even in the aftermath of the financial crisis, some leaders, including former British prime minister Gordon Brown, gushed about how the solidity of international economic cooperation had prevented the crisis turning into a catastrophe. Shrewder observers noted that it was unilateral actions by the United States and China, not multilateral manoeuvres, which stabilised global economic affairs. The significance of actual international cooperation through the G20 meetings is often overstated (Helleiner, 2014, pp. 19–30).

Other astute commentators suggested that the aura of "international economic cooperation" around the financial crisis was sustained only *because* there was very little actual cooperation. Actions taken by individual nations after the crash, dictated by domestic necessities, simply induced a sense of harmony. This was a continuation of the successful "non-cooperation" around the status quo that had emerged after the end of the Cold War (Kahler, 2013, pp. 44–45).

In fact, the congenial international atmosphere leading up to 2008 had mostly been testimony to the relative success of advanced capitalism's coping mechanisms, domestic as well as international. Resilience within the depressed Western economies is tribute to the initially positive impact not only of internationalisation but of financialisation too. The latter is well illustrated by the rapid ascent of all forms of debt dependence – business, household and public.[3]

Together internationalisation, financialisation and their special fusion in cross-border financial flows contributed significantly to offset the impact of the depression on economic life. However, international financialisation in the 1990s and 2000s also generated its nemesis in the financial bubble that burst in 2007–2008. Just like domestic financialisation, increased *international* capital flows have tended to augment domestic credit expansions, fuelling financial instability (Bank for International Settlements, 2017, p. 110). The subsequent crash represented not the *beginning* of "secular stagnation" as some went on to describe it, but the *end* of the period when the palliatives had worked reasonably well.

The economic forces driving conflict between nations were never eliminated, just alleviated. But then the financial crisis exploded the myth of a permanent Great Moderation. Unevenness in national economic development is actually a normal feature of the market system. However, in times of stalling economic growth, unevenness tends to amplify as countries cope with the generalised slowdown with differing levels of success. Divergence between the leading nations of the world increases and, with mitigations becoming exhausted, unevenness spreads and rivalries sharpen.

The result is that the economic internationalisation of trade and foreign investment flows turn from being primarily mitigating forces into additional sources of inter-country tension. In an increasingly cut-throat environment, the internationalisation process sparks frictions between the leading industrial economies as they each try to take maximum advantage from world markets. The advanced countries rival each other over access to export markets, over foreign locations for their businesses to invest as well as in attracting inward investment to give discrete boosts to domestic investment and growth.

While economic internationalisation initially dulls the pace of national decline, this can come at the expense of faster deterioration in other nations. This has been evident in the EU. Germany as its relatively strongest constituent member has used eurozone structures – both its manipulated currency and also the protected Single Market of the wider EU – to bolster its manufacturing and export industries, not least in the production of cars, machine goods and chemicals.

But this has been to the disadvantage of the weaker southern European countries, exemplified by recessions and high unemployment, particularly for young people in Greece, Portugal, Spain and Italy. This illustrates that economic power does not have to take a military form to exert damaging influence. As one international relations scholar noted, "it is not Germany's military power but its economic power that causes fear and resentment in Europe" (Kagan, 2018, p. 126).

Far from assuring us of international calm and harmony, economic interdependence is itself weaponised when states are able to leverage interdependent relations to coerce others. For example, the United States has a range of network tools that can deliver choke point effects and exercise extraterritorial

---

[3]See Chapters 11 and 12 in Mullan (2017).

power (Farrell & Newman, 2019, p. 17). It forced the international financial messaging system SWIFT to disconnect Iranian banks, including by threatening members of SWIFT's board with penalties for sanctions evasion. In turn, under new EU rules that forbid companies from complying with the US sanctions on Iran, SWIFT then faced the threat of punitive action from Europe (Peel, 2018).

Western governments who had thought conflict between them had been permanently relegated to history are unsurprisingly perplexed. They had regarded globalisation as the bearer of a harmonious "convergence" across the world (Baldwin, 2016). Hence, global elites are poorly equipped for this unanticipated revival of rancorous national competition.

Perpetuating illusions about the post-war order being "normal" and "natural" adds to the fateful mix. In the words of Birmingham University international strategy professor Patrick Porter, the nostalgic claim that,

> a unitary "liberal order" prevailed and defined international relations is both ahistorical and harmful. It is ahistorical because it is blind to the process of "ordering" the world and erases the memory of violence, coercion, and compromise that also marked post-war diplomatic history .... such "order" as existed rested on the imperial prerogatives of a superpower that attempted to impose order by stepping outside rules and accommodating illiberal forces.
> (Porter, 2018, p. 1)

Nostalgia is also harmful because framing the world before Trump in absolute moral terms as a "liberal order" makes it harder to consider that it now needs to be transformed. Yet substantial change is necessary in the international settlement to adapt to the qualitative shift that has occurred in the location of economic production. The big risk that ensues from Western elites' nostalgic devotion to old ways is that a combination of complacency and fear leads them to act erratically in response to events. In these circumstances, even economic skirmishes could escalate into wars.

Internationalisation Rebounds

One of the ironies of the national–international interrelationship is how the export of capital undertaken to support old Western economies has helped create new economic competitors for them. Incoming funds from the mature countries has been a source of economic flourishing in other places, boosting the development of the recipients, not least in China. Dependent subsidiaries have been transformed into autonomous competitors.

As a result, declining Western nations are facing economic challenges in world markets not only from each other but also from emerging Asian nations. Those in the West who warn of China as an economic rival conveniently forget the huge contribution that self-interested Western businesses, banks and governments made in speeding up China's economic development. Even during the post-war boom, the West's corporate investments into Asia had set in process the eastward shift in the world's economic centre of gravity (Frankopan, 2016, p. 411).

In the early stages of the Long Depression Western companies looked to investment opportunities in other established markets. More than four out of every five dollars of all foreign investment was destined for developed countries. However, as economic growth and productivity slowed through the 1980s and 1990s, the attraction of "North-North" FDI flows diminished.

With the international opportunities opened up by the end of the Cold War, Western firms searched out profitable locations elsewhere. They didn't stop building cars or televisions or fridges at home, but it was easier to expand their production in other parts of the world than in the already over-capitalised mature parts. Start-up businesses also found it attractive to depart their sluggish domestic conditions.

East Asian countries and China became especially favoured, helping turn this into the most dynamic region in the world. The initial economic interest shown by the West was less as a market for products than as a production base. Once again, the export of capital, rather than of goods, proved to be the dominant force in global economic affairs (see Fig. 9.7).

East Asia's share of global FDI inflows – comprising mainly Korea, Taiwan, Hong Kong and China – was a negligible 1% in 1970 rising to 4% by the end of the Cold War. They then expanded five-fold to about 20% by 2018 (UNCTAD-stat, 2019). The number of foreign business affiliates located in developing countries grew six-fold from 71,000 in 1990 to 425,000 in 2008. Of these, about 16,000,

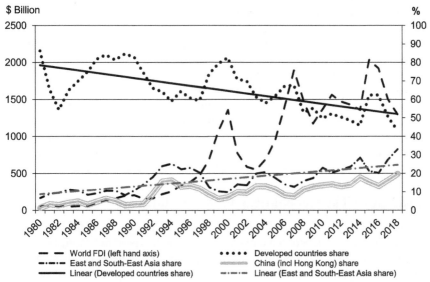

Fig. 9.7.   Asia's Rising Share of Inward Global FDI, 1980–2018
(UNCTADstat, 2019: FDI).

just less than a quarter were in China, growing to 285,000 – two-thirds of the total (Sassen, 2012, p. 53).

Inwards FDI into China has had significant benefits for its economic development. For example, when Western firms set up joint ventures in China, there are positive spillover effects on many Chinese businesses, not just those involved in the new joint ventures. In 2015 alone, foreign companies set up slightly more than 6,000 new joint ventures in China, accounting for nearly US$28 billion of FDI. Such joint venture companies benefitted the most within China; a decade later, their productivity was some 30% higher than other Chinese firms. However, these other businesses in the same sector also gain new technology and achieve absolute productivity improvement (Jiang, Keller, Qiu, & Ridley, 2018).

Thus, the rise of China and other emerging economies is not an autonomous "third world" development. Nor is the shift in the centre of gravity of much of the world's industrial production an inevitable, natural rebalancing. The pace of change is a specific outcome of the over-maturity of capital in the advanced countries and the internationalisation of production that this has propelled. The rise of China is at the same time the rise of *international production in* China.

After many years in which China made a huge contribution in offsetting the West's declining profitability, it has become a timely bogeyman instead. Having supported the Western economies since the turn of the millennium by driving up global growth, China has increasingly become blamed for the West's own economic problems. However, the rapid economic development of China and other Asian beneficiaries of Western investment are the consequence, not the cause, of the West's decay.

Internationalisation is not only a response to economic dysfunctionality in the West. It also sharpens geopolitical rivalries. The initial decades of Asian, including Chinese, economic development was largely "made in the West". From this foundation for growth, several of these countries – led by South Korea, Taiwan and China – are now strong enough to outcompete their previous Western "sponsors".

In 2018, it was symbolic of the economic reordering underway that the world's most valuable company, America's Apple, Inc., fell into third place in the global smartphone market, behind Korea's Samsung and China's Huawei. In newer sectors like AI, robotic machines, electric cars, "new" materials, solar power, high-speed trains and G5 telecommunications equipment, the previous strengths of Western firms are less relevant. Innovating Asian companies have even greater potential to dominate global markets in these cutting-edge industries.

Conclusion: The Geopolitical Tectonic Plates are Creaking

The three pertinent features of recent internationalisation – capital importing, state-led international economic practices and the unexpected delayed return of rivalries – make for a combustible mix. In particular, the dependence of America, the world's hegemonic state, and its closest post-war political ally Britain, on capital from elsewhere makes these countries susceptible to events outside their control and prone to get into confrontations with other nations.

At the end of 2018, foreigners held about 40% of America's national debt, up from less than one tenth in the 1960s, and from about a quarter in the 1970s and 1980s. China alone owned well over US$1 trillion of US government securities, about 5% of the total national debt, Japan another 4% and Middle Eastern oil producers combined up to another 2%.

With international tensions growing, West-West, West-East and North-South, the financial dependence of the number one global power on the second and third largest economies is an unprecedented situation of potential geopolitical flux. It is one thing to have particular export markets closed, or some overseas assets appropriated as a result of foreign political crises. It is a graver matter when funding the national state apparatus that has become so important to sustaining day-to-day economic life is now vulnerable to political decisions taken by other governments.

A revision of political influence is well underway. However, the globalist belief in the permanence of the post-1945 order blinds liberal politicians to how their commitment to the status quo, to the rules-based international order, is itself becoming a source of conflict. The vitriol of their responses to the several popular anti-establishment votes since 2016 is indicative of their difficulty in managing the domestic consequences of change, as well as the geopolitics of economic rebalancing.

Present-day global tensions reflect the post-crash interaction of two now well-established economic trends. The growing rivalries between *and* within the triad of mature nation blocs around North America, Europe and Japan is complicated further by the big global shift in productive weight from the West to the East. A rising China is encroaching on the global hegemony of the United States as the incumbent power. This is not due to China's adoption of particularly aggressive policies. It simply reflects the changing balance of economic power in the world as China's economy expands rapidly and narrows the gap with the United States' lethargic one.

Trust is dissipating; trouble brews. The West's collective reneging on the open economic principles of *their* order is already antagonising China and the other rising economic nations. The double standards practised by the Western nations add to the provocation. Apparently, it is okay for their own states to pursue industrial policies, promote new technologies and protect key sectors, but this is "unfair" and illegitimate when carried out by the Chinese and other emerging country states.

Indeed, by some measures, state intervention is lower in China than in the "free market West". For example, the Chinese state spends less relative to GDP than *every one* of the Group of Seven advanced countries (IMF, 2019). Less surprisingly, environmental policy is not as strict in China as in most Western countries (OECD, 2020a: environmental policy stringency). But the OECD also found that the US government gives extra regulatory protection to existing businesses than does China (OECD, 2020b: regulatory protection of incumbents).

The cultural propaganda war directed against China dodges these inconvenient facts. For many developing countries, this adds the charge of Western hypocrisy to that of unfairness in imposing its own rules and standards as being universal ones (Box 9.1).

Box 9.1.   The West's Dependence on China's Car Market.

As the global car market has slowed, China has become increasingly important for Western producers (see Fig. 9.8). Sales of new passenger cars in
China rose steadily from about five million in 2005 to about 25 million
in 2017. That was the year that China's car purchases for the first time
exceeded those in the United States, Japan and most of Europe combined.
Expansion in China provided an enormous boost to the world's existing car
producers. As one analyst said, it was like finding another planet on which
to sell cars (Alliance Bernstein, 2018). Western companies that were recoil-
ing from investing in new production facilities at home were given an extra
lease of life from supplying this exploding market abroad.

Chinese sales by Western firms, whether imported or produced in China,
have grown hugely in absolute terms, compensating for declining sales and
profits at home. China's 10 million sales for the major western companies
is on a par with the United States and EU, and well ahead of Japan and
South Korea's three million.

General Motors, the United States' top car producer, sells more cars in
China than in its home market. In 2007, the BRICs and other less developed regions accounted for 30% of global profits made by the largest Western car producers. By 2012, that share had doubled to nearly 60% as sales
in these regions rose by two-thirds and outpaced growth in Europe, North
America, Japan and South Korea. More than half of this growth came
from China alone (Mohr et al., 2013).

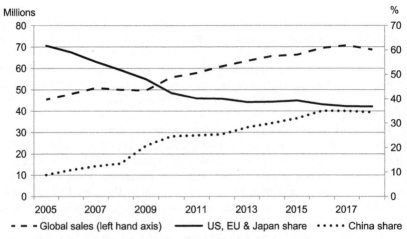

Fig. 9.8.   Global Passenger Car Sales, 2005–2018 (International
Organization of Motor Vehicle Manufacturers, 2020).

The Chinese market has been especially important for luxury brands. In 2017, for example, global sales at nine high-end brands – BMW, Mercedes-Benz, Toyota Motor unit Lexus, Jaguar Land Rover, Volvo Cars, General Motors unit Cadillac, Nissan Motor unit Infiniti and Volkswagen Group

Western carmakers generally do not publish how much of their profits are made specifically in China. However, analysts Evercore ISI estimate that China accounts for about one quarter of the profits made by most large automakers, and in some cases – like Volkswagen – about a half, more than the share of vehicles sold there. China's contribution to profits was particularly high for premium cars that were mainly imported. Evercore found that Mercedes and BMW make double the profit on an S Class or 7 Series sold in China compared to the rest of the world (Clover, 2017).

Growth in China began to slacken in 2016, and in 2018, sales fell for the first time since the early 1990s. There are likely to be a number of contributors: the ending of some government subsidies for vehicle purchases, a larger second hand car market and a secular shift – especially among younger people in the big cities – towards relying on high-quality public transport and other ways of buying mobility-as-a-service.

Regardless of the reasons, and whether the slowdown in sales continues or rebounds, the concerned reaction among commentators reveals the importance of the Chinese market to Western car producers. In the decade since supplanting the United States in 2009 as the world's largest car market, China has become the biggest source of sales and profits for most global carmakers (Hancock, 2018).

The late 2018 slowdown in sales coincided with many Western car companies making a bigger push into China, helped by the government opening up the economy. BMW reported a US$4 billion deal to secure control of its Chinese joint venture, becoming the first automaker to take advantage of China's policy to let foreign companies own a majority holding of their local partnerships. Daimler has considered making a similar move, while other Western brands have been boosting manufacturing capacity in China and expanding local production of models, including electric cars. Tesla, for instance, has announced plans to set up production in Shanghai.

Few in the West publicly applauded China's contribution to their corporate profits and living standards before 2015. However, once Chinese growth spluttered, everyone was attacking China for adding to the troubles of Western car manufacturers. The car industry example is thus typical of the argument made in this chapter as a whole.

Western commentators often present what goes on in the Chinese economy in a jaundiced way. China's substantial assistance to the West in compensating for the impact of its Long Depression is lost in the impassioned blame now attributed to China for its economic woes.

Chapter 10

The Battle Starts at Home

We live in the time of an unusual interaction of intra-West frictions with the tensions arising from the shift in economic weight from the West to the East. This is a combined challenge to the international accord never faced before. How can we prevent today's intensifying economic and political stresses taking a militarised form?

An insistence that everyone respect the rules of the post-war order won't do it. On the contrary, the rigidity of an old regime that thwarts an appropriate role for rising nations has itself become a major source of confrontation. The very structures that for over half a century helped sustain an aura of economic and political cooperation are now the triggers for disagreement.

The rational approach to a changing world is to collectively work out alternative arrangements appropriate to today and to future likelihoods. Negotiation between free, prosperous and independent nations offers the greatest prospect for avoiding another geopolitical breakdown. How can that be envisioned? Can there be, in the evocative phrase of historian Adam Tooze, a "realpolitik of progress" (2015, p. 518)? In the circumstances of uneven development is a collaborative and peaceable settlement feasible? This book contends that this is possible.

We have explained that mounting strains in the world order have both domestic and international roots. Thus, dealing with them requires both domestic and international actions. The starting place is at home. History tells us that countries with a clear and cohesive sense of purpose are much better at handling their international relationships and promoting collaboration than those that are ailing and disorientated. It is telling that the nations that initiated bloody international conflict in the previous century were already riven by grave domestic discord.

Because democracy already has an established *national* basis, domestic politics are not just an historic contributor to global contestation: it can also be the solution. The national polity offers the only proven basis for the flourishing, *public* internationalist movement needed to preserve harmony between nations. Withstanding today's drift towards confrontation *between* states thus needs to start *within* these individual states.

The immediate contribution Western nations can make to a new international settlement is recognition than holding onto the past is counterproductive for

Beyond Confrontation: Globalists, Nationalists and Their Discontents, 151–164
Copyright © 2020 by Phil Mullan
doi:10.1108/978-1-83982-560-620200014

sustained stability. The world is already changing, and it is better to be engaged in creating the future rather than trying to resist it.

National transformation has both economic and political components. The economic dimension of national renaissance is the focus of this penultimate chapter. Chapter 11 that ends the book will enlarge on this to argue that prosperity and peace relies on a fresh, enlightened political vision realised through sovereign nation states.

Relieving the Economic Strains

When domestic economic circumstances are arduous, looking externally for mitigation tends to aggravate rivalries between countries. Since uneven national development is also *combined* development, "nation-first" responses tend to provoke animosities (Tooze, 2018, pp. 614–616). In this regard, despite their expressed opposition to each other, trade blamers and trade boosters have much in common.

Both mercantilists and globalists find it much easier to search for foreign economic solutions. The former blame foreign countries and businesses for job losses; the latter put their hopes in trade agreements and trade promotions to boost depleted wealth creation. By looking to the outside world, both schools of thought not only evade dealing with the domestic roots of production decay – they also inflame rivalries with others. For instance, both mistakenly point the finger of responsibility for Western domestic troubles at China. However, this misleading diagnosis then leads to harmful policy prescriptions that make a tense global environment even grimmer.

Their shared evasive responses to economic entropy at home also generate fiercer national economic competition. Economic nationalist approaches invite confrontation as they squabble over taking their own advantage from the same rest-of-the-world. Nations in economic trouble find themselves jostling over export markets, sources of materials and locations for foreign investments. The world fragments into warring economic blocs.

As countries look to their national interests, they start to object to international, never mind supranational, supervision of their policies (Kahler, 2013, p. 46). Struggling nations wrestle with each other over the very standards and regulations that were supposed to cement international cooperation. For instance, the different applications of state aid rules within the EU, across the Atlantic, as well as between the West and China, have become areas of special rancour because they strike at the heart of national economic policies.

The underlying economic drive towards conflict can only be ameliorated durably, not by diplomacy alone, nor by extra rules, but by reviving the respective national engines of prosperity. Given that the Long Depression has prompted aggressive state protectionist policies, generating economic renaissance at home will directly lower the political temperature.

When countries do better economically, they do not experience the same necessity to externalise their difficulties and rub up against each other. Fixing the deep-rooted sources of Western productive atrophy will both lessen international stresses and help establish the free and autonomous countries that can work cooperatively with each other. Any new international political arrangements will better endure and succeed when based on strong domestic foundations.

Crisis-driven strains between nations are most effectively alleviated by economic renewal within the declining advanced industrial countries. Restructuring these national economies – while pursuing the opportunities that have opened up for them around the world, especially with the rise of Asia – are the best way of achieving that.

A country's state of productive vigour is always primarily a function of domestic factors. Even in a far more interconnected world, economies remain domestically driven. Performance is determined most by the condition of the fundamentals at home – profitability, investment and productivity levels – and by the actions taken by leading domestic players – policy-makers and businesses – to affect these.

Yet it is extremely unlikely that effective solutions to the crisis in production can emerge from the political classes and the associated business elites currently overseeing the Western nations. They are too committed to the status quo to come up with the changes needed to escape the Long Depression. In consequence, economic renewal requires political renewal from the bottom-up, not additional top-down measures that have primarily been about coping with slower growth.

A vital part of regeneration is a citizens' dialogue in each country about the importance of healthier productive growth and how to achieve it. Out of this, we need a programme for economic transformation. As one way of confronting today's pessimistic mood of fatalism, we should popularise the perspective of *national developmentalism* – a term suggested by the business writers Robert Atkinson and Michael Lind (2018, p. 17).

Resetting the economy is a collective activity, which will rely in part on the apparatus of state. To bring about sustained growth, each Western economy needs to go through a phase of *creative destruction*. This is necessary to remove the constraints that have been preventing the higher levels of domestic productive investment requisite to create new sectors and good new jobs. People living in particular localities are ideally placed to guide this activity, setting up transformation task forces that remain independent of central or local state *control*.

Social resources from national taxation or borrowing will be required for the implementation of these plans, and these should be made available via the machinery of state. This requisite role for the state in the programme of change shows that the globalist rejection of national sovereignty is not only anti-democratic: it also obstructs progress. Denigrating the role of the modern nation state denies having a collective agency of economic transformation. Yet there are no other potentially accountable vehicles that men and women can turn to for this crucial project.

National developmental strategies are likely to take different forms in different countries reflecting the particular economic structures, possibilities and constraints. They will also need to reflect regional and local particularities to ensure good jobs for people in all parts of the country. However, three common suppositions underpin the direction of each national change programme.

First, the domestic economic problems across the advanced industrial countries are long-standing and persisting. They precede the 2008–2009 financial

crisis, going back to the 1970s when post-war productivity growth first deceler-
ated. Sluggish growth is now endemic. It cannot be attributed to merely contingent factors.

In particular, weaker growth in one country cannot be explained by the commonly used tautology of weaker growth somewhere else. That sidesteps the home-
grown factors. Nor can languid growth be ascribed to the "declining confidence"
of businesses and consumers, nor to trade or other economic "uncertainties".
These are all consequences, not causes, of the innate slowdown within the system of production across the mature industrialised countries. The depth of the
malaise also means that spontaneous market forces would be unable to fix it:
collective solutions are indispensible.

Second, the crux of anaemic growth is the decline over many decades of business investment in technology and automation. This is what has led to falling
productivity growth. Since productivity measures the output of goods and services from each hour of work, its subdued evolution is the main explanation that
so many people have experienced only slightly increasing, flat or falling incomes.

The inadequacy of investment is itself the result of a dearth of profitable business opportunities. There is no shortage of cash available for corporate investment, either from internal business resources or from borrowing, but there is
an insufficient profit incentive. Too much capital has been accumulated in older
structures and equipment that their business owners are reluctant to write off.
This barrier to profitable investment takes the form of heightened business caution against taking on too much risk – another feature of a troubled society.

Third, and vitally, there *is* a solution. Economic depression is not immutable;
there is much we can do to overcome it. Paramount is rejection of the common
presumption that change is problematic and counterproductive. It is often said
that one of the characteristics of public debate about the economy in recent years
has been a "remarkable degree of fatalism. People have come to believe that 'there
is no alternative'" (Institute for Public Policy Research (IPPR) Commission on
Economic Justice, 2018, p. 82). This observation is only half right.

Predominantly, it is the *politicians* rather than the *people* who have become
fatalistically negative about making change. It is mostly political leaders who have
given up on promoting grand visions about economic advance. Since the 1980s,
traditional political choices on economic policy have narrowed, mainly to who
can best manage implementation.

It is true that lots of potential voters have become disenchanted with politics
as a result of the politicians failing to put forward compelling alternatives to consider. But this is the fault of today's detached political classes, not of the electorate. As a result, it is ordinary men and women – through public discussion and
debate – who will have to come up with transformative ideas. Since politicians
have let them down in so many Western countries, the citizenry will have to take
the lead as advocates and planners of economic change.

Another recognition is crucial for this civic debate. Because the economic rot
has spread so far over the past half-century, there are no easy, pain-free solutions. Doing nothing is not an option, since ongoing decay risks serious economic
breakdowns at home and internationally. Thus, some disruption is unavoidable.

However, initiating our own transformation, unsettling as it will be, is much better than having chaotic disruption inflicted upon us. A central part of any successful transformation plan will be collective support for the many people impacted by the changes. Most workers and their dependents will need financial and practical assistance to make the transition from today's lower productivity, inadequately recompensed, insecure jobs into the newly created, higher productivity, better paying employment that brings greater security.

The Dangers of Enforced Stability

A conundrum of the current economic policy framework is that there is much agreement on the sort of measures that have the *potential* to promote investment-led growth, yet growth remains meagre. Even among "free marketeers", many accept increased public spending on research, on modernising dilapidated infrastructure, and on helping re-skill people for new industries and jobs. Some go further and make the case for business investment allowances, and even enforcing a minimum wage based on "independent" – that is non-political – assessments of the real cost of living.

In the right circumstances, these suggestions could help catalyse a dynamic of business investment in better ideas and technologies. The missing link in realising this potential is businesses having the incentives to take advantage of these initiatives. *Creating these economic conditions* has to be the immediate focus of the transformation programme.

Otherwise, all these well-meaning long-term policies will fail to make much impact. This has been the frustrating case for much of the past quarter-century. The consensus industrial strategy measures have so far been largely ineffective, giving self-perpetuating credence to the fatalist spirit.

Hence, the biggest challenge in reviving economic growth is *taking that initial disruptive step* of clearing away what is holding back innovation and expansion. Because depressed economies are self-reproducing, this rupture will not happen spontaneously. At worst, it could happen from a destructive escalation of geopolitical events. Unfortunately, that is what happened so distressingly in the first half of the last century.

But that history also reminds us that economic atrophy is not forever. By the 1950s and 1960s, the inter-war Great Depression turned into the most dynamic era of economic advance ever. It is not inevitable that total war has to be the catalyst for such a transformation, but what happened in the 1930s and 1940s is an emphatic warning if planned change continues to be put off.

The present class of Western politicians senses that clearing away the preponderance of low-productivity operations is bound to be destabilising, so that nearly all of them have ducked taking on this responsibility. Instead, they have embraced short-termism – muddling through for another few years – while mopping up some, though by no means all, of the detritus as they stumble along. Preservationist measures have been their preference, including high levels of workaday government spending, low interest rates and regulations that sustain incumbents. The result is an increasingly debt-dependent economy that lives beyond its means.

Unintentionally, this attachment to the status quo has been camouflaging the continuing decay of productive capacities. Prolonging economic malaise has inadvertently been augmenting international competitive rivalries. The benign alternative to this is that we take the initiative in clearing the ground to enable something better to be built based around investment in advanced technologies.

The Zombie Block

As the Long Depression became deeply ingrained, a zombie economy has become consolidated. Businesses have become stuck in a sluggish environment that they cannot transform by their individual initiatives. However much the existing healthier – and some start-up – companies might desire to innovate, the wider over-accumulated economy is too slow moving to make these investments sufficiently profitable. The zombie economy becomes a black hole that sucks in dynamism and clogs up activity, thereby frustrating creative impulses.

Zombies in the movies are scary not just because of the way they lurch around wanting to attack you. Even more terrifying is the dread of never being able to terminate them. Collectively, they are so very hard to "kill". The zombie businesses that choke Western economies are similar. They can keep going for ages.

Across the advanced industrial countries, there has been a decline in the pace of business turnover since the 1980s. Fewer low-productivity businesses with dismal growth prospects have been closing down. Many of these businesses may barely cover their costs but are kept on life support, courtesy mostly of unprecedentedly low interest rates (Banerjee & Hofmann, 2018). The survival of low-productivity and mediocre businesses reinforces the debilitating effects of zombie congestion.

The deadweight effect of zombie businesses contributes to lower productivity *levels*, as they push down the national average. Of bigger influence for the *growth* of productivity is the way zombie congestion impedes the *diffusion* of up-to-date technologies across the rest of the economy. It blocks stronger existing firms and start-up businesses from investing in the latest innovations, so that insufficient numbers of businesses using advanced technologies have been replacing the outdated, less efficient ones.

Researchers at the OECD have concluded that the main source of the recent productivity slowdown across the advanced countries is this breakdown of the market's "diffusion machine". They discovered that while the productivity growth of the globally most productive firms remained fairly robust in the twenty-first century, the gap between those high-productivity firms and the rest had widened (Adalet McGowan, Andrews, Criscuolo, & Nicoletti, 2015, p. 12).

Despite some fashionable ideas about "technological exhaustion", it is false to claim humanity has stopped coming up with new ideas. Indeed, a complementary OECD analysis has confirmed a broadening technological and productivity divergence between the top 5% of firms and the other 95% (Andrews, Criscuolo, & Gal, 2016). The deeper challenge has been the barriers hindering the spread of inventions deployed by these frontier firms into innovation investments across other firms and sectors (Adalet McGowan, Andrews, & Millot, 2017).

Stagnation Despite Innovation

This explains the paradox of supposedly living in an era of accelerating technological change, while productivity and wages go nowhere fast. Every day, we read about exciting discoveries that *could* transform manufacturing, agriculture, health services, transport and much more. The problem is that these better ways of working are *not being adopted widely enough*. This is why genuine innovation co-exists with wider stagnation.

As a result, alongside people employed precariously in the weakest zombie firms, a large number are working in mediocre jobs with little technology upgrading. In Britain, for instance, about half of all businesses have experienced zero productivity growth since at least the start of this century. Most of the other half has only averaged growth of around 1% a year (Bank of England, 2018).

Even less recognised is that at the top of the business tree, congestion also drags down the high-productivity elite of firms. For example, in Britain, we can find instances of highly automated car, aerospace or life sciences workplaces that are continuing to invest and raise their productivity. But they are doing so *much more slowly* than their predecessors did.

In fact, there is evidence that the biggest *decline in the rates* of productivity growth over the past couple of decades has been *within* the top-tier innovators (Schneider, 2018). In a stagnant over-accumulated economy accompanied by a culture of fear and uncertainty, few business leaders feel able to write off past investments. Yet this appreciation is the precondition for successfully undertaking the costly replacements in new equipment and processes to develop new products and services.

The Perverse Effect of Supportive State Intervention

The norm over the past three decades has been packages of public measures buttressing incumbency. Existing firms and industries – the weak as well as the stronger – have been propped up at the expense of new and growing ones. State institutions have acted to sustain the zombie economy, not to hasten its demise – even if this happens by contingency rather than by design. In fact, once the zombie economy has emerged, the unintended effect of implementing many "free market" policy recommendations is to entrench it. In the absence of a wider economic shake-up, any pro-business cuts in corporate taxation, or reductions in bureaucratic regulation, would make it even easier for struggling, lethargic firms to keep afloat.

Previously, the practices of the modern state balanced two economic roles: promoting growth and maintaining economic order. In the earlier part of the twentieth century policies to accelerate growth were often regarded as consistent with such stability. They were designed to bring actual growth into line with "potential" growth and ensure "equilibrium".

However, especially since the Second World War, many pro-growth policies were intended to have a deeper impact. Post-war Western states took responsibility for speeding up the expansion of potential output too, by trying to lift productivity. And when boosting productivity turned out to be temporarily a bit disruptive and destabilising, this was accepted. The goal of faster future growth took precedence over short-term stability.

From the end of the post-war boom, and increasingly with the political hollowing out from the latter part of the 1980s, state institutions have shifted again to favour instead the other aspect of the traditional duality: the stabilisation of capitalism. The return of economic crisis in the early 1970s initially prompted government attempts to mitigate the slowdown and to engineer recovery. As weakness persisted, these inadequate efforts to *combat* the crisis gradually gave way to its *containment*, which meant supporting what existed. "Economic stability", "financial stability" and "market stability" have become goals in their own right.

This inclination towards balance and order conformed to the ascendancy of a new post-politics culture of fear and uncertainty. A social preoccupation with safety and a craving for certainty reflected lowered expectations about what could be achieved. The aspiration to keep things the way they were appeared attractive.

In consequence, the state has turned into a *conservator state*, with many public policies working to shield and protect the present condition of economic life (Poynter, 2020). This has had the perverse effect of perpetuating the Long Depression's productivity impasse. Businesses that are mollycoddled by state largesse have less incentive to undertake risky investments in new technologies and innovation.

National state institutions evolved an array of mechanisms that sustain both the economy in general as well as many of its individual businesses. These measures included public–private partnerships, regulatory and other assistance provided to privatised industries, as well as public procurement policies.

Legislative changes, too, have often favoured company survival. For example, the necessity for going fully bankrupt has been mitigated by making it easier for insolvent businesses to manage their debts and keep going. Even state initiatives introduced for other purposes have helped businesses cope better: for instance, in-work welfare benefits have subsidised struggling employers through the reduced cost of payroll.

Such measures have created new problems. Governments have brought about the circumstance of *corporate dependency*. This has proved to be as debilitating for the economy as welfare dependency is for individuals. Regulations, public spending including state procurement policies and the changes to insolvency rules: all these have shored up incumbent businesses, many of which are low productivity.

Most prominently within this framework of measures has been easier monetary policies undertaken by central banks. Ever since the shock of the sharp transatlantic stock market falls of October 1987, the subsequent efforts by state bankers to stabilise economic conditions have made it easier for low-profitability, low-productivity firms to muddle along. This approach was spearheaded then by the US Federal Reserve, under its then recently appointed chair Greenspan but soon spread elsewhere.

The near continuous loosening of monetary policies has enabled politicians and business leaders to evade the difficult decision that eliminating the disease is vital for restoring health. In practice, these policies have instead underpinned the increasing indebtedness that sustains the zombie economy. The implementation of quantitative easing and ultra-low interest rates since the 2008 crash marked an extreme continuation of this trend.

Initially, these loose monetary policies were welcomed as a necessary fix to stabilise the post-crash economy by unfreezing financial markets. Widespread unease about which institutions were holding unreliable and potentially worthless debts led private financial flows to seize up. By pumping liquidity into the financial system through very low interest rates followed by the quantitative easing programme of buying bonds, the leading central banks were taking up one of their traditional counter-crisis roles – as lenders of the last resort.

The new problem was that over the next few years, this emergency intervention turned into a *permanent* market feature. Capitalist resilience now relied upon extreme levels of state sustenance. These super-easy monetary policies became a key aspect of the "new normal" of state-sustained economic torpidity. When, from late 2015, the Federal Reserve led gradual efforts to reverse these measures, renewed signs of economic fragility soon spooked politicians and financial institutions. Fears of another financial crash or economic slowdown meant the Federal in 2019 had to reverse its attempted reversal, long before interest rates or its balance sheet holdings of financial assets returned to previous norms.

Anxieties also spread, initially from central bankers themselves, that there was something fundamentally unhealthy about the acute dependence on such monetary measures. In particular, the mind-boggling arrival of *negative* nominal interest rates was not something that could be ignored. Economic survival was coming at the cost of building up problems and sowing the seeds of the next financial crisis.

Fears grew about new debt and financial asset bubbles being inflated not this time by "greedy bankers" but by the state authorities. Central bankers also worried they would have very limited additional means to intervene when the next recession came. Eventually, by the end of the 2010s, the evident exhaustion of monetary policies led Western governments of all political complexions to look favourably again upon fiscal activism led by their treasuries. This was less the handing of the policy baton from one wing of the state to another than the recognition that the central banks could not be expected to continue as the "only game in town" in trying to preserve economic stability.

Other observers became aware of the even deeper problem. Official policies were not only failing to boost productivity growth but were entrenching its stagnation. Zombie companies, including some banks, were being kept afloat by the extremely low cost of borrowing. These "walking dead" businesses had helped nurture the false idea that the economy was doing okay. By buying and selling things they kept economic output from declining. Also, they employed people thereby underpinning "record" levels of employment.

But at the same time, they were clogging up the economy and tying up resources in low-productivity areas. The resulting congestion added to the chronic constraints discouraging stronger businesses from investing in productivity-enhancing ventures. Hence, the greater awareness by economists since then of *zombification*, even though as we've described this process had already been underway for about three decades (Bank for International Settlements, 2019, pp. 19–26).

The money newly created by the state could not sweep away the barriers resulting from the previous over-accumulation in now outdated equipment and structures. Instead of engaging in productive investment, the borrowing facilitated by the super-loose monetary policies went into share buy-backs and other financial investments, further reinforcing already high asset prices. Debt levels – public and private – soon exceeded those reached before the financial crisis in nominal terms. Within a few years, they were higher relative to GDP. The return of the strains from overindebtedness relative to value creation that had precipitated the 2008–2009 crisis were difficult to overlook. An exact repeat of the latest crisis never happens, but the interlinking of financial markets means that a new catalyst for crisis would emerge in some area at some time.

Breaking the Log-Jam

All the official economic conservation practices have taken political precedence over the turmoil that would be involved in restoring sustained productivity growth. Politicians and their technocrats have in effect traded the possibility of decent, better paying jobs in the future for keeping people in worse paying, unreliable jobs now. This puts one pain – arising from economic insecurity and hardship in work, punctuated by periodic recessions – over the other that comes from losing those jobs through economic restructuring. But people can better absorb the latter pain when they know it brings the opportunity of obtaining other better employment.

In the middle of the last century, the economist Joseph Schumpeter grasped that capitalism could only progress through disruption. He borrowed concepts from Karl Marx and other writers from the nineteenth century to come up with the helpful description that expanding capitalism operates through "creative destruction". This is the way in which older, less productive firms close down and are replaced by newer, productive ones.

This concept recognised that capitalism needs to be changing and renovating continually to ensure social progress. Businesses and organisations that adopt new and improved processes, products and services grow, displacing those that don't. New sectors and businesses provide better, securer employment to replace what has been lost. The withering away of this process is the distinctive characteristic of the Long Depression, expressing itself in reduced business churn and economic zombification.

A prominent feature of the muting of destructiveness has been the "contained" appearance of the crisis, at least between the mid-1980s and the 2008 financial crash. Many went along with describing this period as the "Great Moderation", an unusual description for a time of economic depression (Federal Reserve Board, 2004; Stock & Watson, 2003).

A long period of stable, modest growth can sound like a good thing. Who wants to live in an unsettled rollercoaster of an economy? This is why the muting of capitalism's creative destructive tendencies can appear attractive to politicians and, indeed, to all of us. In the short term, stability seems to be a blessing. It slows the disappearance of jobs in less profitable businesses. Since job loss usually

brings personal insecurity and, sometimes, great hardship, avoiding it has immediate advantages to the people affected.

However, the massive downside of the Great Moderation was the decay of
economic dynamism. The depression since the 1970s has for most of the time
been neither as destructive nor as turbulent as its predecessor in the 1930s. The
relatively shallow recessions of the early 1990s and 2000s illustrate this. The long-
term effect of a less volatile capitalism has been a static economy. Less destructive recessions were also *less cleansing*. The creative aspects of the business cycle
have been contained alongside the destructive ones.

With hindsight, it is easier to see that the Great Moderation period of modest
growth was simply a precursor to the secular stagnation following the financial
crash. The earlier softening of the traditional business cycle was not the sign of
a revived and stronger capitalism as assumed by the Great Moderation thesis.
Resilience is not the same as strength.

Capitalism's coping mechanisms had been effective enough for a couple of
decades to generate the symptoms of the Great Moderation. However, the financial crash of 2008 brought this phase to a close by demonstrating the relative
exhaustion of both financialisation and internationalisation. Neither disappeared
but together they have no longer been enough to camouflage the stagnation in
production.

The Agenda *for* Change is an Agenda *of* Change

Accepting creative destruction again can usher in a different culture and business
climate from that of the past quarter century. Higher productivity businesses will
have the incentive to set up or expand to take the place of the lower productivity
ones. Greater numbers of people will have the opportunity to take higher paid
jobs with extra security, instead of the lower and flat income, insecure ones they
have today.

Sectorally, economic transformation programmes need to cover all the areas
that have seen too little or too narrow advance for many decades: not only manufacturing but also agriculture, mining and extraction, energy production, construction, transport and distribution. For example, much of the latest discussion
about progress in transport is confined to electric cars or autonomous vehicles.
But this mostly amounts to modifying *existing* techniques of mobility using
replacement forms of energy, or additional automation and machine learning.
Instead, we should be going a lot further to explore *new methods* of transport: on
the ground, under the ground and above the ground.

The technologies we need to invest in also need to be much broader than we've
experienced recently. Innovation should not focus so exclusively on *information*
and *communications*. Not everything benefits from additional data flows. Since
the 1960s, there has been only restricted development in other generic technologies, such as materials, forms of propulsion, energy processes such as nuclear
fusion, building techniques, biosciences, nanotechnologies and robotics. We know
all these things are possible, but actual progress over the past half-century has
been slow and protracted.

There is a lot in the area of technological change to inspire people as part of a shared political vision. A return to a broader range of technological advancement will not just make better lives for people in the advanced countries. It can also help address faster than today the *world's* continuing problems of malnutrition, disease, cramped accommodation, lack of power and inadequate living standards. National economic renewal that brings solutions in some of these areas is international in perspective and reach.

Industrial policies that sustain existing weak businesses are worse than doing nothing. They have been reinforcing zombie capitalism. This needs to stop. Preserving the older, muddling through firms and workplaces blocks the force of creative destruction and, by postponing the day of reckoning, can only make it so much worse when it arrives. This is why protectionism, in both old and new forms, is economically harmful. It acts as part of the comfort blanket that props up inefficient and zombie businesses. An *effective* industrial strategy, in the sense of one that revives productivity growth and provides decent jobs, is one that shakes up the economy, not preserves it.

In particular, low productivity, going nowhere firms, offering inadequate job prospects should be allowed to contract or close down. Most people have jobs – employment *is* at record highs in some countries – but many of these do not provide much security, on-the-job training and the prospect of increasing prosperity. An end to state featherbedding of businesses rekindles the incentives for the stronger ones to invest, innovate and provide better employment.

Only with the destruction of the old zombies can a new economy be built, aided by the collective resources of the state. This sequencing is crucial because without first clearing away zombification, the most creative growth policies will make little positive impact. Low-cost public finance or tax credits for transformative investments; lots of additional state-funded basic research that generate new ideas and inventions; an efficient public infrastructure providing cheaper energy, faster transport and comprehensive communications systems – all these are helpful in principle. However, they are neutered as a way to transform a market economy when businesses remain held back by the constraint of inadequate profitability.

It is not the construction of specific industrial policy measures that has resulted in so much failure up to now. It is the absence of economic circumstances propitious for business investment in transformation. This is why the OECD productivity researchers argued that a key implication of their analysis is that weak productivity performance will persist "unless a new wave of structural reforms can revive a broken diffusion machine" (Andrews et al., 2016, p. 8). Such structural reforms should be the primary goal of production change strategies.

Once economic restructuring has restored better conditions of profitability, then targeted state subsidies or tax credits can usefully catalyse firms to invest in innovation. In such a transformed environment, higher public spending on pure research will have greater scope to be commercialised successfully. Publicly funded basic research in government, academic or private institutions will generate the new ideas and inventions to be turned over time into future waves of business innovation. Also, in these improved conditions, better transport networks and energy systems can make a difference. They won't just be helpful for individuals in their everyday lives but can aid businesses to become stronger.

New industrial policies would have nothing to do with "picking winners", or even attempting to anticipate the "next" winners, whether firms or sectors. Instead, the approach should be almost the opposite: acceptance that many state venturing exercises will select "losers" in the sense of firms or new business ventures that fail. Many will flop: that is essential to innovation in a market system. Successful economic growth policies will always have a strong element of trial and error. Just as with private corporate venture financing, nine out of 10 schemes will probably not succeed. But the 10th one makes economic and social progress, and can earn enough return to justify all the venture funding unsuccessful as well as successful.

Many people will have their working lives disrupted through this unsettling process of economic transformation. A return to higher levels of business dynamism *must* go hand in hand with collective measures to assist people during the transition into new jobs, not least when they are already employed in low-productivity workplaces. The new jobs are unlikely to emerge immediately, or to always be in the most convenient locations. State sponsorship will need to be engaged by the local task forces to mitigate effectively the human cost of change, by assisting workers into higher productivity, better paid employment.

Public financial aid to families during the transition would include help to find different employment and, if required, to move home to be near it. State-funded re-skilling should be offered in association with the training provided by the new employers. The costs of these aspects of change can be recouped from the stronger economic growth that would follow.

Such support measures for individuals and families are vital but cannot become a substitute for new employment. Understandably people will be reluctant to give up even insecure low-paying jobs if the alternative seems to be the spread of the welfare dependency that is already blighting so many depressed areas. Providing a state income for people when there is no prospect of getting off benefits provides false hope. That's one problem with the recent suggestions for a universal basic income.

At the same time, training people for jobs that don't exist is demoralising and wasteful – unused skills are soon forgotten. For people to embrace the plans for transforming production, they first need to believe that good jobs, with the opportunity for up-skilling training, will be created by new and expanding businesses.

Conclusion: Popular Engagement is Vital to Success

This brings us back to the key point about economic transformation programmes. Recasting industrial strategy to enable creative destruction to operate will be painful. But for most people, today's employment isn't giving them security, training or the prospect of rising incomes. And there are no painless paths out of this malaise. Civic dialogue in local task forces would explore why such a radical course is needed for economic renewal.

This involves popular understanding and support, as well as a mandate for this direction of change. For instance, the pros and cons of taking monetary policy back under government control could be debated. This could set the claimed dangers of political short-termism against the benefit of policy being set by accountable institutions.

While economic transformation programmes need to be funded centrally, to be successful they have to be organised by people on the ground who appreciate the challenges, who understand best their local economic history and environment and who can most accurately assess their area's existing strengths and weaknesses. What matters more than any specific industrial policy measure is that the populace has the means locally, regionally and nationally to publicly debate, deliberate and choose the next steps. This requires democratic engagement and political courage, backed up subsequently by the institutional infrastructure to put the agreed plans into effect.

Ridding ourselves of the status quo approach of politicians is no simple task. It requires people finding ways to reassert control over their country's political life. Through thrashing out their economic problems and opportunities, the electorate will be experimenting with new democratic mechanisms. In addition to being creative, this is sorely needed now that the old left-right divisions and the traditional political party system are so exhausted.

Lots of people have become disenchanted with politics as a result of elected politicians failing to put forward compelling visions to consider. This is the fault of today's political classes, not of the electorate. Ordinary men and women will have to come up with the transformation ideas themselves, through public discussion and debate. Since politicians have let us down in so many Western countries, the citizenry must take on the roles of advocates and agents of economic change.

Chapter 11

Internationalism, National Sovereignty and Democracy

> The secret to happiness is freedom... And the secret to freedom is courage.
>
> Thucydides, *The History of the Peloponnesian War*

Economic renewal within each mature country will both restore rising prosperity and lessen strains at home and abroad. However, economic dysfunctionality is neither the only source of domestic and international discord, nor is national economic restructuring a total solution. Ultimately, stopping conflict and war is a political rather than an economic undertaking.

At home, for example, cultural factors have recently been far more influential than the economics of austerity or inequality in stirring up divisions. Polarising damage has resulted from governments that have promoted multiculturalism in place of national values. Many indigenous people have felt ignored, patronised or discriminated against. In many of the advanced Western countries, similar fault lines have opened up between native citizens and their cosmopolitan political and cultural leaders (Goodhart, 2017). Resolving this requires a new kind of political leadership, not productivity growth.

In the international sphere too, while economic rivalries are fomented by the decay of Western production, there are other drivers of geopolitical breakdown. For instance, we've explained how divergent attitudes to the old world order have already become a significant arena for battles over power. And since the implications and meaning of laws and regulations are not self-evident, the judicial system itself has become a power play. Differences over the "rule of law" are increasingly sources of conflict, as seen not just in the initiation of multiple legal disputes within post-2016 Britain and America, but notably in west-east clashes between EU member states.

When societies lose inner meaning and start to fragment, foreign scapegoats tend to proliferate. Debates over international relations, economic interests and foreign policy are invariably surrogates for debates about the nation's meaning and identity (Kagan, 2018, p. 138). Without national purpose, countries often become introverted, consumed by a sense of impossibility and stuck in dissension.

Beyond Confrontation: Globalists, Nationalists and Their Discontents, 165–183
Copyright © 2020 by Phil Mullan
All rights of reproduction in any form reserved
doi:10.1108/978-1-83982-560-620200015

It is when countries are drifting and lack direction that wars are liable to happen. As explained earlier, the Second World War was a product of troubled and uncertain national elites, not simply of escalating economic rivalries. Economic crisis does not inexorably end in armies fighting. Responsibility for war lies with the failure of political leaders to successfully manage tensions.

The most perilous consequence of an absence of purpose is the loss of the belief in agency – the conviction that powered the faster developing parts of the world for nearly half a millennium. Writing at the dawn of this age, Shakespeare had Cassius say to Brutus in *Julius Caesar*, "Men at some time are masters of their fates. The fault ... is not in our stars but in ourselves, that we are underlings". This essential Enlightenment message is that people can be masters of their fate. It is not destiny's fault but our own faults, if we've become slaves to a modern Caesar. In international affairs today, losing this belief in mastery underlies the customary fatalistic approach to globalisation. The even greater danger is that the drift to war also becomes regarded as something "in the stars".

In the previous chapter, we argued that the developing an *economic transformation programme* for domestic renewal could help forge a new sense of national meaning. In this final chapter, we marry this with advancing *twenty-first century internationalism* as a parallel means to promote national purpose.

How a nation approaches its relations with others both reflects and can also impact upon its internal life. Striking out in an anti-protectionist, internationalist direction can be a focus for the West to regain direction. For instance, Western countries seizing the economic opportunities from the rise of the East would be to embrace modernity again. Taking advantage of innovation wherever it emerges and extending the productive gains from collaboration with foreigners would be fruitful nationally *and* internationally.

A progressive alternative to the current Western fear of falling behind the East technologically is to invest to a greater extent in cross-border ventures, including with China. This would be a way of expanding the international division of labour, not to prop up a crumbling economic order in the West but to help produce a stronger world economy and polity.

Promoting this vision shakes up Western conservator thinking and has the additional benefit of seeing other nations as partners rather than as beggarly parasites or cheating rivals. By establishing such mutually beneficial connections with China and the rest of East Asia, Western countries would be re-adopting the Enlightenment values of liberty and fraternity.

Trade experts Evenett and Fritz drew attention to some of these cultural opportunities. Explaining that it was futile to rely on international organisations from the G20 to the WTO to resist protectionist trends the "case for openness to trade, investment, expertise, ideas, and data needs to be won at home" (Evenett & Fritz, 2019, p. 16). Remaking a public internationalist sentiment calls upon promoting the values of openness, freedom and progress, which will have liberalising benefits domestically. Since mercantilist and globalist outlooks have increasingly whitewashed these ideals in recent decades, a new internationalism can only emerge through opposition to each of them.

Because these intellectual and political battles take place at home, as well as alleviating international tensions, this perspective should also aid *domestic* cultural renewal. Forging a positive external relationship with the rest of the world offers a country a new spirit while contributing to a harmonious international community.

A precondition for this is to win the argument against the emerging cultural idea in the West that China is today's fascist Germany. While China can expect further domestic political turmoil from its government's efforts to maintain authoritarian control, that is, a problem for the Chinese people to resolve. The best solidarity Western people can offer is to push back on the undemocratic trends in their own countries.

Whither the Nation State?

Mercantilism's distrust of the foreign is self-evident. Its advocates see winning as coming at the expense of others. In the West today, this mostly operates as an explanation for decline – others are winning at our cost. Mercantilist foreign policy seeks to reverse this.

On the surface, globalist ideas appear less anti-foreign. By definition, they espouse the benefits of globalisation and the international order. But in practice, globalism is antagonistic to those who do not respect its ways, abroad as well as at home. Globalists are critical of anyone, foreigners included, who do not adopt its rules-based values. They condemn Brexiteers for being nativist, Trump voters for being nationalistic, and East Europeans in Poland, Hungary and Romania for abandoning the globalist interpretation of the "rule of law".

Defending their interpretation of liberal values makes globalist leaders illiberally intolerant. As much as Trump's White House, globalist politicians condemn China's "state capitalist" ways. While Trump's fight with China is mostly over trade, technology and cross-border investment, globalists have much broader concerns over values and philosophies (Ganesh, 2019). The latter is potentially a lot more dangerous. Economic and trade conflicts can have compromise solutions. In contrast, cultural clashes are harder to allay and can become existential.

The reason globalism is the antithesis of internationalism is that it is grounded in formally rejecting everything to do with the nation. Yet without the nation, there can be no inter*nation*alism, and no rightful inter*nation*al – as well as national – action. Globalists denounce nationalism as regressive and barbaric. The nation state is denigrated as no longer potent, nor relevant. National sovereignty – the ability of a country to make decisions about the lives of its people without having these imposed from outside – is disparaged as an outdated illusion that we should be glad to see the back of.

Globalists think that economic globalisation nullifies the role and effectiveness of national units in boosting growth and prosperity. Technological advances, especially in communications, mean that "territorial boundaries, which once represented natural barriers to communication, now become increasingly artificial" (Camilleri & Falk, 1992, p. 5). The "explosive pressure of economic interdependencies that tacitly permeate national borders" is thought to limit what national governments can do by their own efforts. This shatters the "established relations of solidarity" within national territories, and "compel us" to pursue some form of supranationalism instead (Habermas, 2015, p. 28). Supranational governance is regarded as made inevitable by the emergence of globalisation.

Yet as examined earlier, it is *nation states* that have accelerated the very internationalisation of capital which globalists point to as evidence of globalisation undermining the power and pertinence of the state. Despite such ironies, globalists claim that the nation is past its sell-by date. It is, they say, both too small and too large an entity to operate in the modern world. Under the pressures of "relentless" globalisation a "wide range of subnational and transnational institutions" now confront the outmoded model of a world divided into sovereign nation states (Camilleri & Falk, 1992, p. 7).

The old nation state is thought to be *too small* because larger political associations are needed with the greater resources to deal effectively with today's bigger and more complex problems. It is claimed that the nation can't handle global risks like atomic radiation or environmental depletion that don't respect national borders. But it also *too large* in that national politics has become remote from the interests of local communities. Instead, local subnational entities – regions and big cities – are regarded as assuming a greater importance as centres of politics. Smaller units are thought to be homogeneous, making them better able to agree on actions (Scharpf, 1988, p. 239).

Are Nations Really "Too Small" to Cope?

One of the most common arguments that nation states are today too small is global warming. This is perceived as a global problem that "no nation state can cope with alone" (Beck, 2016, pp. 4–6). What this justification for supranationalism ignores is that most cross-border challenges still emerge out of *national* activities. The human-generated carbon emissions that are believed to contribute to climate change derive from productive activities taking place within national territories or, with international travel and transport between two defined countries. Additionally, the nation state, individually and jointly, remains the best channel to decide, justify and implement any actions needed to reduce the impact of such territorially based activities.

Globalist bodies like the Intergovernmental Panel on Climate Change (IPCC) can make recommendations and set targets but for action to be effective, rather than declaratory, it has to happen *within* actual geographical territory. And, so far, only the nation state has means and legitimacy to act territorially. Not least since emissions control policies are intrusive on people's lives, they can only be agreed, realised, monitored and enforced in an accountable manner through *national* institutions of state.

The IPCC may have a secretariat but – thankfully – it has no autonomous police force that can override national laws. Just because a problem is common to many nations, it does not follow that nation states become anachronistic. Dealing with a shared predicament simply necessitates *cooperative* actions between and across states. The essential point is that there is no working substitute for the national state apparatus in meeting people's collective social needs.

Fundamentally, the globalist rejection of national entities represents an abdication of making change because supranational bodies have neither the means nor the legitimacy to replace the transformative capabilities of nation states. Today, only nation states have the proven potential for democratic accountability. When it comes to practical power, as we've examined earlier, nation states *have* been intervening in their societies including, increasingly, propping up their own capitals. They have the resources to do so from having long achieved the authority to levy taxes and to borrow.

Few people can refute that for about two centuries, nations and nation states have been the chief actors in the world. As two Greek political scientists Daphne Halikiopoulou and Sofia Vasilopoulou described, it is not as individual human beings that we respond to global problems and pressures: "It is nations and national states and their citizens, that determine both the agenda and the action" (Halikiopoulou & Vasilopoulou, 2011, p. 1). In the words of another respected political scientist, the late Stanley Hoffmann, regardless of the post-1945 establishment of many multilateral organisations, nation states remain the ultimate locus of "authoritative decision making regarding most facets of public and private life" (Hoffmann, 2003, pp. 27–35).

Today, although countries are better interconnected than ever before, we all still live in particular national territories, and the nation state remains the only significant territorial actor.[1] The UN itself recognises 195 "sovereign states" today, meaning a place with its own borders and independent government. Governments – elected or otherwise – preside over defined national terrains. Tax revenues and public spending are operated through national budgets.

While states take account of what other states are doing, the vast majority of them retain independent discretion over fiscal, tax, welfare and military policies (with the main exception being members of the EU, especially of the eurozone). Most law and regulation remains national, created by national state entities. Even "international law" is only sanctioned when nation states decide to defer to pan-national bodies, a deferral any nation state can reverse by opting out of the relevant international institution. (Though Britain's protracted departure from the EU underscored the strong status quo forces today that could try to stymie this.)

We might not agree with everything, or even with a lot of what they have done, but the modern nation state has a vigorous track record. Although not always successful, they have still become increasingly active over the course of the past 200 years. National states helped drive industrial revolutions and introduced education, health and welfare systems. Often they have cooperated together for common objectives. Sometimes, tragically, they have fought each other.

---

[1] Some of the world's population does live in disputed territories. In 2019, there were eight significant ones: Taiwan, Kashmir, Kurdistan, Western Sahara, Kosovo, South Ossetia, Abkhazia and Northern Cyprus. All of these are claimed as parts of other countries but aren't controlled by them, at least not completely.

Recent economic crises draw out most clearly the continued reliance on national state intervention. Even where there is strong evidence that the national state apparatus is less effective economically, that hasn't made it less engaged. On the contrary, since the 1970s, states in the advanced industrial countries have been doing much more although achieving less. In fact, the reaction to policy failures has usually been for the state to become interventionist *to a greater extent* rather than wither away. We criticise the damaging consequences of most of this state intervention, but this doesn't deny its reality.

The responses to the 2008–2009 financial crisis revealed how nation states, especially the big ones of the United States and China, remain the key pillars of international economic governance, notwithstanding the façade of global economic cooperation. Despite the amount of "scholarly analysis" in the lead-up to the financial crisis about the growing significance of "transnational non-state actors", post-2008 developments "highlight more than ever the fact that global financial governance continues to rest on very state-centric foundations" (Helleiner, 2014, pp. 16, 20).

Whether they are economically potent or not, whether they have won wars or lost them, whether their public services work well or flounder, nation states remain the predominant agency for collective action. What matters for their power is much less their *scale* of territory than their authority over that space and over its inhabitants. Nation states have been put to question in recent decades, not because of a size or institutional deficiency but because their ruling elites have had extra difficulty in exerting authority (Furedi, 2013).

It is true that failures in effectiveness have made governments keener to wash their hands of their political responsibilities of state. Hence, the vogue for the political classes to voluntarily outsource their authority to unelected technocrats both at home, like central bankers, and to those stationed in international bodies, like the EU. Politicians' giving away power though is not the same as demolishing the nation and replacing it with a legitimate supranational or global body. Global institutions do not have an autonomous existence. They only function with the agreement, and funding, from their national political constituents.

Historically, attempts at creating pan-national institutions – from the League of Nations to the EU – have either collapsed or stumbled when they come into conflict with powerful national interests. One of the few effective international political federations has been the *United States* of America. However, that required the bloodshed of a brutal civil war to establish federal state authority. This is hardly a desirable route to bring about other pan-national entities today. In some ways, a "United States of Europe" parallel to the United States was what Hitler tried in the last century.

The pan-European EU state apparatus is a pale reflection when it comes to act-ing authoritatively and with the power of a traditional nation state. It has, so far at least, no independent, non-nation based, armed force or police. The protracted eurozone crisis since 2010 also exposed the limits of existing EU state institutions. Mario Draghi, the former president of the ECB, might have been able to sooth the eurozone crisis in 2012 with his famous untested pledge that he would do "whatever it takes" but neither the ECB, nor the European Commission, has been able to resolve that crisis. Ultimately, as one respected writer put it, the euro's problem was that it was a "currency without a state" (Eichengreen, 2011, p. 7).

Claims of the emergence of a regional or global consciousness in place of existing national ones also remain hollow. There are no indications of supranational institutions developing a popular legitimacy that overrides national loyalties (Hutchinson, 2011, p. 97). In Europe, for instance, the five-yearly elections to the EU parliament have failed to generate a European sensibility to supersede the national. Beyond the political and cultural elites, there is little collective passion for the European ideal.

On the contrary, the EU is fast becoming a source of polarising national sentiments on issues from migration flows to the economic impact of its single currency. Ironically, it was the repeated delays in Britain leaving the EU that brought greater popular interest to its 2019 European Parliament elections, mostly because many voters wanted to reiterate their earlier vote on Brexit.

National considerations remain a substantial barrier to implementing initiatives coming out of supranational bodies. This is illustrated by European nation states' slowness and incompleteness in complying with EU directives. Despite Britain's eurosceptic reputation, it is striking that it was Germany that delayed implementation of labour law directives beyond the legal deadline for twice as long on average as the UK. Meanwhile, of the 15 core member states, traditionally pro-EU France performed worst of all (Falkner et al., 2005, p. 271).

For example, the implementation of the EU's Working Time Directive remained partial and uneven many years after being approved. This was the directive about a maximum 48-hour working week and a minimum four weeks paid leave. Although in 1993, after three years of debate and modification, Britain was alone in refusing to back it at the Council of Ministers, most of the countries that voted for it failed to implement it in full.

A detailed study published 12 years later found that working time is an area in which "violations of the law are quite widespread" and that "national diversity" remains "very significant". Four-fifths of the 15 original member states implemented the directive no better than "significantly delayed", including "enthusiastic" proponents like France. It seems that national leaders can willingly outsource legislation to supranational bodies, but in the end, national factors retain considerable sway. In most cases of complying with EU directives, national member states follow the "logic of domestic politics" (Falkner et al., 2005, pp. 103–117, 200).

Even the behaviours of global functionaries illustrate how national affiliations remain pertinent. Presumably, most EU commissioners genuinely see themselves as promoting the wider interests of the EU bloc. But these commissioners are not elected by the 500 million EU adults. They are individuals picked from the higher echelons of particular national polities. After their nomination by national governments, the top EU jobs are given out according to national lobbying. And once appointed, the individuals do not receive lobotomies to lose their national identities; they perform their pan-European roles still influenced, maybe unwittingly, by their national heritages.

A study of three decades of data about the EU agricultural commissioners revealed that the commissioners' own countries received more than their fair share of funding. It found that "there is a significant positive relationship between the Commissioners' country of origin and the agricultural fund spending these countries receive during their terms in office" (Gehring & Schneider, 2016). And as the most powerful countries dominate the most influential and big spending commissioner jobs, these practices tend to reinforce existing national power relations in Europe.

The economist Paul Ormerod followed up this analysis. He relayed how in 2007 and 2008, the German EU Commissioner for Enterprise and Industry repeatedly opposed a Commission proposal to reduce new cars' carbon dioxide emissions. This opposition took on a new light with the Volkswagen emissions testing scandal. The Commissioner's "success in weakening the initial proposal was widely perceived as support for the German car industry" (Ormerod, 2018).

Are Nations "Too Large" to be Effective?

The complementary notion that nations are also too big to deal with "local", non-global issues again founders on the matter of authority and legitimacy, not on size. With regard to range, nation states have responsibilities at multiple levels: the local, the national and the international (Hutchinson, 2011, p. 85). As a result, individual nation states *can* be too small or too large for carrying out particular tasks. But who or what determines which issues are purely local and better conducted by subnational entities? The authority to decide this falls best on the nation state.

In practice, local subnational organisations often lack the clout to make a meaningful impact on many issues. However, it doesn't follow that it is desirable to decide everything centrally. On the contrary, devolving decision-making to cities and other localities can produce improved outcomes in specific operational areas like transport, social care or education. However, this will work better for people within the larger fiscal territory of a national polity that is able to offset the public revenue repercussions of economic and social unevenness.

The OECD made the worthwhile suggestion that regional economic development strategies might be most effective when local governments finance expenditure through their own resources by raising their own taxes. This provides an incentive for attracting businesses to increase the local tax base. But while decentralisation may be good for growth on a local basis, the OECD also urged that such arrangements should be implemented carefully.

It noted that a recently reported reduction in regional unevenness, that appeared positive to some commentators, might have been due to a relative decline in top-performing regions rather than catching up growth by the weaker ones – levelling down rather than levelling up. Also, it warned that regional growth initiatives could be detrimental to national ones that might have a bigger positive effect for the country as a whole (Bartolini, Stossberg, & Blöchliger, 2016; Dougherty & Akgun, 2018; OECD, 2017a, p. 93).

Full political secession to localities is also problematic in that it can undermine the coherence and legitimacy of historically developed nations. Since the late 1990s, for example, devolution of UK powers to Scotland and Wales have tended to reinforce political estrangement rather than reverse it.

Practically, local secession can also be damaging economically. When Catalonian separation from Spain seemed a possibility in 2017, scores of businesses in the region announced plans to move their headquarters, or even all their operations, to the rest of Spain. Many businesses showed by these decisions that they preferred the umbrella of an established state than the risk of allying with an unproven entity. Despite Catalonia's relatively high levels of wealth and prosperity, such business departures could soon have had perverse effects on accumulation. The post-fascist Spanish nation state seems to retain substantial importance to its corporations.

The Myth of the Supranational Stateless Corporation

This example from Spain shows the continued dependence of businesses on their national state and contradicts another popular globalist thought: that businesses have now become more important and powerful than many nation states. For instance, we often hear it said that most of the world's "top economies" are corporations. According to the World Bank, 69 out of the top 100 economic units are businesses (Hoornweg, Bhada, Freire, Trejos Gómez, & Dave, 2010).

Even before the post-1970s surge in internationalisation, the earlier expansion of international enterprises had been identified as a decisive agent for undermining national state capabilities. Corporations were said to "sprawl" across national boundaries "linking the assets and activities of different national jurisdictions with an intimacy that seems to threaten the concept of the nation as an integral unit" (Vernon, 1971, p. 5).

Some go further and claim that businesses have become "stateless". The historian Tooze reminds us it is now "commonly accepted" in this age of "deep globalization" that with regard to international trade, national economies no longer matter. Instead, multinational corporations with their GVCs drive trade (Tooze, 2018, p. 8).

However, none of these descriptions establish a qualitative shift, either in businesses or in the validity of the nation state. Businesses have been both national and international ever since they came into existence. A very long time ago, Adam Smith (2012) reported that "A merchant, it has been said very properly, is not necessarily the citizen of any particular country" (Book 3, Chapter 4, paragraph 24, p. 413).

Nor is there anything novel about firms dominating international trade flows, as we illustrated in Chapter 9. Trading is what firms have always done, and many have done it across borders. With regard to production, Smith's discussion in Book 4 of the *Wealth of Nations* about how businesses such as the English, Dutch and French East India companies operated abroad anticipated the extensive internationalisation of production seen in today's GSCs.

Despite the customary depiction of big firms today as being "multinational" or "transnational", as if this represents a distinctive free floating formation, such businesses remain closely tied to their home territory and nation state. Overtly, *international* capital units are national at birth and remain so during their life. Multinationals continue to be rooted in and identify with a single nation.

Capital is a social relationship, and capitalist companies are a way of organising people to produce and distribute the things we need and desire for living. These social relationships are necessarily geographically grounded. A unit of capital begins by establishing itself in one place even if it then moves on to operate in more than one country. This gives it a "nationality" and ties it to the collective body that looks after the interests of the many capitals in that bounded territory: the nation state.

"Home" is usually defined as the place of registration. Take Apple Incorporated, whose international activities we mentioned at the start of this book. It is indisputably a global multinational company, but it is also *American*. Although its manufacturing, sales, shareholders and board members come from all across the world, Apple is universally regarded as a US corporation. Its top group company is registered in the United States, and it has closer links to the US state than to any other national government.

At the dawn of the current phase of internationalisation, Vernon presciently anticipated that

> it is safe to assume that U.S.-controlled multinational enterprises will generally think of themselves as American companies for a long time to come, long after the concept has lost some of its meaning in day-to-day operational terms.

He explained that to accept some measure of confusion about one's national identity is not an easy thing for anyone brought up in a "system of nation states" (Vernon, 1971, pp. 108–109).

Indeed, in their operations, most multinational corporations retain a strong home orientation. The 100 most "global" corporations still have nearly half their sales, assets and employment in their home country (UNCTAD, 2013). While business research facilities have also become further internationalised in recent decades, most firms also retain a strong domestic R&D base. R&D abroad accounted for around 28% of all such spending in 2013, up from 20% in 2001: that means that still almost three-quarters of business R&D each year is at home. Some studies based on patent data even find that R&D internationalisation has been stagnating (Dachs & Zahradnik, 2017).

There are very few genuinely "transnational" firms. The closest are the Anglo-Dutch companies Shell and Unilever. Even those exceptions are better described as bi-national firms. Every so often they debate internally whether they should openly favour one home country over the other. Recently, Unilever considered becoming a "national" Dutch company, partly because Dutch corporate regulation offers extra protection against hostile takeovers. This precise motivation revealed the continued dependence of a big multinational business on national state practices.

Another indication that the real pecking order between business and state remains the opposite of the globalist presumption is that even the biggest of companies are resource-constrained, unlike sovereign governments. When its own internal revenues are limited by a sluggish economy – sales for a business, taxes for a state – most states find it easier and cheaper to borrow on capital markets than the most profitable corporations. In 2018, for example, Apple was paying a yield of 3.5% on 10-year borrowing. Meanwhile, Belgium was paying only 0.8%, while even the hugely debt-burdened Italian state was paying less than 3%.

Many commentators have recently become critical of corporate lobbying efforts as indicative of the undue power of business (Lindsey & Teles, 2017). But this really illustrates the subordination of firms to states, not their dominance over them. Business operations can be sprawling, but wherever they produce they are always subject to the control of that territorial state. A business licence to operate in any place is not absolute. It comes from that state. And what the state provides, the state can withhold or take away. Companies have to spend money on lobbying governments in Washington, Berlin and London because they are subject to state dictates. If businesses really were the superior powers, they could simply ignore their ineffectual governments.

Indeed, greater internationalisation makes businesses not less but *more* reliant on their states precisely because they have to contend with other nation states where they operate. It is governments that arrange official inter-country trading and economic relationships. International capital flows are governed by national laws or by international agreements between sovereign national governments.

The inclusion of "investor-state dispute resolution" provisions in some recent trade agreements has seemed to back up suggestions that corporations are now attaining greater powers relative to governments (Adkins & Grewal, 2016; Mounk, 2018, p. 76). These measures allow individual companies to sue host countries in front of international tribunals for alleged discriminatory practices, regulations and laws, and demand compensation. However, none of this establishes that firms have become more powerful than governments.

All these procedures have to be first agreed by the respective governments, and in principle, as with any trade agreement, the same governments can annul them. These are all international agreements, not "supranational" ones imposed upon nation states. In fact, these dispute provisions illustrate again corporate dependence on their own states. States sometimes insist on these measures against less powerful countries in order to protect their businesses. The unfairness they embody is *between* nations. The firms of the powerful countries are simply the beneficiaries of their states pushing their interests.

It is worth noting that such investment arbitration procedures are not new: they began in the late 1950s and were initiated then by the leading Western powers. At this earlier stage, these mechanisms mostly governed relations between investors from capital-exporting, developed countries and the governments of developing, mainly post-colonial, countries. For example, compensation terms for businesses that were nationalised were set according to international rather than local standards – that is as specified by the Western nations collectively. It is not surprising that recently, it has remained the American government, still the world's most powerful, which has been in the forefront of imposing these provisions on other governments (Dhingra & Datta, 2017).

Although big firms obtain some privileges from these international agreements, national states retain the whip hand. Corporations do not even have direct access to the WTO investor dispute settlement system. That remains with WTO member states. Besides, it is from their own government that firms seek support or redress if they fall foul of another state's actions. As noted earlier, when competition between aircraft manufactures Boeing and Airbus heated up, it was the American government that has fought Boeing's case at the WTO, while the EU has taken the side of Airbus on behalf of its national business subsidiaries.

Some corporations do have huge revenues, larger than some country's national output.[2] But size is not everything. Power is based on authority. Ultimately, it depends on police, courts and armies. This is something all businesses recognise, even the Facebooks and Googles of the world as they find themselves grilled by politicians or paying out regulatory fines. In the pithy words of the international relations expert George Friedman, capitalists live an everyday dependence on the state well before they seek help when "the first bomb destroys their factory" or "the first mob loots them" (Mauldin, 2015).

Business subordination to the state does not need actual blood on the streets to be apparent. When the financial crisis hit in 2008, it was governments that stepped in to bail out banks and other big businesses. Mervyn King, then the Governor of the Bank of England, captured this well when describing how the crisis revealed that banks and other large financial institutions turned out to be "global" in life but "national" in death (Bank of England, 2010, p. 14).

However, much they sell and however many countries they operate in, multinational businesses do not make or apply the law. States do. They – not companies – enforce the laws with their people-in-arms. This absence of corporate coercive power distinguishes even the largest of today's global firms from the likes of the infamous British East India Company.

In 1800, the East India Company had a private army of about 260,000 people, twice the size of the British army. Under the command of Robert Clive, it was this company army that initially took control of most of the territory of the Indian subcontinent, following its victories over the local Indian powers in the Battles of Plassey (1757) and Buxar (1764).

In contrast, today, no firm has such armed wings at its disposal. Modern internal corporate security teams are a pale imitation and are subject to national laws. If extreme circumstances required it, even the biggest corporations would rely upon the military apparatus of the state. We wouldn't expect Walmart or Tesco to put surface-to-air missiles on top of their warehouses to defend against enemy aircraft (Alexander, 2018). Defence is a job for national government. At the Davos global gatherings each year, it is indicative that the business and political leaders in attendance rely not on armed global forces but on Swiss *national* authorities, police and troops to keep them safe from street protestors.

---

[2]Beware that apples are being compared with oranges in World Bank type studies: country GDP is a measure of *value-added*, not of sales.

The Modern Violation of Sovereignty

This reality of continued state supremacy over multinational businesses has not undermined the globalist disparaging of the nation state. Globalists say sovereignty is an illusion in our interconnected world. As an unnamed EU government official said during the Brexit withdrawal saga, "There is no such thing as a sovereign country anymore. It is an illusion the Brits are chasing, but it has gone" (Barker, 2018). With the world being progressively integrated economically, traditional political categories such as sovereignty are seen as no longer relevant.[3]

Efforts made to establish global governance through institutionalised multilateralism have themselves challenged national sovereignty. For instance, even when it lacked any official mandate, the IMF has acted to infringe the sovereignty of its members. By the 1990s, the Fund had evolved to embrace capital movement liberalisation in its interventions in countries. Although its Articles formally respected sovereignty and prevented the IMF's Board from making capital account liberalisation a condition of the use of its resources, the IMF's public "advice" was profoundly influential on states at the receiving end (Abdelal, 2007, pp. 137–138).

The formal infraction of national sovereignty has been taken furthest with the EU. Its original treaty signatories gave it the authority to make decisions for them in limited areas. These pan-European powers over countries have been extended over the decades since (Heartfield, 2013).

But with the important exception of the EU, the existence of international rules over matters like trade and capital flows does not trump national sovereignty. As the most recently established multilateral organisation, the WTO is often seen as the one that most expresses the demise of national sovereignty. However, it is striking that in its authorised history, the WTO denies sovereignty is outmoded. A treaty is defined there as an instrument by which countries "agree to place voluntary limitations on the exercise of their sovereignty", and an international organisation as a body that "states agree to create in order to facilitate the development and execution of these sovereignty-constraining instruments".

The history text notes that any treaty or international organisation necessarily involves some "derogation" in the exercise of sovereignty. But it also explains that "states never abdicate their sovereignty altogether", no matter what the terms of a treaty or the rules of an international organisation may be (VanGrasstek, 2013, p. 202). In addition to signing, states can always annul treaties.

Besides, rules agreed at multilateral level can only be imposed for trade *between* countries, not trade *within* countries. Again with the formal exception of EU members, the latter remains a sovereign matter. When individual producers export, they know they have to follow the rules set by the nation states of their foreign markets. Exporters are rule-takers for each export market, but they are

---

[3]For an incisive critique of these assertions, see Bickerton, Cunliffe, and Gourevitch (2006).

not obligated to sell into that country or region. And this doesn't make entire countries into rule-takers (again with the exception of members of the EU).

It is true that no nation state, even the largest and most powerful ones like China and the United States, are in full autonomous control of their national destinies. Events outside their own borders impinge on them. This reality adds to the rationale for countries working together in fields from scientific experimentation such as CERN, the Geneva-based European Organization for Nuclear Research, to international rescue responses to tsunamis and other natural disasters. But such cooperation with other nations is never an abrogation of sovereignty. It is the exercise of sovereignty.

Sovereignty provides a country with control over its material and immaterial resources, providing a vital means to protect and further its interests. Even from the narrow perspective of the economy, national sovereignty is no less relevant today than it was in the nineteenth and twentieth centuries. As discussed in the previous chapter, Western economic malaise could do with extensive transformative *national* solutions. To meet this challenge effectively, we need political freedom within sovereign entities. Specifically, the fair transfer of technologies between companies of different sovereign countries can help national transformative change.

Despite the claims of globalist commentators, national sovereignty does not invariably lead to regressive economic isolationism. To the contrary, we have seen how state-promoted economic internationalisation is generally progressive in effect, even when it is a response to Western decay. As the economic historian David Edgerton (2006) explained, economic progress relies on international openness.

The internationalisation of production overcomes the parochial barriers restricting an extension to the division of labour. It thereby promotes the benefits of specialisation. The European aerospace industry and the international space station offer just two illustrations of the potential gains from sovereign cooperation, even when pursuing national political agendas. Indeed, successful economic internationalism is most often aided by the actions of nation states.

Sovereign controls can also be valuable in policing damaging instances of outside interference. For example, multinational firms might engage in extreme profiteering in sovereign countries, as much as in their country's colonies, but the advantage of sovereign political independence is that these nations can take actions to curb or even expel these businesses. Such corporate misdeeds might damage a country's prosperity for a time, but only external political intervention through war, or the threat of war, can abrogate a country's sovereignty.

In point of fact, the case for national sovereignty can also be made through the potential economic negative that comes with losing national political autonomy. The absence of sovereignty in countries subjected to colonialism and subordination to imperial powers significantly held back economic development, as was seen in India and parts of Africa in the nineteenth and early twentieth centuries. Furthermore, the creation by imperial dominators of artificial boundaries in areas of Africa, Eastern Europe and the Middle East reveals the importance of legitimate borders. Externally imposed artificial states often lack an economic foundation and remain dependent on outside institutions. As a result, their national illegitimacy is reinforced and helps explain why they are usually presided over by autocratic and corrupt regimes.

Sovereignty, Freedom and Democracy

The positive argument for national sovereignty is that it is the basis for the popular sovereignty of democracy. Popular sovereignty rests on the conviction that the legitimacy of the state is created by the will or consent of its people. From this standpoint, it is the people who are the source of all political power. Today, it is still through the nation state that people can participate with any degree of influence on world affairs.

The modern nation, whatever its other limitations and shortcomings, is the predominant unit for democratic engagement that society has so far developed. It is the most important building block of collectivity. For most men and women, the nation is the foundation of their life's journey. It is in the context of the national community that most people attain cultural identity and meaning (Furedi, 2017, pp. 128–129).

As explained in Part 1, it was the awful experiences of the first half of the twentieth century that informed the turn against both the nation state and the value of national sovereignty. For the West's political leaders, nationalism became identified primarily with national domination and the violent pursuit of interests to the detriment of others. By the end of the Second World War, anti-nationalism had emerged as their dominant outlook.

Over the past 40 years, the increasing loss of faith by the national elites in their own legitimacy reinforced this distaste for the national. Recently, it has fed the transatlantic and intra-European name-calling directed against nationalist populists as being "xenophobes". The uncomfortable irony is that this one-sided assessment of nationalism as always being harmful is what is now fuelling today's international divisions.

In these circumstances, creating a progressive modern internationalism requires us to rehabilitate nationalism and national sovereignty from these partisan negative connotations. The most important argument to win is that democracy still needs national borders to define a collective citizenry.

The political framework of the nation is what offers the electorate the potential through democratic mechanisms for sovereign control over their lives. The nation state is the only foundation that humanity has yet discovered for the institutionalisation of democratic accountability. In the words of the three co-convenors of the Sovereignty and its Discontents working group, the "sovereign state, however imperfect, still provides the best framework for the organisation of collective political life" (Bickerton et al., 2007, p. 1).

Internationalism Through Nationalism

In contrast to today's globalist counterposition of nationalism to internationalism, in the past, the two were assumed to work hand in hand to make the world a better place. Historian Glenda Sluga explained that the concepts of nationalism and internationalism were entwined throughout much of the 100 years leading up to the Second World War. For instance, Giuseppe Mazzini, one of the architects of the national unification of Italy in 1871, spoke positively about republican patriots forging a "world of nations". Nationalists were regarded then as the true internationalists. Of pertinence for today, Mazzini envisioned a world at peace based on an international society of democratic sovereign nations (Mazower, 2013, pp. xii, 48).

Classic expressions of internationalism embraced the idea of self-governing nations that freely cooperated. Political scientist Benedict Anderson astutely explained "nationalism's undivorcible marriage to internationalism" as being central to an understanding of nationalism (Anderson, 2016, p. 207). When colonial political domination remained rife, internationalism manifested itself also through backing indigenous movements battling for national self-determination. This was the legacy of those earlier popular movements seeking freedom in the eighteenth and nineteenth centuries that embraced nationalism as that era's most "powerful transformative political creed" (Anderson, 2016). In the early twentieth century, internationalism involved endorsing the self-determination of national sovereignty as the way of promoting democratic rights. Internationalists argued that without national freedom the people of a territory would not be able to exercise democracy.

As the First World War raged, the concurrent support for national self-determination from US President Wilson and Bolshevik leader Lenin enhanced the legitimacy of nationalism, at least for smaller and dominated countries. Western imperialism lost its self-confidence. While imperial nationalism started to be derided openly as the source of inter-nation conflict and barbarism, nationalist movements within non-imperialist countries gained moral authority. For most of the rest of the twentieth century until the 1980s, it was difficult to oppose intellectually the right of dominated nations to political independence. Colonies and other oppressed nations were widely seen as justified in campaigning for national liberation.

The early twentieth century struggles by, for instance, Irish and Indian people against their colonial domination gave further impetus not only to nationalism's association with national self-government but also to internationalism's bond with the democratic content of national struggles. At the end of the First World War, left-wing internationalists – tellingly mostly located *outside* Britain – supported the Irish struggle for national self-determination and against it being included in the "United Kingdom of Great Britain and Ireland". Between the world wars, internationalist progressives also sided with India's campaign for national independence from Britain.

It was only during the course of the latter part of the twentieth century that the unity of nationalism and internationalism seemed to turn into its opposite. With the rise of the Western elite's anti-nationalist perspective, identification with national struggles in less developed parts of the world became suspect. Especially since the end of the Cold War, Western fears often focussed on "Third World nationalism", which soon morphed into the dangers of terrorism and Islamic fundamentalism.

Some globalist thinkers now construe internationalism, in contrast to nationalism, as a "remnant of Enlightenment-era narratives of the progress of humanity into a global community". For these elites, internationalism has become the outlook of the "liberals" and "progressives", while domestic nationalism is denigrated as the preserve of "racists" and "isolationists" (Sluga, 2015). With the ascendancy of globalist ideas, many now tend to assume that national pride and international harmony are contradictory impulses. This notion seems over the past 30 years to have attained the status of common sense, validated through the academic theories of globalisation.

Yet it was not that long ago that a progressive tradition in Western countries continued to recognise the linkage between nationalism and internationalism. As recently as the 1960s and early 1970s, radicals took sides with the national liberation war in Vietnam against US imperialism. Another particular internationalist outburst occurred in 1974 when warplane engines arrived for repairs at a Rolls Royce factory in the Scottish town of East Kilbride, just outside Glasgow. Factory worker Bob Fulton recognised the engines as coming from Hawker Hunter planes that had attacked Chile's presidential palace the previous year. This assault had helped secure the September 1973 coup that toppled the democratically elected government of Salvador Allende. Fulton refused to work on the engines.

By the end of the day, all 4,000 factory workers had joined him in his act of international solidarity with the Chilean people. Back in Chile, the Scottish boycott became a celebrated moment of internationalist support for their struggle against the Pinochet regime (Gardiner, 2015). The action taken in Scotland was internationalism in practice. They showed that political *inter*nationalism was about people in one nation identifying with and supporting the democratic interests of people in another nation.

To summarise, because globalists reject the value of the political nation, they are also cavalier with its crucial accoutrements of sovereignty and democracy. Most people, though, are sorely diminished without these. There is no possibility for the exercise of popular democratic sovereignty today if national sovereign rights are abandoned.

Reconciling the "Global Trilemma"

The "global trilemma" is Dani Rodrik's oft-cited thesis that globalisation, national sovereignty and democracy are mutually incompatible. Rodrik, a Turkish-born American economist and radical critic of neoliberalism and globalism, calls this the "paradox of globalisation". He has claimed that any two of the three can co-exist, but we can never have all three simultaneously (Rodrik, 2012).

Rodrik argued that any reform of the international economic system must face up to this trilemma, and that if people want further globalisation, they must either give up some democracy or some national sovereignty. He suggested that we really have only three options. We can restrict democracy to gain competitiveness in global markets. We can limit globalisation to rebuild democratic legitimacy at home. Or we can globalise democracy at the cost of national sovereignty. His personal anti-globalist recommendation is the second of these: that we wind back on globalisation.

Significantly, the trilemma has been embraced by many of the globalists it was directed against. They welcomed its implication that at least one of the three had to go. Being committed to increased globalisation, it had to be giving up either sovereignty or democracy, or as it turns out, both. The globalist answer to Rodrik's global trilemma is: "we need to strengthen rules-based globalisation". Or as the Luxembourgish former Commission head Juncker has claimed, national borders are the worst thing ever invented, regardless that British people had recently voted for more control over them; we need "ever-closer union" instead (Crisp, 2017; Hughes & Ferguson, 2016).

The globalist conclusion is that everyone needs to get real and simply recognise that national sovereignty is now meaningless. Although the globalists claim to support democracy – specifically "rule of law" democracy – because democratic popular sovereignty rests on national sovereignty, democracy goes out the window too. For example, most West European governments have chosen the path of maintaining a formal commitment to democracy while assigning much of their power to the undemocratic EU.

In one sense, these European leaders don't make a choice at all and end up rejecting all three options: democracy, national sovereignty and globalisation, if the latter is interpreted as unrestricted economic internationalisation. First, they deny democracy by granting unaccountable authority to the European Council, the European Commission and the ECJ to make overriding decisions for citizens of the EU.

Second, they disparage the legitimacy of particular national peoples' democratic wishes, either ignoring them or getting the electorate to vote again until people come up with the "right result": notably in France, the Netherlands, Ireland and, attempted, in Britain. In the same spirit, they have argued to reject specific national sovereign decisions, in Greece after their austerity bailout referendum, as well as in Italy, Poland and Hungary when the central EU apparatus didn't like what elected governments were mandated to do.

And third, the EU is the antithesis of genuine economic internationalisation since, as described in Chapter 7, the "free trade" Single Market is the most protectionist economic bloc in the world. As a consequence, the peoples of the EU are denied all three: democracy, national sovereignty and the potential benefits of an open internationalised economy.

But Rodrik's thesis is flawed. There is no logical incompatibility between democracy, national sovereignty and "globalisation", in its economic internationalist interpretation. The control of borders – sovereignty – by a democratically accountable government – democracy – does not need to take an isolationist, anti-internationalisation form that stops the flow of goods, services and investment between national territories. We can have a genuinely internationalist, sovereign, national democracy.

This means arguing for international solidarity within the only accountable framework going – that of the nation state. People can make the democratic, sovereign decision to have control over their national laws *and* embrace the opportunities from economic internationalisation. They can manage their borders to promote closer international economic links, to welcome foreign investment and migrant labour and to remove the tariffs and NTBs that impede trade.

While the famous 1846 repeal of the Corn Laws did not, as we described in Chapter 7, bring about truly free trade it did illustrate the falsity of the Rodrik trilemma. Corn Law repeal expressed, first, democratic advance: the Chartists supported repeal as part of their campaign for greater democratisation. Second, it was pro-internationalisation, because it reduced barriers to the cross-border flow of goods and helped extend the international division of labour. And third, it was a unilateral act of sovereign decision-making by the British parliament. So, the act of repeal was a sovereign decision that advanced both democracy and internationalisation.

Conclusion: Popular Sovereignty as Bulwark Against World War

Ronald Findlay and Kevin O'Rourke ended their mammoth study of trade, war and the world economy across the second millennium with the words, "As in all human affairs, the choices that individual human beings make will matter, for better and for worse" (Findlay & O'Rourke, 2007, p. 545). In a similar vein, Preet Bharara, the US district attorney renowned for going after Wall Street insider traders and later being sacked by Trump, reiterated that "Freedom comes from human beings, rather than laws and institutions" (Bharara, 2019, as cited in Luce, 2019). However, in the West today, the particular challenge is that humans are not trusted to act together to make such free choices.

With respect to worldwide technical developments this is especially anomalous. Greater cross-border interconnectedness should mean that man's universal features are less hidden than previously. Our technologically connected world is more amenable than ever before to people acting cooperatively. These are great advances for realising the scope of human collaboration to meet our many remaining common wants and aspirations, as well as to maintain peace.

But having great potential is very different to believing these interconnections have automatic effects. What actually flows from cross-border possibilities depend on political and social circumstances. War or peace is a matter of human choice. This choice is a global one that is best exercised through accountable national polities (Abdelal, 2007, p. 216).

Unfortunately, today's globalist political influence in the West disparages such human possibilities and mechanisms. Making the right choices now starts with securing democratic control over the apparatus of nation states that the globalists vilify and the mercantilists vulgarise.

The democratic path to peace and prosperity is truly internationalist *because* it upholds the national sovereignty of all countries. National sovereignty and international cooperation are not the opposites that we have been told they are. On the contrary, there is much truth in the proverb that "good fences make good neighbours". Inter*national* cooperation works when we have cohesive and dynamic states with assured national borders. Such nation states are what we need in order to make strong and effective commitments to cross-border collaboration and international harmony.

References

Abdelal, R. (2007). *Capital rules: The construction of global finance*. Cambridge, MA: Harvard University Press.

Acemoglu, D., & Robinson, J. (2012). *Why nations fail: The origins of power, prosperity and poverty*. New York, NY: Penguin Random House.

Acharya, R., & Keller, W. (2008). *Estimating the productivity selection and technology spillover effects of imports*. NBER Working Paper No. 14079, National Bureau of Economic Research, Cambridge, MA.

Adalet McGowan, M., Andrews, D., Criscuolo, C., & Nicoletti, G. (2015). *The future of productivity*. Paris: OECD Publishing.

Adalet McGowan, M., Andrews, D., & Millot, V. (2017, January). *The walking dead? Zombie firms and productivity performance in OECD countries*. OECD Economics Department Working Paper No. 1372, OECD Publishing, Paris.

Adkins, C., & Grewal, D. S. (2016, June). Democracy and legitimacy in investor-state relations. *Yale Law Journal Forum*, 126. Retrieved from http://www.yalelawjournal.org/forum/democracy-and-legitimacy-in-investor-state-arbitration

Aggarwal, V., & Evenett, S. (2012). Industrial policy choice during the crisis era. *Oxford Review of Economic Policy, 28*(2), 261–283.

Aggarwal, V., & Evenett, S. (2013). A fragmenting global economy: A weakened WTO, mega FTAs, and murky protectionism. *Swiss Political Science Review, 19*(4), 550–557.

Aggarwal, V., & Evenett, S. (2014). Do WTO rules preclude industrial policy? Evidence from the global economic crisis. *Business and Politics (De Gruyter), 16*(4), 481–509.

Ahn, J., Dabla-Norris, E., Duval, R., Hu, B., & Njie, L. (2016, March). *Reassessing the productivity gains from trade liberalization*. IMF Working Paper No. 16/77, International Monetary Fund, Washington, DC.

Alexander, K. (2018). A transatlantic alliance is crucial in the cyber war era. *Financial Times*, September 5.

Al-Haschimi, A., Gächter, M., Lodge, D., & Steingress, W. (2016, October 14). The great normalisation of global trade. *Vox CEPR Policy Portal*. Retrieved from https://voxeu.org/article/great-normalisation-global-trade

Ali, S., & Dadush, U. (2011, February 9) Trade in intermediates and economic policy. *VOX CEPR Policy Portal*. Retrieved from https://voxeu.org/article/rise-trade-intermediates-policy-implications

Alliance Bernstein. (2018, June 6). All time record profits! So why are investors so worried about the auto industry? – Speech by Max Warburton. At the Research Automotive News Congress 2018, Turin. Retrieved from https://europe.autonews.com/assets/pdf/ane-congress/speakers2018/MaxWarburtonpresentation.pdf

Allison, G. (2017). *Destined for war: Can America and China escape Thucydides's Trap?* London: Scribe UK.

Almond, G. (1989, April) Review Article: The International–National Connection. *British Journal of Political Science, 19*(2), 237–259.

Amadeo, K. (2019, June 25). Doha round of trade talks: The real reason why it failed. *The Balance*. Retrieved from https://www.thebalance.com/what-is-the-doha-round-of-trade-talks-3306365#why-doha-failed

Amsden, A., & Hikino, T. (2000). The bark is worse than the bite: New WTO law and late industrialization. *The Annals of the American Academy of Political and Social Science, 570*(1), 104–114.

Anderson, B. (2016). *Imagined communities: Reflections on the origin and spread of nationalism*. New York, NY: Verso.

Andrews, D., Criscuolo, C., & Gal, P. (2016, September). *The global productivity slowdown, technology divergence and public policy: A firm level perspective*. Hutchins Center Working Paper No. 24, Brookings Institution, Washington, DC.

Angell, N. (1910). *The great illusion: A study of the relation of military power in nations to their economic and social advantage*. New York, NY: G.P. Putnam's.

Anghie, A. (2004). *Imperialism, sovereignty and the making of international law*. Cambridge: Cambridge University Press.

Annan, K. (1999). Two concepts of sovereignty. *The Economist*, September 18.

Ashcroft, L. (2016). How the United Kingdom voted on Thursday ... and why. Retrieved from https://lordashcroftpolls.com/2016/06/how-the-united-kingdom-voted-and-why/

Atkinson, R., & Lind, M. (2018). *Big is beautiful: Debunking the myth of small business*. Cambridge, MA: MIT Press.

Autor, D., Dorn, D., & Hanson, G. (2013, October). The China syndrome: Local labor market effects of import competition in the United States. *American Economic Review, 103*(6), 2121–2168.

Autor, D., Dorn, D., & Hanson, G. (2016). The China shock: Learning from labor-market adjustment to large changes in trade. *Annual Review of Economics, 8*, 205–240.

Babones, S. (2018). *The new authoritarianism: Trump, populism, and the tyranny of experts*. Cambridge: Polity Press.

Bagwell, K., Bown, C., & Staiger, R. (2016). Is the WTO passé? *Journal of Economic Literature, 54*(4), 1125–1231.

Baker, P. (2017, January 23). Trump abandons Trans-Pacific Partnership, Obama's signature trade deal. *New York Times*. Retrieved from https://www.nytimes.com/2017/01/23/us/politics/tpp-trump-trade-nafta.html

Baldwin, R. (2012). *Global supply chains: Why they emerged, why they matter, and where they are going*. CEPR Discussion Papers No. 9103, Centre for Economic Policy Research, London.

Baldwin, R. (2016). *The great convergence: Information technology and the new globalization*. Cambridge, MA: Harvard University Press.

Banerjee, R., & Hofmann, B. (2018, September). The rise of zombie firms: Causes and consequences. *Bank for International Settlements Quarterly Review*, 67–78.

Bank for International Settlements. (2017, June). *Understanding globalisation*. 87th Annual Report: 2017, chapter 6. Basel: Bank for International Settlements.

Bank for International Settlements. (2019, June). *Annual economic report: 2019*. Basel: Bank for International Settlements.

Bank of England. (2010, October 25). Banking: From Bagehot to Basel, and back again – Speech by Mervyn King. At the Second Bagehot Lecture, Buttonwood Gathering, New York City. Retrieved from https://www.bankofengland.co.uk/speech/2010/banking-from-bagehot-to-basel-and-back-again-speech-by-mervyn-king or https://www.bankofengland.co.uk/-/media/boe/files/speech/2010/banking-from-bagehot-to-basel-and-back-again-speech-by-mervyn-king.pdf?la=en&hash=87D5017B64002660244F6ED8B33CFA48EDF902CF

Bank of England. (2017, June 20). A fine balance – Speech by Mark Carney. At the Mansion House, London. Retrieved from https://www.bankofengland.co.uk/speech/2017/a-fine-balance

Bank of England. (2018, June 28). The UK's productivity problem: Hub no spokes – Speech by Andy Haldane. At the Academy of Social Sciences Annual Lecture, London. Retrieved from https://www.bankofengland.co.uk/speech/2018/andy-haldane-academy-of-social-sciences-annual-lecture-2018

Barber, T. (2019). The EU struggles to speak with a single voice. *Financial Times*, April 6.

Barker, A. (2018). Brexiters fear biggest loss of sovereignty since 1973. *Financial Times*, July 10.

Bartolini, D., Stossberg, S., & Blöchliger, H. (2016). *Fiscal decentralisation and regional dispari-ties.* OECD Economics Department Working Paper No. 1330. Paris: OECD Publishing.

BBC News. (2001, June 28). GE-Honeywell deal 'back on'. Retrieved from http://news.bbc.co.uk/1/hi/business/1411366.stm

Beattie, A. (2019). Eyes on the prize. *Financial Times,* July 25.

Beck, U. (2016). *The metamorphosis of the world.* Cambridge: Polity Press.

Berman, P. (2007). *Power and the idealists: Or, the passion of Joschka Fischer and its after-math.* New York, NY: W. W. Norton.

Bernard, A., Jensen, B., & Schott, P. (2006). Survival of the best fit: Exposure to low-wage countries and the (uneven) growth of US manufacturing establishments. *The Journal of International Economics, 68,* 219–237.

Bernard, A., Jensen, B., Redding, S., & Schott, P. (2012). The empirics of firm heterogene-ity and international trade. *Annual Review of Economics, 4,* 283–313.

Bhagwati, J., Greenaway, D., & Panagariya, A. (1998, July). Trading preferentially: Theory and policy. *Economic Journal, 108*(449), 1128–1148.

Bickerton, C., Cunliffe, P., & Gourevitch, A. (Eds.). (2007). *Politics without sovereignty.* London: University College London Press.

Blackhurst, R., Marian, N., & Tumlir, J. (1977, November). Trade liberalization, protec-tionism and interdependence. *GATT Studies in International Trade, 5,* 1–79.

Blair, T. (2005, September 28). Tony Blair's speech in full. *Independent.* Retrieved from https://www.independent.co.uk/news/uk/politics/tony-blairs-speech-in-full-5348100.html

Bonefeld, W. (2017, July). Authoritarian liberalism: From Schmitt via ordoliberalism to the euro. *Critical Sociology, 43*(4–5), 747–761.

Bordo, M., & Kydland, F. (1995). The gold standard as a rule: An essay in exploration. *Explorations in Economic History, 32,* 423–464.

Bown, C., & Crowley, M. (2013). Import protection, business cycles, and exchange rates: Evidence from the Great Recession. *Journal of International Economics, 90*(1), 50–64.

Bown, C., & Irwin, D. (2015, December). *The GATT's starting point: Tariff levels circa 1947.* NBER Working Paper No. 21782, National Bureau of Economic Research, Cambridge, MA.

Boyce, R. (1989). World war, world depression: Some economic origins of the Second World War. In R. Boyce & E. Robertson (Eds.), *Paths to war: New essays on the ori-gins of the Second World War* (pp. 55–95). New York, NY: St. Martin's Press.

Brailsford, H. (2012). *A league of nations.* Lexington, KY: Ulan Press (Original work pub-lished in 1917).

Bremmer, I. (2018). *Us vs. them: The failure of globalism.* New York, NY: Portfolio Penguin.

Brennan, J. (2016). *Against democracy.* Princeton, NJ: Princeton University Press.

Brinkley, J. (2018, March 21). What Trump calls nationalism looks more like isolationism. *Forbes.* Retrieved from https://www.forbes.com/sites/johnbrinkley/2018/03/21/what-trump-calls-nationalism-looks-more-like-isolationism/#389657d928f1

Brooks, D. (2016). The grand delusion. *New York Times,* September 28.

Brown, W. (2018). Who is not a neoliberal today? *Tocqueville 21,* January 18.

Brusse, W. (1997). *Tariffs, trade, and European integration, 1947–1957.* New York, NY: St. Martin's Press.

Busse, M., & Königer, J. (2012). *Trade and economic growth: A re-examination of the empirical evidence.* Hamburg Institute of International Economics Research Paper No. 123. Hamburg Institute of International Economics, Hamburg, Germany.

Camilleri, J., & Falk, J. (1992). *The end of sovereignty? The politics of a shrinking and frag-menting world.* Aldershot: Edward Elgar.

Carlsen, L. (2009, February 12, updated 2011, May 25). Obama reaffirms promise to rene-gotiate NAFTA. *HuffPost.* Retrieved from https://www.huffpost.com/entry/obama-reaffirms-promise-t_b_157316

Caryl, C. (2016). The end of politics as we know it. *Foreign Policy,* May 3.

Chalmers, M. (2019, April). *Which rules? Why there is no single rules-based international system.* RUSI Occasional Paper, Royal United Services Institute, London.

Chang, H. (2008). *Bad samaritans: The myth of free trade and the secret history of capitalism.* New York, NY: Bloomsbury.

Chipman, J. (1965, July). A survey of the theory of international trade: Part 1, the classical theory. *Econometrica, 33*, 477–519.

Claude, I. (1984). *Swords into plowshares: The problems and process of international relations.* New York, NY: McGraw-Hill Publishing (Original work published in 1956).

Clemens, M., & Williamson, J. (2001, September). *A tariff-growth paradox? Protection's impact the world around 1875–1997.* NBER Working Paper No. 8459, National Bureau of Economic Research, Cambridge, MA.

Clover, C. (2017). China increasingly vital to big car groups' profits. *Financial Times*, August 13.

Coe, D., & Helpman, E. (1995). International R&D spillovers. *European Economic Review, 39*, 859–887.

Collins, L. (2019). Can Emmanuel Macron stem the populist tide? *The New Yorker*, June 24. Retrieved from https://www.newyorker.com/magazine/2019/07/01/can-emmanuel-macron-stem-the-populist-tide

Conner, T. (2004). Introduction. In T. Conner & I. Torimoto (Eds.), *Globalization redux: New name, same game* (pp. 1–34). Lanham, MD: University Press of America.

Conrad, J. (1995). *Heart of darkness.* London: Penguin.

Constantinescu, C., Mattoo, A., & Ruta, M. (2015, January). *The global trade slowdown: Cyclical or structural?* World Bank Policy Research Working Paper No. 7158, World Bank Group, Washington, DC.

Cooper, R. (1968). *The economics of interdependence: Economic policy in the Atlantic community.* New York, NY: McGraw-Hill/Council on Foreign Relations.

Costello, S. (2019). Where is the iPhone made? *Lifewire*, April 8. Retrieved from https://www.lifewire.com/where-is-the-iphone-made-1999503

Crafts, N. (2018). Walking wounded: The British economy in the aftermath of World War I. In S. Broadberry & M. Harrison (Eds.), *The economics of the Great War: A centennial perspective* (pp. 119–125). A VoxEU.org book, CEPR Press. Retrieved from https://voxeu.org/content/economics-great-war-centennial-perspective

Crisp, J. (2017). Jean-Claude Juncker unveils vision for bigger, more powerful EU and warns Britain will 'regret' Brexit. *The Telegraph*, September 13. Retrieved from https://www.telegraph.co.uk/news/2017/09/13/jean-claude-junker-claims-uk-will-regret-brexit-vows-create/

Cross, M. (2018). We shouldn't celebrate a protectionist GDPR. *The Law Society Gazette*, May 23.

Crowley, M. (2003). An introduction to the WTO and the GATT. *Federal Reserve Bank of Chicago Economic Perspectives, 27*(Q4), 42–57.

Cummings, W. (2018, November 12). 'I am a nationalist': Trump's embrace of controversial label sparks uproar. *USA Today*. Retrieved from https://eu.usatoday.com/story/news/politics/2018/10/24/trump-says-hes-nationalist-what-means-why-its-controversial/1748521002/

Dachs, B., & Zahradnik, G. (2017, October 9). Recent trends in the internationalisation of Business R&D [Blog post]. Retrieved from https://blogs.lse.ac.uk/gild/2017/10/09/recent-trends-in-the-internationalisation-of-business-rd/

D'Alisa, G., Demaria, F., & Kallis, G. (Eds.). (2014). *Degrowth: A vocabulary for a new era.* London: Routledge.

De Backer, K., & Miroudot, S. (2013). *Mapping global value chains.* OECD Trade Policy Paper No. 159. Paris: OECD Publishing.

DeLong, B. (1998). Trade policy and America's standard of living: A historical perspective. In S. M. Collins (Ed.), *Imports, exports, and the American workers* (pp. 348–388). Washington, DC: Brookings Institution.

Dhingra, S., & Datta, N. (2017). How not to do trade deals. *London Review of Books*, September 21.

DiCaprio, A., & Gallagher, K. (2006). The WTO and the shrinking of development space: How big is the bite? *Journal of World Investment and Trade, 7*(5), 781–803.

Donnan, S. (2018a). The tech war behind trade moves. *Financial Times*, July 6.

Donnan, S. (2018b). US Car Industry. *Financial Times*, April 16.

Dougherty, S., & Akgun, O. (2018). Globalisation, decentralisation and inclusive growth. In J. Kim & S. Dougherty (Eds.), *Fiscal decentralisation and inclusive growth* (pp. 49–73). Paris: OECD Publishing. Retrieved from https://doi.org/10.1787/9789264302488-5-en.

Dudley S., & Warren, M. (2016, May). *Regulators' budget from Eisenhower to Obama: An analysis of the U.S. budget for fiscal years 1960 through 2017*. Washington, DC: George Washington University Regulatory Studies Center and the Weidenbaum Center on the Economy, Government, and Public Policy.

Dunning, J., & Lundan, S. (2008). *Multinational enterprises and the global economy.* Aldershot: Edward Elgar.

Eatwell, R., & Goodwin, M. (2018). *National populism: The revolt against liberal democracy*. London: Pelican Books.

Economist Intelligence Unit. (2018, January). *Democracy index 2017: Free speech under attack*. London: The Economist Group.

Edel, C. (2018). The China challenge. *The American Interest*, August 24.

Ederington, J., & Ruta, M. (2016, May). *Non-tariff measures and the world trading system*. World Bank Trade and Competitiveness Global Practice Group Policy Research Working Paper No. 7661. World Bank Group, Washington, DC.

Edgerton, D. (2006). *The shock of the old: Technology and global history since 1900*. London: Profile Books.

Eichengreen, B. (1986, August). *The political economy of the Smoot-Hawley tariff*. NBER Working Paper No. 2001, National Bureau of Economic Research, Cambridge, MA.

Eichengreen, B. (1992). *Golden fetters: The gold standard and the Great Depression 1919–39*. Oxford: Oxford University Press.

Eichengreen, B. (2011). *Exorbitant privilege*. Oxford: Oxford University Press.

Eichengreen, B., & Irwin, D. (2009, July). *The slide to protectionism in the Great Depression: Who succumbed and why?* NBER Working Paper No. 15142, National Bureau of Economic Research, Cambridge, MA.

Encyclopaedia Britannica. (n.d.). Opium trade: British and Chinese history. Retrieved from https://www.britannica.com/topic/opium-trade

Estevadeordal, A., Frantz, B., & Taylor, A. (2003). The rise and fall of world trade, 1870–1939. *The Quarterly Journal of Economics, 118*(2), 359–407.

European Centre for International Political Economy. (2015, March 9). *The New World of Trade – Lecture by Pascal Lamy*. Giving the Third Jan Tumlir Lecture, Brussels. Retrieved from https://ecipe.org/publications/new-world-trade/

European Commission. (2004, April 1). Europe and peace – Speech by Romano Prodi president of the European Commission. At the University of Ulster, Derry. Retrieved from https://ec.europa.eu/commission/presscorner/detail/en/SPEECH_04_170

European Commission. (2016, June). *European Union global strategy for foreign and security policy – Shared vision, common action: A stronger Europe*. Brussels: European Commission.

European Commission. (2019, March 12). *EU-China – A strategic outlook*. Brussels: European Commission.

European Court of Justice. (1964, July 15). *Flaminio Costa v E.N.E.L* (Judgment of the Court, Case 6-64). Luxembourg City: European Court of Justice.

Evenett, S. (Ed.). (2017). *Cloth for wine? The relevance of Ricardo's comparative advantage in the 21st century*. Washington, DC: CEPR Press.

Evenett, S., & Fritz, J. (2015). Crisis-era trade distortions cut LDC export growth by 5.5% per annum. In B. Hoekman (Ed.), *The global trade slowdown: A new normal* (pp. 267–278). Vox.EU.org Ebook, CEPR Press. Retrieved from https://voxeu.org/sites/default/files/file/Global%20Trade%20Slowdown_nocover.pdf

Evenett, S., & Fritz, J. (2017). *Will awe Trump rules?* The 21st global trade alert report. Washington, DC: CEPR Press.

Evenett, S., & Fritz, J. (2018). *Going spare: Steel, excess capacity, and protectionism.* The 22nd global trade alert report. Washington, DC: CEPR Press.

Evenett, S., & Fritz, J. (2019). *Jaw jaw not war war: Prioritising WTO reform options.* The 24th global trade alert report. Washington, DC: CEPR Press.

Falkner, G. (Ed.). (2011). *The EU's decision trap: Comparing policies.* Oxford: Oxford University Press.

Falkner, G., Treib, O., Hartlapp, M., & Leiber, S. (2005). *Complying with Europe: EU harmonisation and soft law in the member states.* Cambridge: Cambridge University Press.

Fallon, R. (1997). The rule of law as a concept in constitutional discourse. *Columbia Law Review, 97,* 1–56.

Farley, R. (2019, May 14) Economists: Tariffs not boosting GDP. *FactCheck.org.* Retrieved from https://www.factcheck.org/2019/05/economists-tariffs-not-boosting-gdp/

Farnsworth, K. (2015, July). *The British corporate welfare state: Public provision for private businesses.* SPERI Paper No. 24, Sheffield Political Economy Research Institute. Sheffield: University of Sheffield.

Farrell, H., & Newman, A. (2019). Weaponized interdependence: How global economic networks shape state coercion. *International Security, 44*(1), 42–79.

Fassin, D. (2019, July 4). Macron's war. *London Review of Books, 41*(13). Retrieved from https://www.lrb.co.uk/the-paper/v41/n13/didier-fassin/macron-s-war

Federal Reserve Board. (2004, February 20). Remarks by Governor Ben S. Bernanke: The Great Moderation. At the meeting of the Eastern Economic Association, Washington, DC. Retrieved from https://www.federalreserve.gov/boarddocs/speeches/2004/20040220/

Financial Times editorial. (2020). The EU needs to learn the language of power. *Financial Times,* January 2.

Findlay, R., & O'Rourke, K. (2007). *Power and plenty: Trade, war, and the world economy in the second millennium.* Princeton, NJ: Princeton University Press.

Franck, T. (2018, March 2). Trump doubles down: 'Trade wars are good, and easy to win'. *CNBC.* Retrieved from https://www.cnbc.com/2018/03/02/trump-trade-wars-are-good-and-easy-to-win.html

Frankel, J., & Romer, D. (1999, June). Does trade cause growth? *American Economic Review, 89*(3), 379–399.

Frankopan, P. (2016). *The silk roads: A new history of the world.* New York, NY: Bloomsbury.

Frankopan, P. (2019). *The new silk roads: The present and future of the world.* New York, NY: Bloomsbury.

Freund, C. (2016, April 20). *The global trade slowdown and secular stagnation.* Washington, DC: Peterson Institute for International Economics.

Froud, J., Johal, S., Law, J., Leaver, A., & Williams, K. (2011). *Rebalancing the economy (or buyer's remorse).* CRESC Working Paper No. 87, Centre for Research on Socio-Cultural Change. Manchester: University of Manchester.

Fukao, K. (2018). Chinese buyers spur rise in global luxury car sales. *Nikkei Asian Review,* February 18.

Fukuyama, F. (2017). On why liberal democracy is in trouble. *National Public Radio,* April 4, Morning Edition.

Furedi, F. (2013). *Authority: A sociological history.* Cambridge: Cambridge University Press.

Furedi, F. (2014). *First World War: Still no end in sight.* New York, NY: Bloomsbury Continuum.

Furedi, F. (2016). The spectre of democracy. *Spiked,* February. Retrieved from https://www.spiked-online.com/2016/03/31/the-spectre-of-democracy/

Furedi, F. (2017). *Populism and the European culture wars: The conflict of values between Hungary and the EU*. London: Routledge.

Furedi, F. (2018). Why the people must be sovereign. *Spiked*, March. Retrieved from https://www.spiked-online.com/2018/03/02/why-the-people-must-be-sovereign/

Furnivall, J. (1948). *Colonial policy and practice: A comparative study of Burma and Netherlands India*. Cambridge: Cambridge University Press.

Ganesh, J. (2018a). An era of estrangement distracts western allies. *Financial Times*, November 15.

Ganesh, J. (2018b). Donald Trump drops the pretence on American exceptionalism. *Financial Times*, November 28.

Ganesh, J. (2019). Trump's trade obsession keeps the peace with China. *Financial Times*, April 11.

Gardiner, K. (2015, April 21). *Nae Pasaran* shares the story of Scottish laborers standing against Chile's Pinochet regime. *Vice.com*. Retrieved from https://www.vice.com/en_us/article/avywx8/nae-pasaran-shares-an-untold-story-of-chilean-solidarity-415

Gash, N. (1986). *Sir Robert Peel: The life of Sir Robert Peel after 1830*. Upper Saddle River, NJ: Prentice Hall Press.

Gaulier, G., Santoni, G., Taglioni, D., & Zignago, S. (2015). The power of the few in determining trade accelerations and slowdowns. In B. Hoekman (Ed.), *The global trade slowdown: A new normal* (pp. 93–108). Vox.EU.org Ebook, CEPR Press. Retrieved from https://voxeu.org/sites/default/files/file/Global%20Trade%20Slowdown_nocover.pdf

Gehring, K., & Schneider, S. (2016, March 7). *Towards the greater good? EU Commissioners' nationality and budget allocation in the European Union*. Zürich CIS Working Paper No. 86, Center for Comparative and International Studies.

General Accounting Office. (2000). *Report to the Chairman, Committee on Ways and Means, House of Representatives – World Trade Organization: Issues in Dispute Settlement*. NSIAD-00-210. Washington, DC: US General Accounting Office.

Gereffi, G. (2011, Spring). Global value chains and international competition. *The Antitrust Bulletin, 56*(1), 37–56.

Ghodsi, M., Grübler, J., Reiter, O., & Stehrer, R. (2017, May). *The evolution of non-tariff measures and their diverse effects on trade*. Wiiw Research Report No. 419, Vienna Institute for International Economic Studies, Vienna.

Gill, S. (1998, February). New constitutionalism, democratisation and global political economy. *Pacifica Review Peace Security & Global Change, 10*(1), 23–28.

Gilpin, R. (1987). *The political economy of international relations*. Princeton, NJ: Princeton University Press.

Goddard, C. R., Cronin, P., & Dash, K. (Eds.). (2003). *International political economy: State-market relations in a changing global order*. Basingstoke: Palgrave Macmillan.

Goodhart, D. (2017). *The road to somewhere: The new tribes shaping British politics*. London: Penguin.

Greenfeld, L. (1992). *Nationalism: Five roads to modernity*. Cambridge, MA: Harvard University Press.

Grossman, G., & Helpman, E. (1991). *Innovation and growth in the global economy*. Cambridge, MA: MIT Press.

Grossman, G., & Rossi-Hansberg, E. (2008). Trading tasks: A simple theory of offshoring. *American Economic Review, 98*, 1978–1997.

Grossmann, H. (1992). *The law of accumulation and breakdown of the capitalist system*. London: Pluto Press.

Grundke, R., & Moser, C. (2014, December). *Hidden protectionism? Evidence from non-tariff barriers to trade in the United States*. CESifo Working Paper No. 5142, Center for Economic Studies and Information and Forschung Institute Group, Munich.

Guzman, A. (2002, December). A compliance-based theory of international law. *California Law Review, 90*(6), 1823–1887.

Habermas, J. (2015). *The lure of technocracy*. Cambridge: Polity Press.

Halikiopoulou, D., & Vasilopoulou, S. (Eds.). (2011). *Nationalism and globalisation: Conflicting or complementary?* London: Routledge.

Hall, P. (2013). The political origins of our economic discontents: Contemporary adjustment problems in historical perspective. In M. Kahler & D. Lake (Eds.), *Politics in the new hard times: The Great Recession in comparative perspective* (pp. 129–149). Ithaca, NY: Cornell University Press.

Hancock, T. (2018). Car sales in China set for first annual fall since early 1990s. *Financial Times*, December 15.

Hansen, A. (1939, March). Economic progress and declining population growth. *The American Economic Review, 29*(1), pp. 1–15.

Harding, R., & Harding, J. (2017). *The weaponization of trade: The great unbalancing of politics and economics*. London: London Publishing Partnership.

Hardt, M., & Negri, A. (2000). *Empire*. Cambridge, MA: Harvard University Press.

Harley, K. (1994). Foreign trade: Comparative advantage and performance. In R. Floud & D. McCloskey (Eds.), *The economic history of Britain since 1700, volume 1: 1700–1860* (pp. 300–331). Cambridge: Cambridge University Press.

Harrison, A. (1995). *Openness and growth: A time-series, cross-country analysis for developing countries*. NBER Working Paper No. 5221, National Bureau of Economic Research, Cambridge, MA.

Hartwich, O. (2009, May 21). *Neoliberalism: The genesis of a political swearword*. CIS Occasional Paper No. 114, The Centre for Independent Studies, Sydney.

Haugh, D., Kopoin, A., Rusticelli, E., Turner, D., & Dutu, R. (2016, September). *Cardiac arrest or dizzy spell: Why is world trade so weak and what can policy do about it?* OECD Economic Policy Paper No. 18, OECD Publishing, Paris.

Hayakawa, K. (2007). Growth of intermediate goods trade in East Asia. *Pacific Economic Review, 12*(4), 511–523.

Hayek, F. (1979). *Law, legislation and liberty*. London: Routledge.

Hayek, F. (1981). An interview. *El Mercurio*, April 12.

Heartfield, J. (2013). *The European Union and the end of politics*. Alresford: Zero Books.

Held, D., & McGrew, A. (Eds.). (2003). *The global transformations reader: An introduction to the globalization debate*. Cambridge: Polity Press.

Held, D., McGrew, A., Goldblatt, D., & Perraton, J. (1999). What is globalization? Retrieved from http://www.polity.co.uk/global/research.asp

Helleiner, E. (1994). *States and the reemergence of global finance: From Bretton Woods to the 1990s*. Ithaca, NY: Cornell University Press.

Helleiner, E. (2014). *The status quo crisis: Global financial governance after the 2008 financial meltdown*. Oxford: Oxford University Press.

Herbert, J., McCrisken, T., & Wroe, A. (2019). *The ordinary presidency of Donald J. Trump*. Basingstoke: Palgrave Macmillan.

Herghelegiu, C. (2017). The political economy of non-tariff measures. *The World Economy*, November 16.

Hewitt, G. (2015, February 1). Greece: The dangerous game. Retrieved from https://www.bbc.co.uk/news/world-europe-31082656

Hilferding, R. (2007). *Finance Capital: A Study in the Latest Phase of Capitalist Development*. London: Routledge (Original work published in 1910).

Hingstman, D., & Goodnight, G. T. (2001). From the Great Depression to the Great Recession: The 1932 Hayek-Keynes debate: A study in economic uncertainty, contingency, and criticism. *Poroi, 7*(1). Retrieved from https://s-lib012.lib.uiowa.edu/poroi/poroi0701-05.htm

Hobson, J. (2011). *Imperialism: A study*. Nottingham: Spokesman Books (Original work published in 1902).

Hoekman, B. (Ed.). (2015). *The global trade slowdown: A new normal?* A VoxEU.org eBook, CEPR Press. Retrieved from https://voxeu.org/sites/default/files/file/Global%20Trade%20Slowdown_nocover.pdf

Hoffmann, S. (2003). World governance: Beyond Utopia. *Daedalus, 132*(1), 27–35.

Hoornweg, D., Bhada, P., Freire, M., Trejos Gómez, C., & Dave, R. (2010). *Cities and climate change: An urgent agenda.* Washington, DC: World Bank Group.

Hornby, L. (2018). Beijing hands US an olive branch over global trade. *Financial Times,* July 17.

Horwitz, M. (1977). The rule of law: An unqualified human good? *Yale Law Journal, 86,* 584–587.

Howard, M. (1972). *The continental commitment.* London: Temple Smith.

Howe, A. (1998). *Free trade and liberal England, 1846–1946.* Oxford: Oxford University Press.

Hudec, R. (1990). *The GATT legal system and world trade diplomacy.* Oxford: Butterworth Legal Publishers.

Hufbauer, G., Schott, J., Cimino, C., Vieiro, M., & Wada, E. (2013). *Local content requirements: A global problem.* Washington, DC: Peterson Institute for International Economics.

Hughes, D., & Ferguson, K. (2016). National borders are 'the worst invention ever', says EC Chief Jean-Claude Juncker. *Independent,* August 22. Retrieved from https://www.independent.co.uk/news/world/europe/national-borders-are-the-worst-invention-ever-says-ec-chief-jean-claude-juncker-a7204006.html

Hummels, D., Ishii, J., & Yi, K. (2001). The nature and growth of vertical specialization in world trade. *Journal of International Economics, 54*(1), 75–96.

Huntington, S. (1999). The lonely superpower. *Foreign Affairs,* March–April.

Hutchinson, J. (2011). Globalisation and nation formation in the *longue duree.* In D. Halikiopoulou & S. Vasilopoulou, (Eds.), *Nationalism and globalisation: Conflicting or complementary?* (pp. 84–99). London: Routledge.

Ikenberry, J. (2004). Illusions of empire: Defining the new American order. *Foreign Affairs,* March/April.

IMF. (2014, February 3). *A new multilateralism for the 21st century: The Richard Dimbleby Lecture – By Christine Lagarde.* London. Retrieved from http://www.imf.org/en/News/Articles/2015/09/28/04/53/sp020314

IMF. (2016, October). Global trade: What's behind the slowdown? In IMF, *World economic outlook.* Washington, DC: International Monetary Fund.

IMF. (2018, April 19). *Transcript of managing director's press briefing – Christine Lagarde.* Washington, DC. Retrieved from https://www.imf.org/en/News/Articles/2018/04/19/tr041918-transcript-of-managing-directors-press-briefing

IMF. (2019, October). *World economic outlook database.* Retrieved from https://www.imf.org/external/pubs/ft/weo/2019/02/weodata/weorept.aspx?pr.x=46&pr.y=11&sy=2010&ey=2020&scsm=1&ssd=1&sort=country&ds=.&br=1&c=156%2C924%2C132%2C134%2C136%2C158%2C112%2C111&s=GGX_NGDP&grp=0&a=

Institute for Public Policy Research Commission on Economic Justice. (2018). *Prosperity and justice: A plan for the new economy.* Cambridge: Polity Press.

International Organization of Motor Vehicle Manufacturers (OICA). (2020). Passenger car sales [Data file]. Retrieved from http://www.oica.net/category/sales-statistics/

Ip, G. (2017). We are not the world. *The Wall Street Journal,* January 7.

Irwin, D. (1993, March). Free Trade and Protection in Nineteenth Century Britain and France Revisited: A Comment on Nye. *The Journal of Economic History, 53*(1).

Irwin, D. (1996). *Against the tide: An intellectual history of free trade.* Princeton, NJ: Princeton University Press.

Irwin, D. (2011). *Peddling protectionism: Smoot-Hawley and the Great Depression.* Princeton, NJ: Princeton University Press.

Irwin, D. (2015). *Free trade under fire.* Princeton, NJ: Princeton University Press.

Ismay, H. (n.d.) Retrieved from https://www.nato.int/cps/en/natohq/declassified_137930.htm

Jiang, K., Keller, W., Qiu, L., & Ridley, W. (2018, May). *International joint ventures and internal vs. external technology transfer: Evidence from China.* NBER Working Paper No. 24455, National Bureau of Economic Research, Cambridge, MA.

Jones, G. (2005). *Multinationals and global capitalism: From the nineteenth to the twenty-first century.* Oxford: Oxford University Press.

Juncker, J.-C. (2013). Interview: The demons haven't been banished. *Der Spiegel*, March 11.

Kagan, R. (2018). *The jungle grows back: America and our imperiled world.* New York, NY: Alfred A. Knoff.

Kahler, M. (2013). Economic crisis and global governance: The stability of a globalized world. In M. Kahler & D. Lake (Eds.), *Politics in the new hard times: The Great Recession in comparative perspective* (pp. 27–51). Ithaca, NY: Cornell University Press.

Kant, I. (2016). *Essay on perpetual peace: A philosophical sketch.* Scotts Valley, CA: CreateSpace Independent Publishing Platform (Original work published in 1795).

Karacaovali, B., & Limão, N. (2008). The clash of liberalizations: Preferential vs. multilateral trade liberalization in the European Union, *Journal of International Economics, 74*(2), 299–327.

Kee, H., Nicita, A., & Olarreaga, M. (2009). Estimating trade restrictiveness indices. *Economic Journal, 119*, 172–199.

Kennan, G. (1947, July). The sources of Soviet conduct. *Foreign Affairs.* Retrieved from https://www.foreignaffairs.com/articles/russian-federation/1947-07-01/sources-soviet-conduct

Kennedy, D. (1987). The move to institutions. *Cardoza Law Review, 8*(5), 841–988.

Keohane, R. O., & Nye, J. S. (1977). *Power and interdependence: World politics in transition.* Boston, MA: Little, Brown.

Kershaw, I. (2001). *Hitler, 1889–1936: Hubris.* London: Penguin.

Keynes, J. M. (2012). *The collected writings of John Maynard Keynes* (Vol. 20). Cambridge: Cambridge University Press.

Kinsella, D. (2005). No rest for the democratic peace. *American Political Science Review, 99*, 791–807.

Kissinger, H. (2001). The pitfall of universal jurisdiction. *Foreign Affairs*, July–August.

Krauss, M. (1978). *The new protectionism: The welfare state in international trade.* New York, NY: New York University Press.

Krueger, A. (Ed.). (1996). *The political economy of American trade policy.* Chicago, IL: University of Chicago Press.

Krugman, P. (1995). Growing world trade: Causes and consequences. *Brookings Papers on Economic Activity, 1*, 327–377.

Krugman, P. (2009). Protectionism and the Great Depression. *New York Times*, November 30.

Krugman, P. (2016). Trade plateaus (wonkish). *New York Times*, October 31.

Lanz, R., & Miroudot, S. (2011). *Intra-firm trade: Patterns, determinants and policy implications.* OECD Trade Policy Paper No. 114, OECD Publishing, Paris.

Lee, J., & Swagel, P. (1997, August). Trade barriers and trade flows across countries and industries. *The Review of Economics and Statistics, 79*(3), 372–382.

Lenin, V. (1996). *Imperialism: The Highest Stage of Capitalism.* London: Pluto Press (Original work published in 1916).

Levitt, T. (1983). The globalization of markets. *Harvard Business Review*, May.

Lindsey, B., & Teles, S. (2017). *The captured economy: How the powerful become richer, slow down growth, and increase inequality.* Oxford: Oxford University Press.

Luce, E. (2017). *The retreat of Western liberalism.* Boston, MA: Little, Brown.

Luce, E. (2019). Doing justice by Preet Bharara. *Financial Times*, May 27.

Maddison, A. (2003). *The world economy: Historical statistics.* Paris: OECD Publishing.

Maier, C. (1981). The two postwar eras and the conditions for stability in twentieth-century Europe. *American Historical Review, 84*(2), 327–352.

Mangone, G. (1954). *A short history of international organization.* New York, NY: Greenwood Press.

Marx, K. (1973). *Grundrisse: Foundations of the critique of political economy* (Trans. by M. Nicolaus). Harmondsworth: Penguin.

Mauldin, J. (2015). George Friedman's world of geopolitics. *Mauldin Economics*, December 11. Retrieved from https://www.mauldineconomics.com/frontlinethoughts/george-friedmans-world-of-geopolitics

Maurer, A., & Degain, C. (2010, June). *Globalization and trade flows: What you see is not what you get!* WTO Staff Working Paper ERSD-2010-12, WTO, Geneva, Switzerland.

Mazarr, M. (2018). The real history of the liberal order: Neither myth nor accident. *Foreign Affairs*, August 7.

Mazower, M. (2008). *No enchanted palace: The end of empire and the ideological origins of the United Nations.* Princeton, NJ: Princeton University Press.

Mazower, M. (2013). *Governing the world: The history of an idea.* London: Penguin.

Mazower, M. (2019). Capitalism vs democracy: Europe's hard problem. *New Statesman*, August 28.

McAdams, D. (2016, June). The mind of Donald Trump. *The Atlantic*. Retrieved from https://www.theatlantic.com/magazine/archive/2016/06/the-mind-of-donald-trump/480771/

McBride, S. (2011). The new constitutionalism: International and private rule in the new global order. In S. McBride & G. Teeple (Eds.), *Relations of global power: Neoliberal order and disorder* (pp. 19–40). Toronto: University of Toronto Press.

McNair, L. A. (Ed.). (1928). *International law: A treatise by L. Oppenheim, Vol. I. Peace.* Harlow: Longmans, Green & Co.

McNamara, K. (2019, October). When the banal becomes political: The EU in the age of populism. *Polity, 51*(4), 654–667.

Mével, J.-J. (2015). Jean-Claude Juncker: "Pas question de supprimer la dette grecque". *Le Figaro*, January 28.

Miles, T. (2018). China partially wins WTO case over Obama-era U.S. tariffs. *Reuters Business News*, March 21.

Mill, J. S. (1848). *The principles of political economy with some of their applications to social philosophy.* Farnham: John W. Parker.

Mills, C. (2019, October 30). *EU defence: Where is it heading?* Briefing Paper No. 8216, House of Commons Library, London.

Miravete, E., Moral, M., & Thurk, J. (2015). *Innovation, emissions policy, and competitive advantage in the diffusion of European diesel automobiles.* CEPR Discussion Paper No. 10783, Centre for Economic Policy Research, Washington, DC.

Miroudot, S., Lanz, R., & Ragoussis, A. (2009). *Trade in intermediate goods and services.* OECD Trade Policy Working Paper No. 93. Paris: OECD Publishing.

Mohr, D., Müller, N., Krieg, A., Gao, P., Kaas, H., Krieger, A., & Hensley, R. (2013, August). *The road to 2020 and beyond: What's driving the global automotive industry?* Washington, DC: McKinsey.

Momtaz, R. (2019). Macron, Europe's wannabe president. *Politico*, November 7. Retrieved from https://www.politico.eu/article/emmanuel-macron-europe-president-china-trade/

Morris, M., & Kibasi, T. (2019, January). *State aid rules and Brexit.* London: Institute for Public Policy Research.

Mounk, Y. (2018). *The People vs. Democracy: Why Our Freedom Is in Danger and How to Save It.* Cambridge, MA: Harvard University Press.

Mullan, P. (2017). *Creative destruction: How to start an economic renaissance.* Bristol: Policy Press.

Muller, J.-W. (2012). Beyond militant democracy. *New Left Review, 73*, 39–47.

Murphy, J. (2004). *The United States and the rule of law in international affairs.* Cambridge: Cambridge University Press.

Naess-Schmidt, H., Harhoff, F., & Hansen, M. (2011). *State aid crisis rules for the financial sector and the real economy.* Brussels: European Parliament.

National Intelligence Council. (2017, January). *Global trends: Paradox of progress.* Washington, DC: Office of the US Director of National Intelligence.

Narlikar, A. (2018). A trade war on the poor. *Foreign Affairs*, March 5.

Noland, M., Hufbauer, G., Robinson, S., & Moran, T. (2016, September). *Assessing trade agendas in the US presidential campaign*. PIIE Briefing 16-6, Peterson Institute for International Economics.

Nordås, H. (2003). *Fragmented production: Regionalisation of trade?* WTO Staff Working Paper No. ERSD-2003-01, WTO, Geneva, Switzerland.

Nye, J. (1991, March). The myth of free-trade Britain and fortress France: Tariffs and trade in the nineteenth century. *The Journal of Economic History*, *51*(1), 146–152.

OECD. (2017a, June 30). How to make trade work for all. In *OECD economic outlook* (Vol. 2017, Issue 1). Paris: OECD Publishing.

OECD. (2017b, June 7–8). *Key issue paper. For the meeting of the council at ministerial level*. Paris: OECD Publishing.

OECD. (2018, November). *Current trends in investment policies related to national security and public order*. Paris: OECD Publishing.

OECD.Stat. (2020a). Environmental Policy Stringency Index, Variable: Environmental Policy Stringency. [Data file]. Paris: OECD. Retrieved on 9 April 2020 from https:// stats.oecd.org/Index.aspx?DataSetCode=EPS#.

OECD.Stat. (2020b). Product Market Regulation 2013, Indicator: PMR: Product market regulation [Data file]. Paris: OECD. Retrieved on 9 April 2020 from https://stats. oecd.org/viewhtml.aspx?datasetcode=PMR&lang=en#

Office for National Statistics (UK). (2019a). Economy. Gross domestic product [Data file]. Retrieved from https://www.ons.gov.uk/economy/grossdomesticproductgdp/time-series/ybha/qna

Office for National Statistics (UK). (2019b). Economy. National accounts. Balance of payments [Data file]. Retrieved from https://www.ons.gov.uk/economy/nationalaccounts/ balanceofpayments/datasets/balanceofpayments

Oh, S.-Y. (2014). Shifting gears: Industrial policy and automotive industry after the 2008 financial crisis. *Business and Politics*, *16*(4), 641–665.

Ormerod, P. (2018). In their national interest? How European commissioners really allocate EU funding. *City A.M.*, February 7.

O'Rourke, K. (2000, April). Tariffs and growth in the late 19th century. *The Economic Journal*, *110*, 456–483.

O'Rourke, K. (2017). *Two great trade collapses: The interwar period & Great Recession compared*. Oxford University Economic and Social History Discussion Paper No. 159. University of Oxford, Oxford.

Palen, M.-W. (2017). Protectionism 100 years ago helped ignite a world war. Could it happen again? *Washington Post*, June 30.

Panic, M., & Joyce, P. (1980, March). UK manufacturing industry: International integration and trade performance. *Bank of England Quarterly Bulletin*, *20*(1), 42–55.

Parker, G., Chassany, A.-S., & Dyer, G. (2015). Europeans defy US to join China-led development bank. *Financial Times*, March 16.

Patrick, S. (2008). *The best laid plans: The origins of American multilateralism and the dawn of the Cold War*. Lanham, MD: Rowman & Littlefield Publishers.

Pavia, W., & Philp, C. (2018). UN general assembly: Macron challenges Trump's world view. *The Times*, September 26. Retrieved from https://www.thetimes.co.uk/article/ un-general-assembly-macron-challenges-trump-s-world-view-fpqcsp3vz

Peel, M. (2018). Swift to comply with US sanctions on Iran in blow to EU. *Financial Times*, November 5.

Pérez, C. (2017). Jean-Claude Juncker: 'Nationalism is poison'. *El Pais*, November 20. Retrieved from https://elpais.com/elpais/2017/11/20/inenglish/1511177283_048948.html

Pohl, J. (2019, February 25). Is international investment threatening or under threat? *Columbia FDI Perspectives*, *246*. Retrieved from http://ccsi.columbia.edu/ files/2018/10/No-246-Pohl-FINAL.pdf

Polillo, S., & Guillén, M. (2005). Globalization pressures and the state: The worldwide spread of central bank independence. *American Journal of Sociology, 110*(6), 1764–1802.

Pop, V. (2011). Eurogroup chief: 'I'm for secret, dark debates'. *EUobserver*, April 21.

Porter, P. (2018, June). *A world imagined: Nostalgia and liberal order*. Policy Analysis No. 843. Cato Institute, Washington, DC.

Poynter, G. (2020). *Conserving capital: State intervention and the long depression*. London: Routledge.

Rajan, A. (2018). Tariffs and populism put 'long-term' back in vogue. *Financial Times*, July 2.

Reissl, S., & Stockhammer, E. (2016, March). The euro crisis and the neoliberal EU policy regime: Signs of change or more of the same? *Europe at a Crossroads – Near Futures Online, 1*. Retrieved from https://www.academia.edu/23091749/_Europe_At_a_Crossroads_Near_Futures_Online

Ricardo, D. (1973). *On the principles of political economy and taxation*. New York, NY: Everyman Paperback Dent Dutton (Original work published in 1815.

Ricardo, D. (1997). *On protection to agriculture*. In C. Schonhardt-Bailey (Ed.), *The rise of free trade, volume 1: Protectionism and its critics, 1815–1837*. London: Routledge (Original work published in 1822).

Robbins, L. (1939). *The economic causes of war*. London: Jonathan Cape.

Robbins, L. (1963). *Politics and economics: Papers in political economy*. Basingstoke: Macmillan.

Roberts, J. (2017, October 13). *NAFTA's investor dispute (ISDS) provisions are good for Americans*. The Heritage Foundation. Retrieved from https://www.heritage.org/economic-and-property-rights/report/naftas-investor-dispute-isds-provisions-are-good-americans

Roberts, M. (2018). Imperialism, globalization and the profitability of capital. *Rupture Magazine, 1*. Retrieved from https://rupturemagazine.org/2018/01/25/imperialism-globalization-and-the-profitability-of-capital/

Rodríguez, F., & Rodrik, D. (2001). Trade policy and economic growth: A skeptic's guide to the cross-national evidence. In *NBER macroeconomics annual 2000* (Vol. 15). Cambridge, MA: MIT Press.

Rodrik, D. (2012). *The globalization paradox: Why global markets, states and democracy can't coexist*. Oxford: Oxford University Press.

Rosenberg, E., & Saravalle, E. (2018). China and the EU are growing sick of U.S. financial power: They are trying their best to erode Washington's rules. *Foreign Policy*, November 16.

Rosenboim, O. (2017a). Globalism and nationalism. *Foreign Affairs*, July 10.

Rosenboim, O. (2017b). *The emergence of globalism: Visions of world order in Britain and the United States, 1939–1950*. Princeton, NJ: Princeton University Press.

Ruggie, J. (1982, Spring). International regimes, transactions, and change: Embedded liberalism in the postwar economic order. *International Organization, 36*(2), 379–415.

Samuelson, P. (2004, Summer). Where Ricardo and Mill rebut and confirm arguments of mainstream economists supporting globalisation. *Journal of Economic Perspectives, 18*(3), 135–146.

Sandbu, M. (2017). The battles of ideology that will define our age. *Financial Times*, December 26.

Sanyal, K., & Jones, R. (1982). The theory of trade in middle products. *American Economic Review, 72*(1), 16–31.

Sassen, S. (2012). *Cities in a world economy*. Thousand Oaks, CA: Sage.

Scharpf, F. (1988). The joint-decision trap: Lessons from German federalism and European integration. *Public Administration, 66*(3), 239–278.

Schneider, P. (2018, July). *Decomposing differences in productivity distributions*. Bank of England Staff Working Paper No. 740, Bank of England, London.

Schonhardt-Bailey, C. (2006). *From corn laws to free trade: Interests, ideas, and institutions in historical perspective*. Cambridge, MA: MIT Press.

Sellars, K. (2002). *The rise and rise of human rights*. Stroud: Sutton Publications.
Sellars, K. (2010). Imperfect justice at Nuremberg and Tokyo. *European Journal of International Law*, *21*, 1085–1102.
Silva, R. (2019). Amazon inferno is a threat to us all — and the UN must lead the intervention. *Evening Standard*, August 30. Retrieved from https://www.standard.co.uk/comment/comment/amazon-inferno-is-a-threat-to-us-all-and-the-un-must-lead-the-intervention-a4225006.html
Skinner, A. (1990, May). The shaping of political economy in the Enlightenment. *Scottish Journal of Political Economy*, *37*, 145–165.
Slobodian, Q. (2018). *Globalists: The end of empire and the birth of neoliberalism*. Cambridge, MA: Harvard University Press.
Sluga, G. (2015). *Internationalism in the age of nationalism*. Philadelphia, PA: Pennsylvania Studies in Human Rights.
Smith, A. (2012). *An Inquiry into the nature and causes of the wealth of nations*. Ware: Wordsworth Editions (Original work published in 1776).
Statement From G20 Summit. (2008). *New York Times*, November 15. Retrieved from https://www.nytimes.com/2008/11/16/washington/summit-text.html
Stigler, G. (1976). The successes and failures of Professor Smith. *Journal of Political Economy*, *84*(6), 1199–1213.
Stock, J., & Watson, M. (2003). Has the business cycle changed and why? In *NBER macroeconomics annual 2002* (Vol. 17). Cambridge, MA: MIT Press.
Strange, S. (1986). *Casino capitalism*. Oxford: Basil Blackwell.
Strange, S. (1996). *The retreat of the state: The diffusion of power in the global economy*. Cambridge: Cambridge University Press.
Streeck, W. (2014). *Buying time: The delayed crisis of democratic capitalism*. New York, NY: Verso.
Stuenkel, O. (2016). *Post-western world: How emerging powers are remaking global order*. Cambridge: Polity Press.
Subramanian, A., & Kessler, M. (2013, July). *The hyperglobalization of trade and its future*. Peterson Institute for International Economics Working Paper No. 13-6, Peterson Institute for International Economics, Washington, DC.
The Economist. (2013). A cut above the rest. *The Economist*, April 8.
The Economist. (2015). Why everyone is so keen to agree new trade deals. *The Economist*, October 6.
The Economist. (2016a). The new political divide. *The Economist*, July 30.
The Economist. (2016b). Review of Richard Baldwin's *The Great Convergence*. *The Economist*, November 19.
Thucydides. (2000). *The history of the Peloponnesian War*. London: Penguin.
Timmer, M., Erumban, A., Los, B., Stehrer, R., & de Vries, G. (2014). Slicing up global value chains. *Journal of Economic Perspectives*, *28*(2), 99–118.
Timmer, M., Los, B., Stehrer, R., & de Vries, G. (2016). *An anatomy of the global trade slowdown based on the WIOD (World Input–Output Database) 2016 release* (GGDC Research Memorandum No. 162). University of Groningen.
Tooze, A. (2015). *The deluge: The Great War and the remaking of the global order, 1916–1931*. London: Penguin.
Tooze, A. (2018). *Crashed: How a decade of financial crises changed the world*. London: Allen Lane.
Trimble, P. (1990, February). Review: International law, world order, and critical legal studies. *Stanford Law Review*, *42*(3), 815.
Tucker, P. (2018). *Unelected power: The quest for legitimacy in central banking and the regulatory state*. Princeton, NJ: Princeton University Press.
Tumlir, J. (1983a). International economic order and democratic constitutionalism. *Ordo*, *34*, 71–86.

Tumlir, J. (1983b). Strong and weak elements in the concept of European integration. In F. Machlup, G. Fels, & H. Muller-Groeling (Eds.), *Reflections on a troubled world economy: Essays in honour of Herbert Giersch* (pp. 29–56). New York, NY: St. Martin's Press.

UK Government. (2019, June 19). Economic talks to boost UK–China relations. Retrieved from   https://www.gov.uk/government/news/economic-talks-to-boost-uk-china-relations

UN. (2004, August). *The rule of law and transitional justice in conflict and post-conflict societies: Report of the Secretary-General: S/2004/616.* New York, NY: United Nations.

UN Charter. (1945). United Nations. Retrieved from https://www.un.org/en/sections/un-charter/un-charter-full-text/

UNCTAD. (1996, October 8). UNCTAD and WTO: A common goal in a global economy – Address by the Director-General of the World Trade Organization Renato Ruggiero. At the UNCTAD Trade and Development Board. Retrieved from http://unctad.org/en/pages/PressReleaseArchive.aspx?ReferenceDocId=3607

UNCTAD. (2013). *World investment report 2013 – Global value chains: Investment and trade for development.* New York, NY: United Nations.

UNCTAD. (2014, September 16). Industrial policy – Better, not less: Development strategies in a globalized world: Policymaking in an evolving framework of global governance – Speech by Robert Wade. At the sixty-first session of UNCTAD's Trade and Development Board, Geneva. Retrieved from https://unctad.org/meetings/en/Presentation/tdb61_Rwade_item8_en.pdf

UNCTAD. (2018). *World investment report 2018 – Investment and new industrial policies.* New York, NY: United Nations.

UNCTAD. (2019). *World investment report 2019 – Special economic zones.* Annex Table 1. New York, NY: United Nations. Retrieved from https://unctad.org/en/Pages/DIAE/World%20Investment%20Report/Annex-Tables.aspx

UNCTADstat. (2019). Retrieved from https://unctadstat.unctad.org/wds/ReportFolders/reportFolders.aspx?sCS_ChosenLang=en

US Bureau of Economic Analysis. (2019a). International Investment Position. Table 1.1 [Data file]. Retrieved from https://apps.bea.gov/iTable/iTable.cfm?ReqID=62&step=1

US Bureau of Economic Analysis. (2019b). National Income and Product Accounts. GDP. Table 1.1.5 [Data file]. Retrieved from https://apps.bea.gov/iTable/iTable.cfm?reqid=19&step=2#reqid=19&step=2&isuri=1&1921=survey

US Bureau of Economic Analysis. (2019c). National Income and Product Accounts. US Corporate Profits Pre-tax. Table 6.17 [Data file]. Retrieved from https://apps.bea.gov/iTable/iTable.cfm?reqid=19&step=2

US Census Bureau. (2018). Related Party Database [Data file]. Retrieved from https://relatedparty.ftd.census.gov

US International Trade Commission. (2019, March). US imports for consumption, duties collected, and ratio of duties to value, 1891–2018. Table 1 [Data file]. Retrieved from https://www.usitc.gov/documents/dataweb/ave_table_1891_2018.pdf

Vamvakidis, A. (1997). *GATT was right: Historical evidence on the growth-openness connection and discriminatory versus non-discriminatory liberalization.* Economics Department mimeo. Cambridge, MA: Harvard University.

VanGrasstek, C. (2013). *The history and future of the World Trade Organization.* Geneva, Switzerland: World Trade Organization.

Varoufakis, Y. (2016). Yanis Varoufakis: Why we must save the EU. *The Guardian,* April 5. Retrieved from https://www.theguardian.com/world/2016/apr/05/yanis-varoufakis-why-we-must-save-the-eu

Vernon, R. (1971). *Sovereignty at bay: The multinational spread of U.S. enterprises.* New York, NY: Basic Books and London: Longman.

Viner, J. (1947). Conflicts of principle in drafting a trade charter. *Foreign Affairs,* January.

Wade, R. (2017). Empire spawned a new economic paradigm. *Financial Times*, April 3.
Walt, S. (2015). The U.N. security council. What's up with that? *Foreign Policy*, April 7.
Walt, S. (2018). Why I didn't sign up to defend the international order. *Foreign Policy*, August 1.
Washington, G. (1796). *Farewell address*. Yale Law School Lillian Goldman Law Library. Retrieved from https://avalon.law.yale.edu/18th_century/washing.asp
Wertheim, S. (2012). The League of Nations: A retreat from international law? *Journal of Global History, 7*(2), 210–232.
Wijen, F. (2015). Banning child labour imposes naive western ideals on complex problems. *The Guardian*, August 25. Retrieved from https://www.theguardian.com/sustainable-business/2015/aug/26/ban-child-labour-developing-countries-imposes-naive-western-ideals-complex-problems
Williams, J. (1929). *Chapters on current international law and the League of Nations*. London: Longmans.
Wilson, C., & Wood, D. (2016, September). *Growing together: Economic ties between the United States and Mexico*. Washington, DC: The Wilson Center.
World Bank. (1993). *The East Asian miracle: Economic growth and public policy*. Oxford: Oxford University Press.
World Bank. (1997). *World development report 1997: The state in a changing world*. Washington, DC: World Bank Group.
World Bank. (2005). *Global economic prospects: Trade, regionalism and development*. Washington, DC: World Bank Group.
World Bank. (2017). *Global economic prospects, Special focus 2: Arm's-length trade: A source of post-crisis trade weakness*. Washington, DC: World Bank Group.
World Bank World Development Indicators. (2020). Retrieved from https://databank.worldbank.org/source/world-development-indicators
World Bank World Integrated Trade Solution. (2020). World all product and intermediate goods imports [Data files]. Retrieved from https://wits.worldbank.org/CountryProfile/en/Country/WLD/StartYear/1988/EndYear/2017/TradeFlow/Import/Indicator/MPRT-TRD-VL/Partner/WLD/Product/Total and https://wits.worldbank.org/CountryProfile/en/Country/WLD/StartYear/1988/EndYear/2017/TradeFlow/Import/Indicator/MPRT-TRD-VL/Partner/WLD/Product/UNCTAD-SoP2
WTO. (2015). *Understanding the WTO*. Geneva, Switzerland: World Trade Organization.
WTO. (2019). Regionalism: Friends or rivals? Retrieved from https://www.wto.org/english/thewto_e/whatis_e/tif_e/bey1_e.htm
WTO. (2020). Evolution of RTAs, 1948–2020. Regional Trade Agreements Information System [Data file]. Retrieved from http://rtais.wto.org/UI/charts.aspx#
Young, K. (2014). The complex and covert web of financial protectionism. *Business and Politics, 16*(4), 579–613.
Zakaria, F. (2018). The new dividing line in Western politics. *Washington Post*, December 13.
Zammit-Lucia, J. (2017). Liberalism dies when it becomes the Establishment (letter). *Financial Times*, December 29.
Zhong, S. (a pen name often used by the *People's Daily* Chinese Communist Party publication to express official views on foreign policy). (2019). US should not duck responsibilities as major country. *People's Daily*, August 8.

Index

Note: Page numbers followed by "*n*" indicate footnotes.

Absolute advantage, 80
Accountability, 14, 35, 38
Acheson, Dean, 46
Acquisitions (*see* M&A)
Administrative state, 49
Aerospace, 157
Africa, 4, 44, 49, 88, 178
Agency, 3, 36, 47, 153, 166, 170
Agriculture, 103, 105–106, 157, 161
Airbus, 125, 135, 176
Allende, Salvador, 181
Allison, Graham, xxxvi
Amazon, 62
Anderson, Benedict, 180
Angell, Norman, xviii, xix, 142
Anghie, Antony, 4–5, 9, 12, 18, 89
Annan, Kofi, 17–18
Anti-Corn Law League, 86, 102
Anti-crisis measures, 92
Anti-democracy, 182
Anti-politics, 35–39, 51
Anti-semitism, 24
Anti-state, 35–39, 47, 51
APEC [Asia-Pacific Economic
        Cooperation], xxi
Apple, xvii, 62, 174, 175
    iPhone, xvii
Apple Inc., 146
Aristocracy, 86
Armed conflict, 6, 89
Artificial intelligence (AI) (*see also*
        Machine learning), xxxi,
        32, 98
Asgill, John, 118
Asia, 4, 44–45, 60, 96, 98, 153
Asian Infrastructure Investment Bank
        (AIIB), 60
Athens, 11, 64

Atkinson, Robert, 153
Audi, 149
Austerity, 7, 31, 165, 182
Austria, 6
Austrian school, 41, 46–47
Austro-Hungarian Hapsburg empire,
        42
Automation, 154, 161
Automobile industry (*see* Car
        industry)
Autonomy, 4, 7, 12, 14, 23–24, 38, 178
Autor, David, 120

Bailouts, 107–108, 126
Balanced budgets, 157
Baldwin, Richard, 70, 91, 94, 135, 144
Balkans, 18, 26, 60
Bank for International Settlements,
        137, 143
Bank of England, 7, 13, 74, 140, 176
Banking sector, 35, 108
Banks, 25, 31, 35, 62, 100, 144,
        158–159, 176
Barber, Tony, 31
Barroso, José Manuel, 22
Batteries, 98
Beck, Ulrich, xxiv, 168
Beggar-thy-neighbour policies, xxxii,
        91–92, 117
Behind the border. (*see* Non-tariff
        barriers)
Belgium, 112, 175
Berlin Conference, 88
Berlin Wall, 27, 57, 113
Bharara, Preet, 183
Big Bang, 141
Biosciences, 161
Blair, Tony, 33

Blueberries, xvii
BMW, 149
Boeing, 125, 176
Bolshevik Revolution (*see* Russian
    Revolution)
Bonefeld, Werner, 43
Borrell, Joseph, 65
Borders, 10, 18, 23, 24, 30–31, 34, 84,
    107, 121, 131, 135, 137, 139,
    170, 174, 179–180, 182–184
Borrowing, 153–154, 159–160, 175
Bosnia, 18
Bourgeoisie, 77
Boyce, Robert, 90
Brailsford, Henry, 5–6, 65
Brandeis, Louis, 11
Branding, 100
Brazil, 106, 137
Bretton Woods, 9, 25, 45, 47, 99, 132
Brexit, 21–22, 28–29, 58–59, 70, 85,
    87, 171, 177
BRICs, 149
Britain, 5–7, 15, 24, 55, 58, 61, 64,
    70, 80, 85, 88–90, 92, 171,
    180, 182
    economic policy, 90
    empire, 36
    EU referendum vote, 65
    imperialism, 24
    outward FDI, 73
    protectionism, 32, 37, 70, 77
    trade, 88, 132, 141
British East India Company, 176
Broadcom, 97
Brown, Gordon, 142
Brown, Wendy, 48
Bubbles (*see* Financial bubbles)
Burma, 12
Bush, George H W, 116
Bush, George W, 116
Business, 78, 100, 156, 158, 160, 173,
    175–176
    churn, 160
    dynamism, 163
    R&D, 97
    stateless, 173–176

Business cycle, 84, 161
Business investment (*see* Corporate
    investment)

California, 48
Canada, 15, 93, 110, 112
Capital, 9, 42, 58, 111, 174
    accumulation, 173
    exports, 73
    flows, 10, 64, 133, 143, 175, 177
    imports, 139–140
    investment, 82–83
    markets, 175
    stock, 90
Capitalism, 24, 27, 30, 35, 43, 46–47,
    52, 59, 71–72, 76, 78, 86,
    94–95, 101–103, 115, 142,
    158, 160, 162
    in crisis, 46–47
Capitalist breakdown, 46
Car industry, 150, 172
Carney, Mark, 140
Carter, Jimmy, 17, 116
Cecil, Lord (Robert), 45
Central and Eastern Europe, 41
Central banking, 35, 100, 158–159
    independent, 25
CERN (European Organization for
    Nuclear Research), 178
Change, 31–33, 146–147, 154
Chartists, 183
Chemical industries, 136, 143
Chicago school, 41, 78
Chile, 39, 181
China, xxv–xxxiv, 31, 59–64, 70, 83,
    98, 112, 137, 142, 146–147,
    167, 170
    car market, 148–149
    economic policy, 90, 95, 126
    inward FDI, 146
    protectionism, 31, 70, 81
    trade, 26, 60–61, 83, 87, 98
Chipman, John, 79
Christian democracy, 22
Chrysler, 108
Churchill, Winston, 23

Civilisation, 6, 9
Civilising mission, 9, 19, 88
Class, 7, 8, 21, 48, 86, 101–102, 149,
    155
Class conflict, 46
Classical political economy, 76, 81, 87
Claude, Inis, 46
Clausewitz, Carl von, xviii
Clemens, Michael, 93
Climate change (*see also* Global
    warming), 19, 26, 29, 168
Clinton, Bill, 33
Clinton, Hillary, xxiv$n$, 85
Clive, Robert, 176
Cloth, 78–80
Cold War, 17, 34, 48, 56–59, 64, 73,
    84, 95, 113, 142, 145, 180
Colonialism, 4, 9, 49, 88, 178
Colonies, 12, 49, 178, 180
Committee on Foreign Investment
    in the United States
    (CFIUS), 63
Communications, 34, 141,
    161–162, 167
Communism, 48, 56
Comparative advantage, 78–80
Competition, 63, 77, 126–127, 176
Competition authorities, 63
Complexity, 47, 127
Comprehensive and Progressive
    Agreement for Trans-
    Pacific Partnership, 127
Congo, 62
Conrad, Joseph, 88
Conservator state, 100, 158
Constitution, 10, 25
Construction sector, 161
Consumer products, 109
Consumer protection, 109, 117
Consumption, 76, 83, 137
Containment, 56, 158
Conventional wisdom, 34, 80, 82
Corn, 76, 80–81
Corn Laws repeal, 80, 86, 102, 183
Corporate dependency, 158
Corporate investment, 126, 145, 154

Corporate profits, 132–134, 149
Corporate taxes, 59, 126
Cotton, 76, 81
Council of Europe, 17
Counteracting forces, 72, 84
Covid-19, xiii–xv
Creative destruction, 72n1, 73n3,
    100n1, 118n1, 131n1, 132n2,
    153, 160–163
Credit (*see also* Debt), 143, 162
Crisis of profitability, 72–73, 131
Culture, 22, 29, 81, 161
    of fear, 157–158
    wars, 95
Currency devaluation, 107, 116
Current account deficits, 139
Czechoslovakia, 43

Daimler, 149
Davos (*see also* World Economic
    Forum), 22, 61, 176
Debt, 5, 34, 50
    bubble, 159
    business, 143
    economy, 133
    foreign, 140
    household, 143
    public, 100
Decay, 72, 82, 84, 97, 113, 119–120,
    132, 140, 146, 152, 154,
    156, 161, 165, 178
Decolonisation, 7n1, 55–56
Deglobalisation, 69, 81
Delor, Jacques, 124
Democracy, xxiii–xxv, 4, 7, 12–14,
    16, 18, 24, 27–29, 32–33,
    36–39, 47–52, 66, 85, 135,
    151, 165–183
Democratic deficit, 53
Democratic Party (US),
    28, 85
Democratic peace theory, 142
Democratic rights, 19, 49,
    51, 180
Demos, 49–50
Depoliticisation, 35, 42

Depression (*see also* Great
    Depression; Long
    Depression), 44, 46, 91–93,
    97, 100, 117, 143, 161
Deregulation, 100
Destabilisation, 37, 47, 55, 155, 158
Determinism, 70, 74, 76–81
Discrimination, 107, 116–117, 125
Disputes settlement systems, 10, 26,
    43, 61, 106, 110, 175, 176
Division of labour, 42, 77–78, 178
    international, 30, 132, 135,
        166, 183
    technical, 77
Doha round (WTO), 3, 109, 113
Dorn, David, 120
Double government, 42, 53
Draghi, Mario, 170
Duisenberg, Wim, xxiii
Dulles, John Foster, 49
Dumping of goods, 107–108
Dunning, John, 80
Dynamism, 60, 132, 156, 161, 163

East Asia, 83, 119, 145, 166
East Asian "Miracle", 75
East Indies, 101
East Timor, 17
Eastern Europe, 41, 178
Economic and Monetary Union (*see*
    European Union)
Economic crisis, 55, 57, 131, 136, 158,
    166
Economic decay, effect of, 29, 92, 118
Economic development, 12, 31, 41,
    60, 77, 79, 83, 87, 96, 118,
    127, 133, 143, 146, 172, 178
Economic dynamism, 161
Economic growth, 34, 47, 69–71,
    74–75, 81, 83, 87, 89, 116,
    132, 143, 145, 155, 163
Economic policy, 34, 38, 42, 90, 95,
    126, 154–155
    counter-crisis, 159
    discrediting of, 34
    fiscal (*see* Fiscal policy)

industrial (*see* Industrial policy)
    Keynesian (*see also* Keynesian
        economics), 22, 34, 47–48
    monetary (*see* Monetary policy)
    outsourcing of, 135
Economic renewal, xxxii, xxxv, 97,
    100, 119, 153, 162–163, 165
Economic restructuring, xxxi, 47, 108,
    118, 153, 160, 162, 165
Economic transformation, xx, xxxv,
    119, 153, 155, 161–164, 166
Economicisation, 29–30
Economics, 28–30, 32, 41–42, 48,
    51–52, 87–88, 96, 121, 165
Economies of scale, 132
Economist Intelligence Unit, 28
Edgerton, David, 178
Education, 30, 169, 172
Eichengreen, Barry, 91
Eisenhower, Dwight D., 49
Elections, 13, 28, 50, 171
Electric cars, 146, 149, 161
Electronic industries, 137
Embedded liberalism, 47
Emerging economies, 119, 146
Emissions control policies, 168
Empire, 41–42, 55, 113
Employment, 18, 35, 80, 100,
    117–121, 155, 159–160,
    162–163, 174
Energy industries, 161–163
Engineering industries, 62, 136
Enlightenment, 6, 23, 27, 32, 77,
    81, 166, 181
Entertainment industries, 127
Epistocracy, 29
Equality, 24
Eucken, Walter, 43, 52
Europe, 5, 8, 17, 22–24, 27, 31, 41, 43,
    45, 48, 54, 61–62, 95, 110,
    125, 144, 147–149,
    171–172
European Central Bank (ECB), xxiii,
    27, 43, 170
European Coal and Steel Community
    (ECSC), xxii, 111

European Commission, 16, 22, 26–27, 31, 58, 62–63, 65, 108, 111, 124, 126, 170, 182
European Community, 43, 54, 85
European Council, 89, 182
European Council of Ministers (the Council of the EU), 171
European Court of Human Rights, 17
European Court of Justice (ECJ), 10–11, 63
European Defence Fund, 65
European Parliament, 16, 112, 171
European Union (EU), xxii, xxv, xxix, xxx, xxxii–xxxiii, 3, 15–16, 27, 31, 50, 59–61, 65, 70, 110–111, 171, 182
    Common External Tariff, 111
    Common Security and Defence Policy, 65
    Customs Union, 85, 111–112
    directives, 171
    Economic and Monetary Union, 43
    protectionism, 31
    regulations, 15
    Single Market, 42
    state aid, 15, 26
    Working Time Directive, 171
Eurozone, 22, 31, 50, 59, 143, 169–170
    crisis, 31, 59, 170
Evenett, Simon, 117, 125, 166
Evercore ISI, 149
Exchange rates, 47, 90, 142
Expectations, lowering of, 158
Exports, 71, 73, 76, 83–84, 91, 92, 107, 119, 136
    capital, 76
    goods, 73–74, 82
    incentives, 123
    promotion, 87
    services, 73–74, 82

Facebook, 62–63, 176
Factory closures, 97, 108
Falkner, Gerda, 10–11
Farming (*see also* Agriculture), 127

Fascism, 6, 8, 23, 45, 48, 90
Fatalism, 34, 65, 153–154
Fear (*see* Culture of fear)
Federal Reserve, central banking system of the US; also the 'Fed', 159
Feld, Lars, 43
Feudalism, 101
Finance Capital (Hilferding), 132
Financial bubbles, 143
Financial crash (2008), 33, 35–36, 57, 81, 108, 133, 142, 143, 159, 161, 170
Financial crises, 100
Financial investment, 160
Financial markets, 123, 159–160
Financial services, 141
Financialisation, 133, 143, 161
Findlay, Ronald, 64, 91, 106–107, 136, 183
First World War, 5, 8, 23, 65, 72, 90, 93, 107, 132, 180
Fiscal policy, 7, 92, 169
Fischer, Joschka, 18
5G, xxxi
Ford, Gerald, 63
Foreign direct investment, 72–73, 126, 132–134, 141, 145–146
    greenfield, 72n2, 133–134
    inward, effect of, 146
Foreign Investment Risk Review Modernization Act, 63
Foreign trade (*see* Trade)
France, 5–7, 21–22, 26, 54–55, 61, 88, 90, 93, 103, 112, 135, 171, 182
    empire, 110
Franco, 48
Frankel, Jeffrey, 75
Frankfurter, Felix, 11n3
Fraternity, 24, 166
Free market, 22, 34, 37, 39, 43, 51–52, 61, 77, 80, 88, 95, 99–100, 102, 122, 157
Free market ideas, 35–36

Free trade, 30, 51, 61, 70–71, 80,
        86–87, 92–93, 98–99,
        101–104, 108, 111, 113,
        115, 117, 183
Free trade agreements (FTAs), 70,
        99, 110
Freedom, 5, 11, 24–25, 27, 32, 43, 51,
        61, 101–103, 106, 109–110,
        179, 183
Freiburg school, 43
French Revolution, 24
Friedman, George, 176
Friedman, Milton, 41
Fritz, Johannes, 117
Fukuyama, Francis, 12
Fulton, Bob, 181
Furedi, Frank, 95, 179
Furnivall, John Sydenham, 12

Ganesh, Janan, 26, 61
GATT (General Agreement on Tariffs
        and Trade), 10, 25, 43, 45,
        49, 56, 93, 95, 104–107,
        109, 112–113, 116–117,
        121–122, 125
GDP (gross domestic product), 26,
        73, 75, 81, 83–84, 108, 132,
        137, 141, 147, 160
General Agreement on Trade in
        Services (GATS), 106, 109
General Data Protection Regulation
        (GDPR), xxx, 62
General Electric, 63
General Motors (GM), 108, 149
Genomics, 98
Geopolitics, 90, 96, 128, 147
Germany, 5–7, 9, 18, 26, 28, 44, 61,
        90, 92–93, 95, 112, 125,
        135, 143, 167, 171
    empire, 110
Gilets jaunes, 21
GlaxoSmithKline, 62
Glencore, 62
Global commodities, xxxii
Global frameworks under strain,
        xxv–xxviii

Global supply chain (GSCs), 134
Global Trade Alert (GTA), 121
Global trade slowdown, 81–84
Global value chain (GVCs), 82–84, 134
Global warming, 123, 168
Globalisation, xx–xxi, 3, 18, 23,
        32–36, 38, 41, 47, 69–70,
        72–73, 80, 98, 113, 131,
        142, 144, 166–168, 181–182
Globalisation 1.0, 132
Globalisation 2.0, 134–139
Globalism, xiii–xiv, xix–xx, xxxii–
        xxxiii, xxxv, 18, 21–39,
        44–46, 48, 51–53, 65–66,
        79, 124–125, 132, 167–171,
        181–182
*Globalists: The End of Empire and
        the Birth of Neoliberalism*
        (Slobodian), 36
Gold standard, 7, 91–93
Google, 62–63, 176
Governance, 3, 6, 13, 17, 21, 39, 47,
        59, 104, 168, 170, 177
Governments, 4, 13, 15, 18, 35, 82, 89, 92,
        97, 116, 122, 141, 158, 169
Great Depression (1930s), 12, 91–92,
        104, 155
Great Moderation, 143, 160–161
Great War, 5, 44, 46n2
Greece, 8, 26–27, 31, 143, 182
Green growth, 116
Greenfeld, Liah, 24
Greenspan, Alan, 32–33, 35–36, 158
Grossman, Gene, 75
Grossmann, Henryk, 72
Grotius, Hugo, 101
Growth (*see* Economic growth)
Gulf War (*see* Iraq invasion (1990))

Halikiopoulou, Daphne, 23, 169
Hansen, Alvin, 94
Hanson, Gordon, 120
Harding, Rebecca, 87
Harley, Knick, 75
Hayek, Friedrich, 37–38, 41–43,
        45–46, 48, 51–52

Health, 116, 122, 124, 158, 169
  and safety regulations, 122
Healthcare, 18, 100
Heart of Darkness (Conrad), 88
Held, David, xx–xxi
Helpman, Elhanan, 70, 75
High-speed trains, 146
Hilferding, Rudolf, 132
Hitler, Adolf, 44, 48, 95, 170
Hobson, John, 132
Hoffmann, Stanley, 169
Holocaust, 6, 8
Honda, 141
Honeywell, 63
Hoover, Herbert, 5
Howe, Anthony, 102
Huawei, 62–63, 146
Hull, Cordell, 95
Human agency, 3, 36
Human rights, 13, 16–19
Humanity, 19, 29, 32, 156, 179, 181
Hungary, 59, 167, 182
Huskisson, William, 80

IMF (International Monetary Fund),
    xxix, 9, 22, 27, 34, 43, 45,
    54–56, 70, 74–75, 82–83,
    100, 147, 177
Imperialism, 24, 72, 132, 180–181
Imperialism: A Study (Hobson), 132
*Imperialism: The Highest Stage of
    Capitalism* (Lenin), 132
Imperialist nations, 24
Import tariffs, 30, 92, 101–104, 116, 121
Imports, 26, 30, 70, 72, 75–76, 80–81,
    103, 107, 117, 121, 126
  capital, 71
  goods, 71, 83
  services, 71
Income, 35, 71, 75, 91, 100, 119, 140,
    154, 161, 163
India, 85, 106, 128, 178
Industrial policy, xxvii, xxxii, xxxv,
    15, 98, 100, 107–108,
    122–125, 147, 155, 162–164
Industrial revolution, 70, 169

Industrialists, 86
Inequality, 27, 41, 165
  income, 119
Information and communications
    technologies, 141
Infrastructure, 56, 60, 83, 141, 155,
    162, 164
Innovation, 71, 74–75, 118,
    155–156, 163
  wars, 98
Insecurity, 160–161
Insolvencies, 158
Instability, 32, 58
Institutions, 3–4, 6, 8, 13–18, 22, 25,
    27, 36, 38, 43, 50–57, 64,
    66, 108, 113, 159, 164, 176,
    179, 183
Intel, 62
Intellectual property (IP), 61, 109
  intellectual property rights (IPR), 126
  theft, 98
Interconnectedness, xviii–xx
Inter-war years, 41, 48, 90–91, 96
Interest rates, 92, 159
  low, 36, 155–156, 159
  negative, 159
Intergovernmental Panel on Climate
    Change (IPCC), 168
International Bank for
    Reconstruction and
    Development, 43
International cooperation, 7, 45, 47,
    54, 59, 125, 142, 152, 183
International Court of Justice (ICJ),
    9–10
International Criminal Court (ICC), 26
International division of labour (*see*
    Division of labour)
International law, 4, 6–7, 9–11, 15–19,
    32, 50, 54, 56, 169
International order, xvii–xix, xxv–
    xxxi, 3–19, 22–23, 25,
    42–46, 48, 50, 53–61,
    64–65, 96, 98–99, 103, 113,
    124–125, 144, 147, 165,
    167, 177

International relations, 4, 9–11, 58–59, 90, 104, 125, 143–144, 151, 176
  neoconservatism, 48
  neorealism, 58
International Whaling Commission, 16
Internationalisation, 9, 69, 73–74, 84, 131–150, 161, 178
  capital flows, 143, 175
  international economic cooperation, 104, 142
  trade flows, 122, 173
Internationalisation 1.0, 132, 141
Internationalisation 2.0, 139–144
Internationalism, 23, 131, 165–183
Internet, 64
Inventions, 156, 162
Investment, 82–83, 153, 155, 182
  business, 71, 82, 94, 97, 154–155, 162
  financial, 160, 186
  incentives, 107, 126
  international, 140
  public, 166
Inward investment controls, 63, 127, 141, 143
Iran, 62, 144
  nuclear deal, 62
  sanctions against, 101
Iraq, 14, 18, 60
Iraq invasion (1990–01 Gulf War), 60
Iraq invasion (2003), 26
Ireland, 26, 59, 126, 180, 182
Irish famine, 17
Iron, 76
Irwin, Douglas, 71
Islam, 180
Ismay, Lord (Hastings), 56
Isolationism, 21, 86, 178, 181
Italy, 5, 31, 90, 93, 112, 125, 143, 180, 182

Jaguar Land Rover, 149
Japan, 5, 14, 44, 56, 63, 90, 93, 95–97, 104, 113, 127, 147–149
Jevons, William Stanley, 88

Jobs
  insecurity, 155
  and investment, 120, 153
  technology, effect of, 119
  trade, effect of, 119
Johnson, Lyndon, 116
Juncker, Jean-Claude, 22–23, 27, 182
Juridification, 9–10, 19

Kagan, Robert, 48
Kant, Immanuel, 9, 32
Kellogg-Briand Pact, 14
Kennan, George, 56
Keohane, Robert, xxii
Kershaw, Ian, 44n1
Keynes, John Maynard, 7, 46, 92–93
Keynesianism/Keynesian economics, 22, 34, 41, 48, 99
Kissinger, Henry, 19
Knowledge (and the economy), 70
Kosovo, 17, 26, 169n1
Krugman, Paul, 75, 91
Kuwait, 60

Labour, 30, 77, 79–80, 111, 135, 166, 171, 183
Labour Party (UK), 33
Labour theory of value, 88
Lagarde, Christine, 34, 74
Laissez-faire ideas, 35, 46, 102
Lamy, Pascal, 124
Landowners, 76, 86, 107
Law, 4, 10–11, 13
League of Nations, 5–6, 14, 42, 45, 54, 170
Legalism, 38, 51
Lenin, Vladimir, 132, 180
Levitt, Theodore, xx
Leyen, Ursula von der, 22, 65
Liberalisation, 81, 99, 100
  trade, 60, 70, 87, 101, 106, 113
Liberalism, 11–12, 27, 31, 43, 48, 52, 66, 104
Liberty, 11, 24–25, 37, 43, 166
Libya, 14, 18
Lind, Michael, 153

Liquidity, 133, 159
Living standards, 31, 82, 149, 162
Lloyd George, David, 5–6
Loans, 31
Long Depression, 113, 121, 132, 136,
    139, 142, 145, 150, 152–
    153, 156, 158, 160
Luce, Edward, 27
Lundan, Sarianna, 80

M&A (mergers and acquisitions),
    133–134
Machine learning, 161
Machinery (for production), 49, 72,
    77, 83, 136, 153
Macron, Emmanuel, 21–22
"Made in China 2025", 98
Manchuria, 14
Mandate System (League of Nations), 9
Manufacturing, 83, 119–120, 136,
    143, 149, 157, 161, 174
Marginal utility-based theory of
    value, 88
Marginalist revolution, 88
Market fundamentalism, 36
Market system, 66, 101, 143, 163
Marshall Plan, 34
Marx, Karl, xxxiii, 88, 160
Marxism, 48
Mazower, Mark, 57
Mazzini, Giuseppe, 180
McNair, Lord (Arnold Duncan), 9
Medicines industry, 128
Menger, Carl, 41, 88
Mercantilism, xxxi–xxxii, 65, 76, 132, 166
Mercedes-Benz, 149
Mergers (*see* M&A)
Mexico, 110
Microsoft, 62
Middle East, 178
Migration, 59, 95, 171
Militarisation, 65
Militarism, 8, 90, 97
Military, 10, 14, 18, 25–26, 37, 39, 49,
    55–56, 65, 89, 94, 143, 169,
    176

Mill, John Stuart, 81, 102
Mining, 62, 161
Mises, Ludwig von, 41–42, 46
Missouri v Holland ruling, 15
Mitrany, David, 96
Mixed economy, 34, 47–48
Mobility, 161
Mobility-as-a-service, 149
Monetarism, 22
Monetary policy, 7, 52, 164
    quantitative easing, 159
    ultra-low interest rates, 156
    unconventional mechanisms, 36
Monnet, Jean, 53
Monopolies, 101
Mont Pelerin Society, 42
Montesquieu, 81
Most favoured nation (MFN), 45, 91,
    107, 112
Motorola, 63
Mounk, Yascha, xxiii, 27
Multifibre Arrangement, 107
Multilateralism, 61, 98, 177
Multinational business, 73, 120, 134,
    174, 176–177
Murky protectionism, 122–124, 128
Mussolini, Benito, 48
Myopia, 32

Nanotechnologies, 161
Nation state, 3–4, 23–25, 12, 16–17,
    33–36, 38, 42, 44–47, 51,
    66, 96, 100, 107, 109, 119,
    126–127, 142, 152–153,
    167–168, 171, 174–175,
    177, 179, 182–183
National developmentalism, 153
National independence, 180
National political activity, xxii
National security, 26, 62–63, 86, 141
National self-determination, 18, 34, 180
National socialism, 44, 48
National sovereignty, xxiii
Nationalism, 6, 8, 21–24, 27, 46, 51,
    94–95, 115, 137, 179–181
    Third World, 180

Navarro, Peter, 98
Nazism, 41
Negative nominal interest rates, 159
Neoclassical economics, 102
Neoliberalism (*see also*
    Ordoliberalism), 4, 22,
    36–38, 41–52, 181
  'renaissance' (1980s onwards), 34,
    141
Netherlands, 93, 112, 182
New Deal, 12, 13, 93
New normal, 35, 159
New Zealand, 104, 112
Newman, Abraham, 144
Nigeria, 62
Night watchman role, 47
Nissan, 141
Nixon, Richard, 116
Non-tariff barriers (NTBs), xxxi–
    xxxii, 122
  sanitary and phytosanitary rules,
    122, 124
  technical barriers to trade, 30, 122,
    124
  behind the border, 106, 122, 124,
    126
Norman, Montagu, 7
North American Free Trade
    Agreement (NAFTA), 86,
    97, 99, 110, 115, 126
North Atlantic Treaty Organisation
    (NATO), 26, 56–57
Nuclear fusion, 161
Nuremburg war crimes trials, 10
Nye, Joseph, xxii, 103

O'Neill, Paul, 63
O'Rourke, Kevin, 75, 183
Obama, Barack, 26, 127
OECD (Organisation for Economic
    Co-operation and
    Development), 54, 81, 100,
    118, 120, 137, 139, 141,
    147, 156, 162, 172
Oil, 97, 147
Opium War, 103

Order, 3–4, 7, 14, 23, 25, 32, 37, 48,
    53, 56–58, 60, 66, 113, 144,
    175, 177
Ordoliberalism, 43, 52
Organisation for Economic
    Co-operation and
    Development, 54
Ormerod, Paul, 172
Osborne, George, 61
Ottoman empire, 9, 42
Outsourcing of production, 135
Over-accumulation, 160
Overindebtedness, 160
Overseas earnings, 133–134

Patents, 127, 174
Patriotism, 23
Pax Americana, 55
Pearl Harbor attack, 97
Peloponnesian War, 165
Perpetual peace, 9, 58
Peru, 104
Peterloo Massacre, 17
Peugeot, 108
Pharmaceuticals, 127
Pinochet, Augusto, 39, 52
Poland, 41, 167, 182
Political independence, 6, 49, 178, 180
Political renewal, 153
Politicisation, 86
Politics, 6, 8–10, 21–39, 48, 51, 96
Popular pressures, 48, 50
Populism, 22
Porter, Patrick, 144
Portugal, 26, 31, 78–79, 143
Post-war boom, 34, 56, 59, 73, 116,
    132, 158
Post-war order, 4, 45–46, 53–66, 103,
    144, 151
Pound, Ezra, 6
Poverty, 70, 117
Precarious employment, 35
Precaution, 124–125
Precautionary principle, 125
Preferential trade agreements (*see also*
    Free trade agreements), 110

Privacy, 62
Private property, 41
Prodi, Romano, 58
Production
    domestic, 70, 72, 81, 96, 102–103,
        117, 120, 137
    international, 73, 83, 145
    outsourcing, 135
Production decay, 152 (*see also*
        Decay)
Productivity
    diffusion, 156, 162
    slowdown, 156
Profitability
    crisis, 132
    falling, 131
Profits, corporate, 132–133, 149
Progress, 23–24, 27, 31–32, 53, 65,
        76, 80, 88, 94, 98, 115, 119,
        128, 153, 160–161, 163,
        166, 178
Protectionism, xix–xx, xxxi–xxxiii,
        22, 30–32, 36, 61–62, 70,
        75, 76–77, 81, 85, 87, 89,
        90–98, 101, 103, 105–113,
        115–128, 141, 162, 182
Public debt, 100
Public infrastructure, 141, 162
Public procurement, 108, 158
Public spending, 41, 100, 155, 158,
        162, 169
Public-private partnerships, 158
Purchasing power parity (PPP),
        xxvi$n$5

Qualcomm, 97
Quantitative easing (QE), 36, 159
Quotas, 92, 101, 107, 111, 116, 121,
        124, 126

R&D (research and development), 97,
        108, 122, 174
Racism, 24
Rajan, Amin, 90
Rawls, John, 116
Reagan, Ronald, 26, 99

Recessions, 29, 34, 132, 143, 160–161
    cleansing role of, 161
Reciprocal Trade Agreements Act
        (US), 93, 95
Referendum
    Britain (2016), 65
    Greece (2015), 278
Regional segregation, xxxi
Regional trade agreements (*see also*
        Free trade agreements),
        107, 111
Regulation (*see* State)
Reissl, Severin, 36
Renault, 108
Reparations, 5, 90
Resource allocation, 70
Responsibility to Protect (R2P), 18
Restructuring (*see* Economic
        restructuring)
Revolution of 1688 ('Glorious
        Revolution'), 12
Ricardo, David, 76, 78–81, 102
Risk, 50, 54, 94, 144, 173
Risk management, 128
Rivalries, xviii, xxvi, xxiv, 24, 94, 139,
        142-144, 146, 147, 152,
        165–166
    intra-Western, 60
    West-East, 60
Robbins, Lionel, 37, 95
Robotics, 98, 161
Rodrik, Dani, 181–183
Rolls Royce, 62, 181
Roman Republic, 11
Romania, 167
Romer, David, 75
Roosevelt, Franklin Delano (FDR),
        12–13, 93, 95
Röpke, Wilhelm, 43
Rosenboim, Or, xx–xxi, 44, 66, 95
Ruggie, John, 47
Ruggiero, Renato, 25
Rule of law, 3–4, 11–14, 18, 26, 58–60,
        165, 167, 182
Rules, 3, 7, 12–13, 15, 25–26, 50,
        58–59, 61–64, 177

Rules-based international order,
     xxviii, 3–19, 99, 147
Russia, 5
  Empire, 42
Russian Revolution, 41, 44, 132
Rustow, Alexander, 46
Rwanda, 17–18

Safety, 116, 122, 124, 128, 158
Samsung, 146
Samuelson, Paul, 117
San Francisco, 45
Sanctions, 14, 62, 101, 117, 144
Sanitary and phytosanitary rules,
     122–123
Schäuble, Wolfgang, 28, 50
Schonhardt-Bailey, Cheryl, 86
Schuman, Robert, 53
Schumpeter, Joseph, 160
Science, 125, 157
Scotland, 173, 181
Scramble for Africa, 88
Second World War, 3, 7–8, 10, 14,
     23–24, 42, 44, 48, 53, 64,
     90–91, 94–95, 99, 110, 115,
     142, 157, 166, 179–180
Secular stagnation, 94, 143, 161
Security, 24, 93, 95, 124, 155, 161–
     162, 176
Self-determination (*see* National
     self-determination)
Serbia, 14
Service industries, 123
Services sector, 141
Short-termism, 155, 164
Silicon Valley, 62
Skilling, 163
Skills, 163
Skinner, Andrew, 77
Slavery, 17
Slobodian, Quinn, 36, 42, 50, 52
Sluga, Glenda, 180
Slump, 41, 44, 83
  1930s, 46, 59
Smartphone market, 146

Smith, Adam, 76–79, 81, 95, 102, 115,
     173
Smoot-Hawley Act (US), 90
Social media, 63
Socialism, 34, 48, 50
Solar power, 146
Somalia, 14
South Korea, 96, 146, 149
Southern Europe, 31
Sovereignty
  national, 3, 10, 16, 18–19, 33–34,
     41–42, 44, 53, 63, 66, 153,
     165–183
  popular, 13, 16, 23, 48, 179,
     182–183
Soviet Union (USSR), 23, 34, 48, 56,
     59, 96, 110
Spain, 31, 90, 104, 125, 135, 143, 173
Sparta, 64
Specialisation, 70, 77–79, 84, 135, 178
Stability
  economic, 158–159
  geopolitical, 57
Stagflation, 34
Stagnation, 3, 35, 94, 118, 143, 157,
     159, 161
Stalinism, 41
Start-up, 145, 156
State
  discrediting of, 34
  intervention, 34, 36, 38, 42, 46–47,
     51, 62, 92, 97, 99–101, 104,
     116, 122, 147, 157–160, 170
  regulation, 77, 88, 102
  spending, 100
State aid, 15, 26, 107–108, 125, 152
State internationalisation, 141–142
State socialism, 48
State subsidies, 26, 125, 162
Status quo, 3, 21, 32, 57, 59, 64, 79,
     118, 142, 147, 153, 156, 169
Steam power, 77
Steel industry, 116
Steuart, James, 118
Stigler, George, 78
Stock market crash 1929, 90

Stockhammer, Engelbert, 36
Strange, Susan, xxii, 101
Structural reform, 162
Suez crisis, 55
Support for those affected, 143
Supranational bodies, 3, 17, 53,
        169, 171
Supranationalism, 168
Supreme Court (US), 11–13, 15
Sustainability, 124
SWIFT, 144
Switzerland, 22
Syria, 14, 18, 22

Taiwan, 96, 145–146, 169n1
Tariff protectionism, 91, 94, 121
Tariffs (*see* Import tariffs)
Taxation, 37, 76, 117, 119, 125, 153, 157
Technical barriers to trade (*see* Non-
        tariff barriers)
Technical services, 49
Technocratic governance, 59
Technological change, 78, 117, 157, 162
Technological exhaustion, 156
Technology, 61, 96, 98, 119, 146, 154,
        167
    effect of, 119
Telecommunications, 39, 62, 146
Terrorism, 180
Tesla, 149
Textiles, 105–107
Thatcher, Margaret, 37, 99, 141
Thatcherism, 37
*The Emergence of Globalism: Visions
        of World Order in Britain
        and the United States*, 44,
        1939–1950 (Rosenboim)
The Great Illusion (Angell), xviii, 142
The left, 21, 34
The Retreat of the State (Strange),
        xxii, 39
The Retreat of Western Liberalism
        (Luce), 27
The right, 17, 43, 48, 155, 180, 183
The Road to Serfdom (Hayek), 37
Third way politics, 21

Third World nationalism, 180
"Third world" development, 146
Thucydides, xvii, xxv, xxxvi, 165
TINA ('there is no alternative'), xxvii,
        50
Tokyo round (GATT), 105, 109
Tokyo war crimes trials, 10
Tooze, Adam, 151, 173
Toyota, 141, 149
Trade, 3, 30, 54, 60, 62, 69–98,
        120–121
    effect of, 119
    deficits, 139
    determinism, 70, 74, 76–81
    finance, 107, 123, 126
    wars, 65, 70, 82, 86, 89–90, 94,
        96–97–98, 115
Trade Facilitation Agreement, 109
Trade-related intellectual property
        rules (TRIPs), 109
Trade-related investment measures
        (TRIMs), 109
Training, 162–163
Trans-Pacific Partnership (TPP), 60,
        86, 113, 127
Transatlantic Trade and Investment
        Partnership, 127
Transformation (*see* Economic
        transformation)
Transnational business, 22, 124, 173–174
Transport, 83, 91, 102, 157, 161–162,
        168, 172
Trump, Donald, 21–22, 25–26, 28,
        31, 56, 60–62, 64, 85–87,
        96–98, 106, 112, 115, 127,
        144, 167, 183
Trust, lack of, 6
Trusteeship System (UN), 9
Tucker, Paul, 13
Tumlir, Jan, 10–11, 43, 49–50
Tusk, Donald, 89

Ukraine, 41
UN (United Nations), xxix, 45
    Educational, Scientific and
        Cultural Organization, 26

UN Charter, 17–18, 45, 49
UN General Assembly, 17, 22, 55
UN Human Rights Council, 17
UN Security Council, xxix, 4, 17–18, 26, 55
Uncertainty, 32, 73, 157–158
UNCTAD (United Nations Conference on Trade and Development), 25, 135
Unemployment, 29, 92, 117–121, 143
Unilateralism, 61
United Kingdom (UK) (*see* Britain)
United States (USA), xxv–xxxiv
   economic policy, 90
   imperialism, 180
   outward FDI, 73
   protectionism, 30–31
   trade, 93, 98, 120, 136
United States-Mexico-Canada Agreement, 126
Universal Declaration of Human Rights, 18
Uruguay round (GATT), 105–106, 109
USSR (*see* Soviet Union)

Varoufakis, Yanis, 28
Vasilopoulou, Sofia, 23, 169
Venezuela, 62
Vernon, Raymond, 34, 73, 120, 136, 173–174
Versailles Treaty, 5
Vietnam, 113, 181
Viner, Jacob, 103–104
Volkswagen, 149, 172
Voltaire, 110
Volvo, 149

Wade, Robert, 72
Wages, 86–87, 119, 157
Walras, Léon, 88

Walt, Stephen, 43, 57–58
Walter Eucken Institute, 43
Walter Lippmann, 46*n*2
Walter Lippmann Colloquium, 46
War, 4–14, 42–44, 56–59, 65, 89–92, 94–96, 165, 183
   debts, 90
Warfare, 4, 6, 44, 90, 95
Washington, George, 54
Wealth, 41, 69–71, 74, 76, 173
Wealth of Nations (Smith), 77, 115, 173
Weaponisation, 87–89
Welfare, 9, 48–49, 158, 163, 169
   dependency, 158, 163
   state, 48, 158
Welfarism, 34
Western Europe, 48, 57–58, 65, 104
WhatsApp, 63
Williamson, Jeffrey, 93
Wilson, Woodrow, 5–6, 46*n*2
Wine, 78–80
Working class, 21
   militancy, 8
World Bank, xxiv, 9, 38–39, 43, 45, 50, 56, 75, 106, 173
World Economic Forum, 22, 61
World Health Organization, xiii
World War I (*see* First World War)
World War II (*see* Second World War)
WTO (World Trade Organization), xxi
   Appellate Body, 10, 109
   Disputes Settlement Body, 10

Xi Jinping, 61

Zombie businesses, 156, 162
Zombie economy, 100, 156–157, 159
Zombification, 159–160, 162